MW00533970

TAREK - VINCENT POMPETTI

# CONQUEST

## JULIUS CAESAR'S GALLIC WAR

Translated by Cecile Bohard & Andrew Benteau

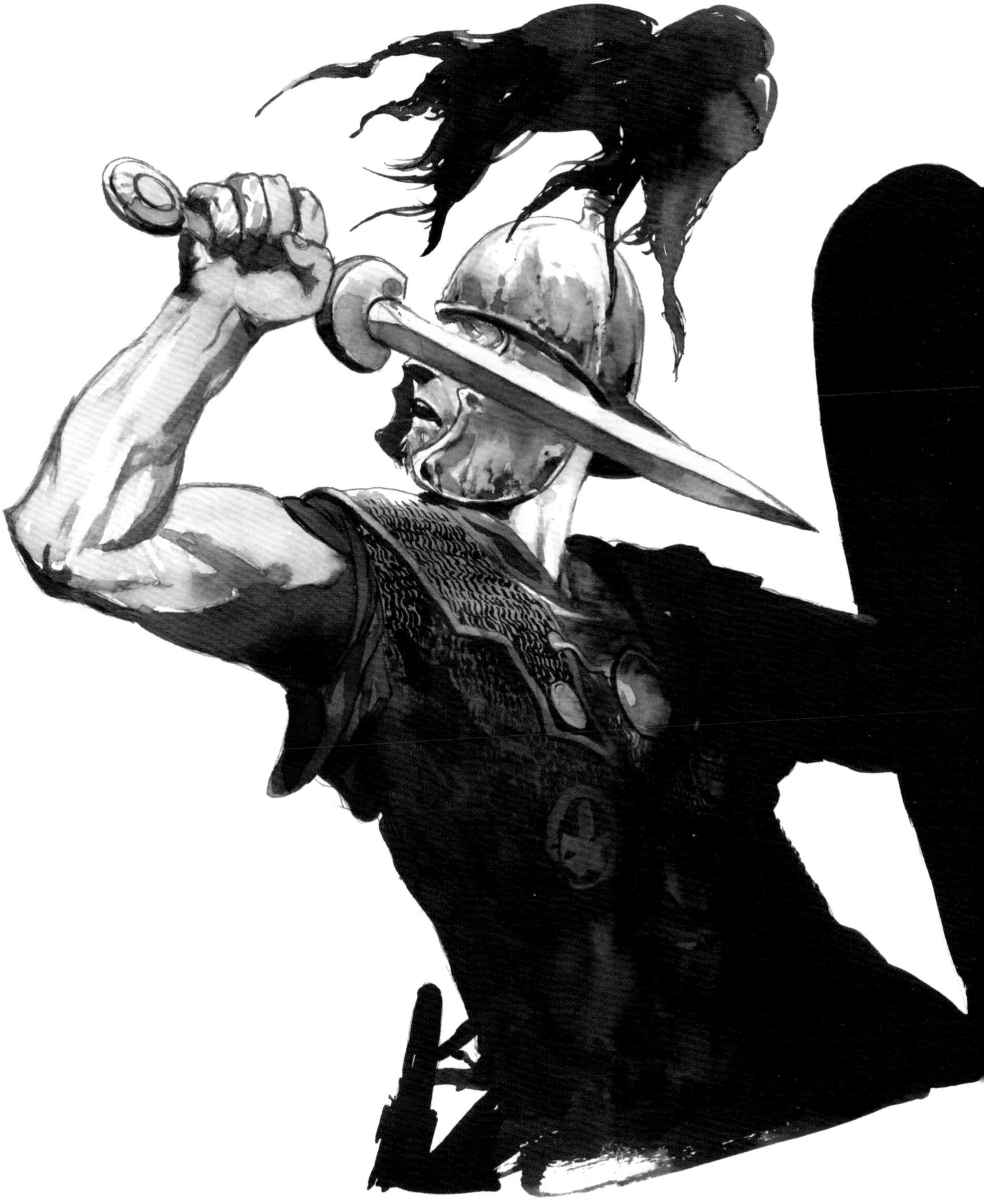

## JULIUS CAESAR'S GALLIC WAR

Black Panel Press
Toronto, ON
Canada

www.blackpanelpress.com
www.tartamudo.com (Original French Version)
Tarek: www.tarek-bd.fr
Vincent Pompetti: http://pompetti.wordpress.com

First Edition

Originally published in French by Tartamudo Editions.


ISBN: 978-1-7751015-4-3 (Print)
ISBN: 978-1-9994704-0-1 (E-book)


**Printed in China.**

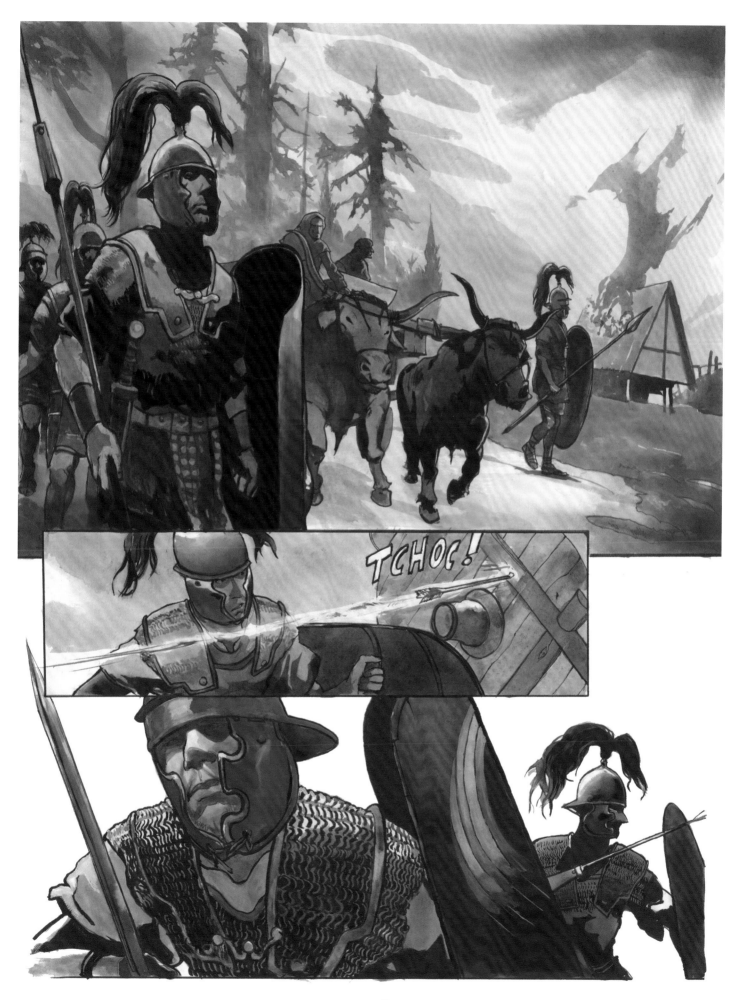

TCHOC!

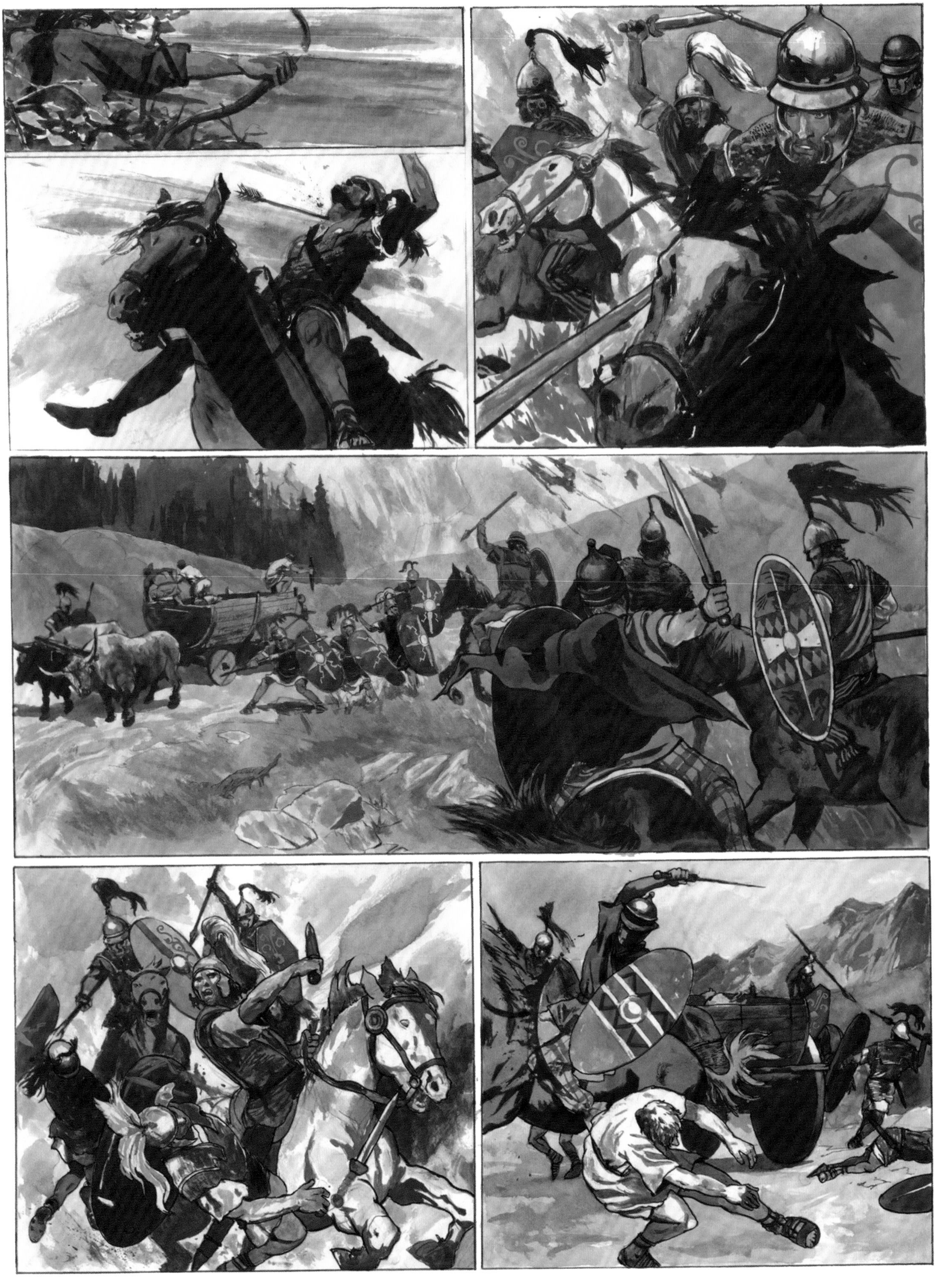

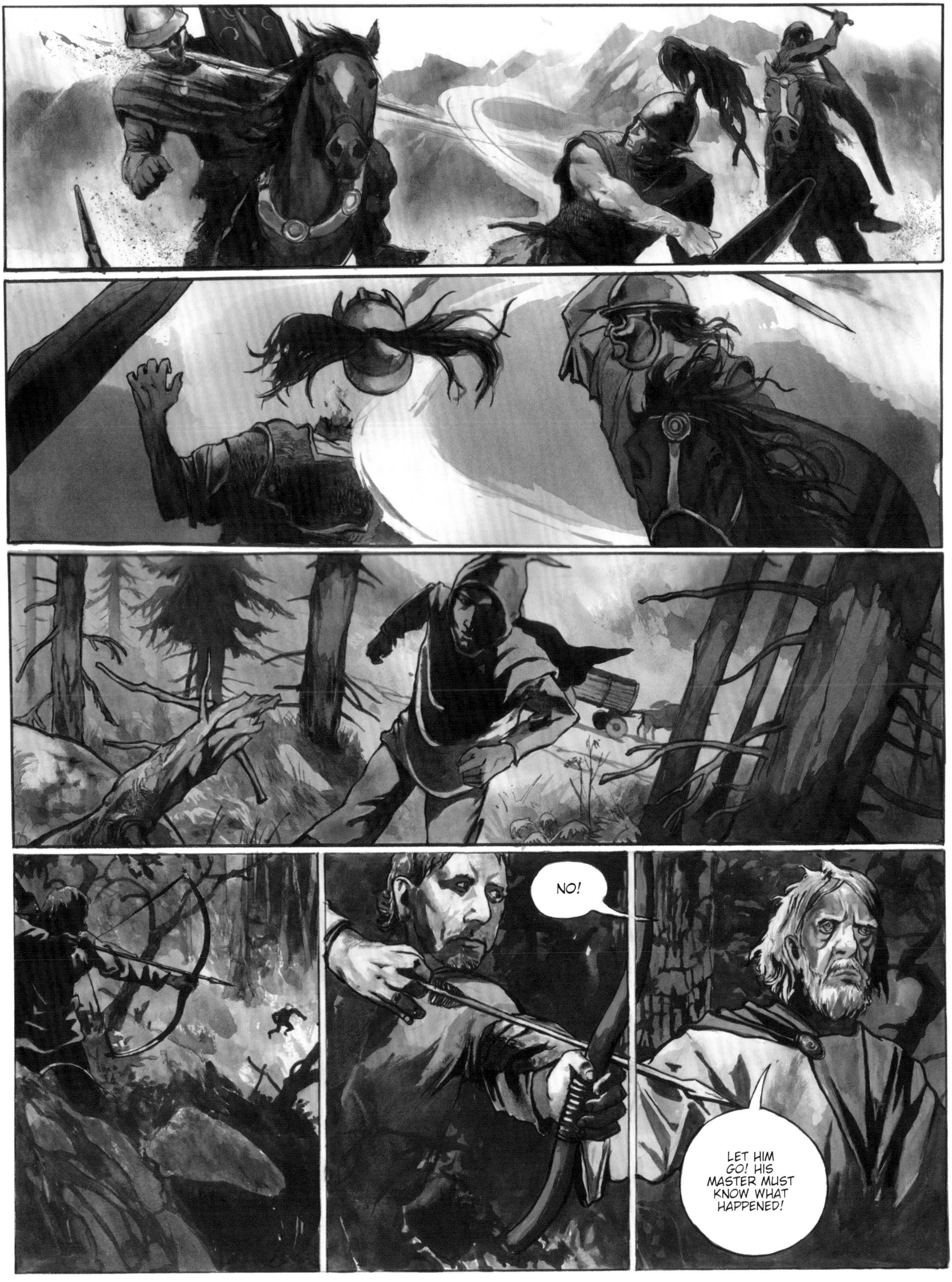
NO!
LET HIM GO! HIS MASTER MUST KNOW WHAT HAPPENED!

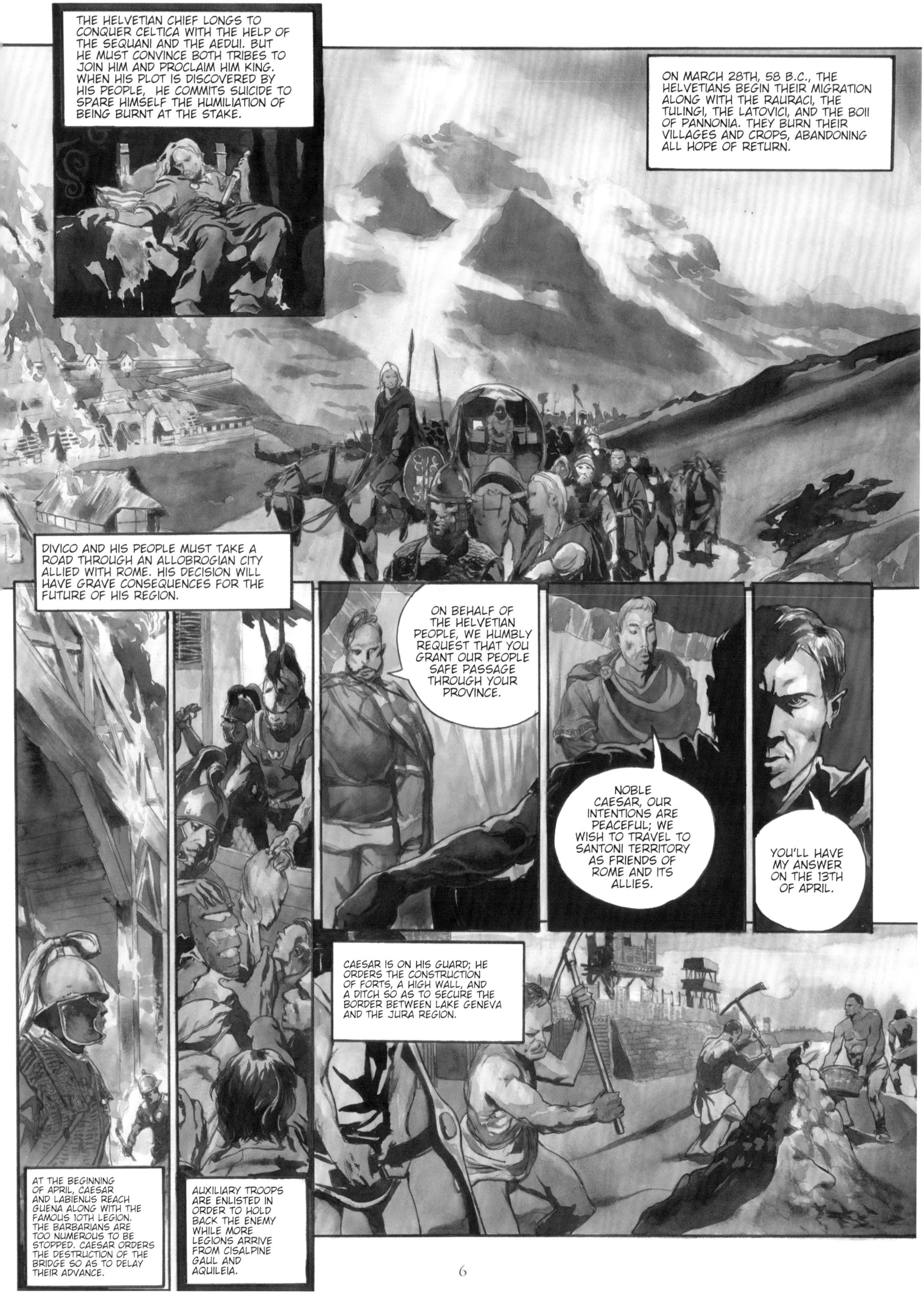
THE HELVETIAN CHIEF LONGS TO CONQUER CELTICA WITH THE HELP OF THE SEQUANI AND THE AEDUI. BUT HE MUST CONVINCE BOTH TRIBES TO JOIN HIM AND PROCLAIM HIM KING. WHEN HIS PLOT IS DISCOVERED BY HIS PEOPLE, HE COMMITS SUICIDE TO SPARE HIMSELF THE HUMILIATION OF BEING BURNT AT THE STAKE.
ON MARCH 28TH, 58 B.C., THE HELVETIANS BEGIN THEIR MIGRATION ALONG WITH THE RAURACI, THE TULINGI, THE LATOVICI, AND THE BOII OF PANNONIA. THEY BURN THEIR VILLAGES AND CROPS, ABANDONING ALL HOPE OF RETURN.
DIVICO AND HIS PEOPLE MUST TAKE A ROAD THROUGH AN ALLOBROGIAN CITY ALLIED WITH ROME. HIS DECISION WILL HAVE GRAVE CONSEQUENCES FOR THE FUTURE OF HIS REGION.
AT THE BEGINNING OF APRIL, CAESAR AND LABIENUS REACH GUENA ALONG WITH THE FAMOUS 10TH LEGION. THE BARBARIANS ARE TOO NUMEROUS TO BE STOPPED. CAESAR ORDERS THE DESTRUCTION OF THE BRIDGE SO AS TO DELAY THEIR ADVANCE.
AUXILIARY TROOPS ARE ENLISTED IN ORDER TO HOLD BACK THE ENEMY WHILE MORE LEGIONS ARRIVE FROM CISALPINE GAUL AND AQUILEIA.
ON BEHALF OF THE HELVETIAN PEOPLE, WE HUMBLY REQUEST THAT YOU GRANT OUR PEOPLE SAFE PASSAGE THROUGH YOUR PROVINCE.
NOBLE CAESAR, OUR INTENTIONS ARE PEACEFUL; WE WISH TO TRAVEL TO SANTONI TERRITORY AS FRIENDS OF ROME AND ITS ALLIES.
YOU'LL HAVE MY ANSWER ON THE 13TH OF APRIL.
CAESAR IS ON HIS GUARD; HE ORDERS THE CONSTRUCTION OF FORTS, A HIGH WALL, AND A DITCH SO AS TO SECURE THE BORDER BETWEEN LAKE GENEVA AND THE JURA REGION.

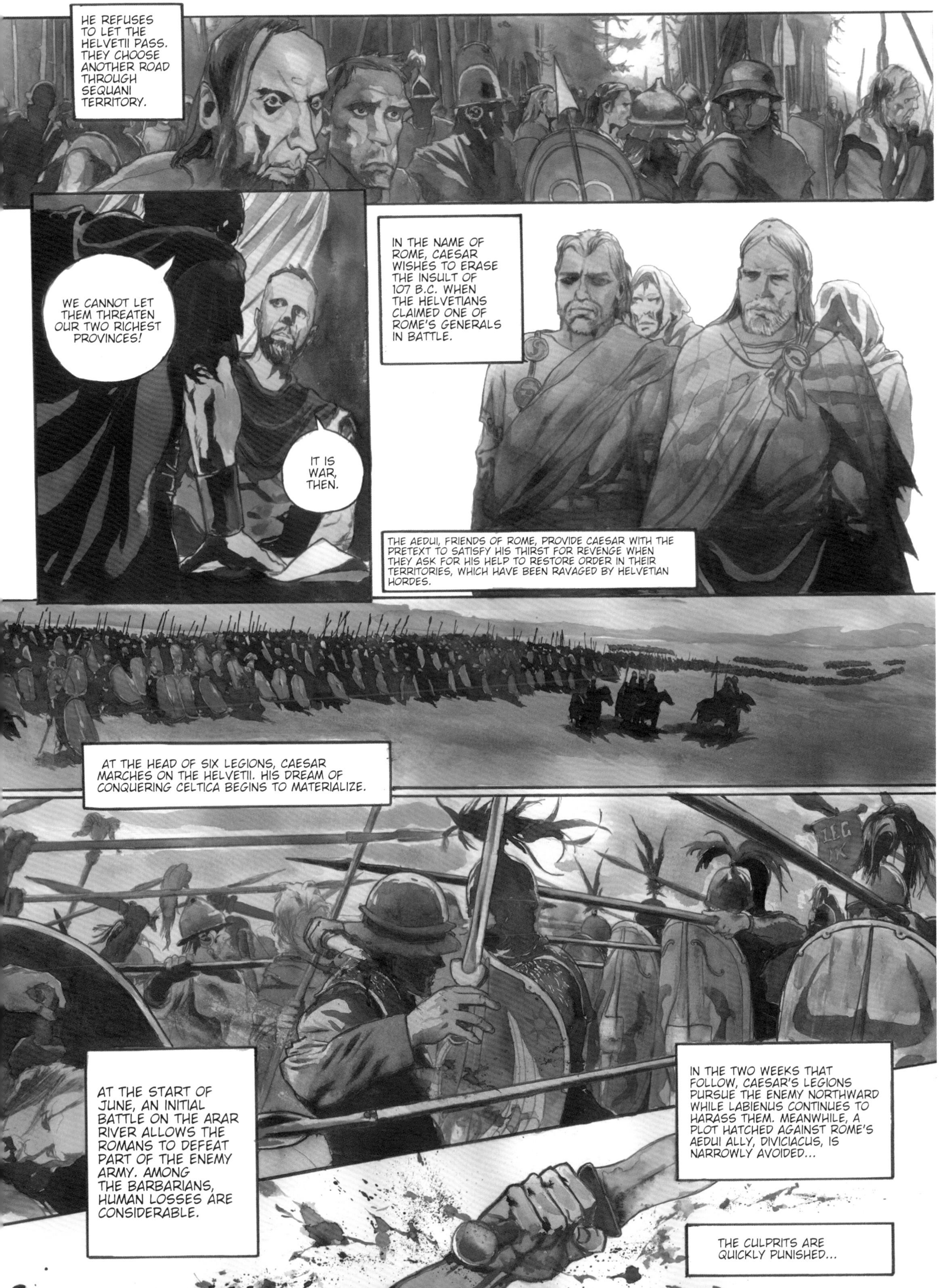

HE REFUSES TO LET THE HELVETII PASS. THEY CHOOSE ANOTHER ROAD THROUGH SEQUANI TERRITORY.
WE CANNOT LET THEM THREATEN OUR TWO RICHEST PROVINCES!
IT IS WAR, THEN.
IN THE NAME OF ROME, CAESAR WISHES TO ERASE THE INSULT OF 107 B.C. WHEN THE HELVETIANS CLAIMED ONE OF ROME'S GENERALS IN BATTLE.
THE AEDUI, FRIENDS OF ROME, PROVIDE CAESAR WITH THE PRETEXT TO SATISFY HIS THIRST FOR REVENGE WHEN THEY ASK FOR HIS HELP TO RESTORE ORDER IN THEIR TERRITORIES, WHICH HAVE BEEN RAVAGED BY HELVETIAN HORDES.
AT THE HEAD OF SIX LEGIONS, CAESAR MARCHES ON THE HELVETII. HIS DREAM OF CONQUERING CELTICA BEGINS TO MATERIALIZE.
LEG IX
AT THE START OF JUNE, AN INITIAL BATTLE ON THE ARAR RIVER ALLOWS THE ROMANS TO DEFEAT PART OF THE ENEMY ARMY. AMONG THE BARBARIANS, HUMAN LOSSES ARE CONSIDERABLE.
IN THE TWO WEEKS THAT FOLLOW, CAESAR'S LEGIONS PURSUE THE ENEMY NORTHWARD WHILE LABIENUS CONTINUES TO HARASS THEM. MEANWHILE, A PLOT HATCHED AGAINST ROME'S AEDUI ALLY, DIVICIACUS, IS NARROWLY AVOIDED...
THE CULPRITS ARE QUICKLY PUNISHED...

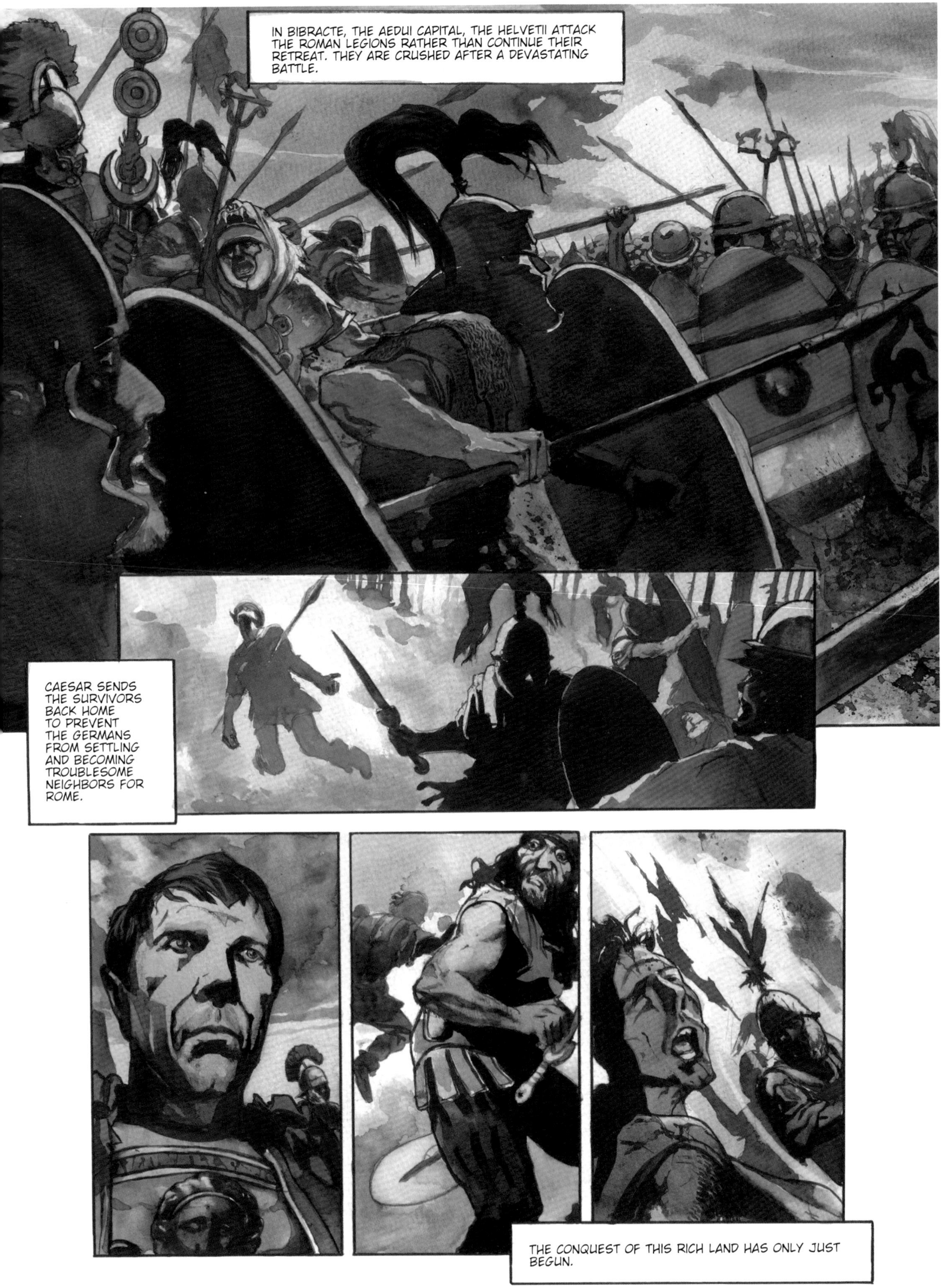
IN BIBRACTE, THE AEDUI CAPITAL, THE HELVETII ATTACK THE ROMAN LEGIONS RATHER THAN CONTINUE THEIR RETREAT. THEY ARE CRUSHED AFTER A DEVASTATING BATTLE.
CAESAR SENDS THE SURVIVORS BACK HOME TO PREVENT THE GERMANS FROM SETTLING AND BECOMING TROUBLESOME NEIGHBORS FOR ROME.
THE CONQUEST OF THIS RICH LAND HAS ONLY JUST BEGUN.

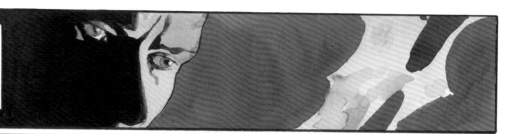

IN THE SUMMER OF 58 B.C., GAIUS JULIUS CAESAR, MEMBER OF THE RENOWNED JULII FAMILY, WHOSE ANCESTOR ASCANIUS WAS THE SON OF AENEUS, DESCENDANTS OF THE LAST TROJANS, MUST FIGHT AGAINST AN EVEN MORE THREATENING ENEMY THAN THE HELVETII...

AS PROCONSUL OF CISALPINE AND ILLYRIA, HE AGREES TO HELP THE ALLIED GALLIC TRIBES.

THE GERMAN THREAT IS CLEARLY GROWING. THEIR KING WILL SOON CROSS THE RHINE WITH A POWERFUL ARMY.

AVE CAESAR!

ONE OF OUR PATROLS HAS BEEN DECIMATED BY REBELS IN SEQUANI TERRITORY. THEY OBEY A DRUID WHO VOWS TO KILL US ALL. OUR SPIES HAVEN'T MANAGED TO GET NEAR HIM YET.

SHOULD I SEND SOLDIERS TO FIND THEM?

WE'LL TAKE CARE OF THIS TRIBE LATER, GENERAL CALPURNIUS. FOR NOW, GIVE OUR LEGIONS THE ORDER TO PREPARE FOR DEPARTURE...

9

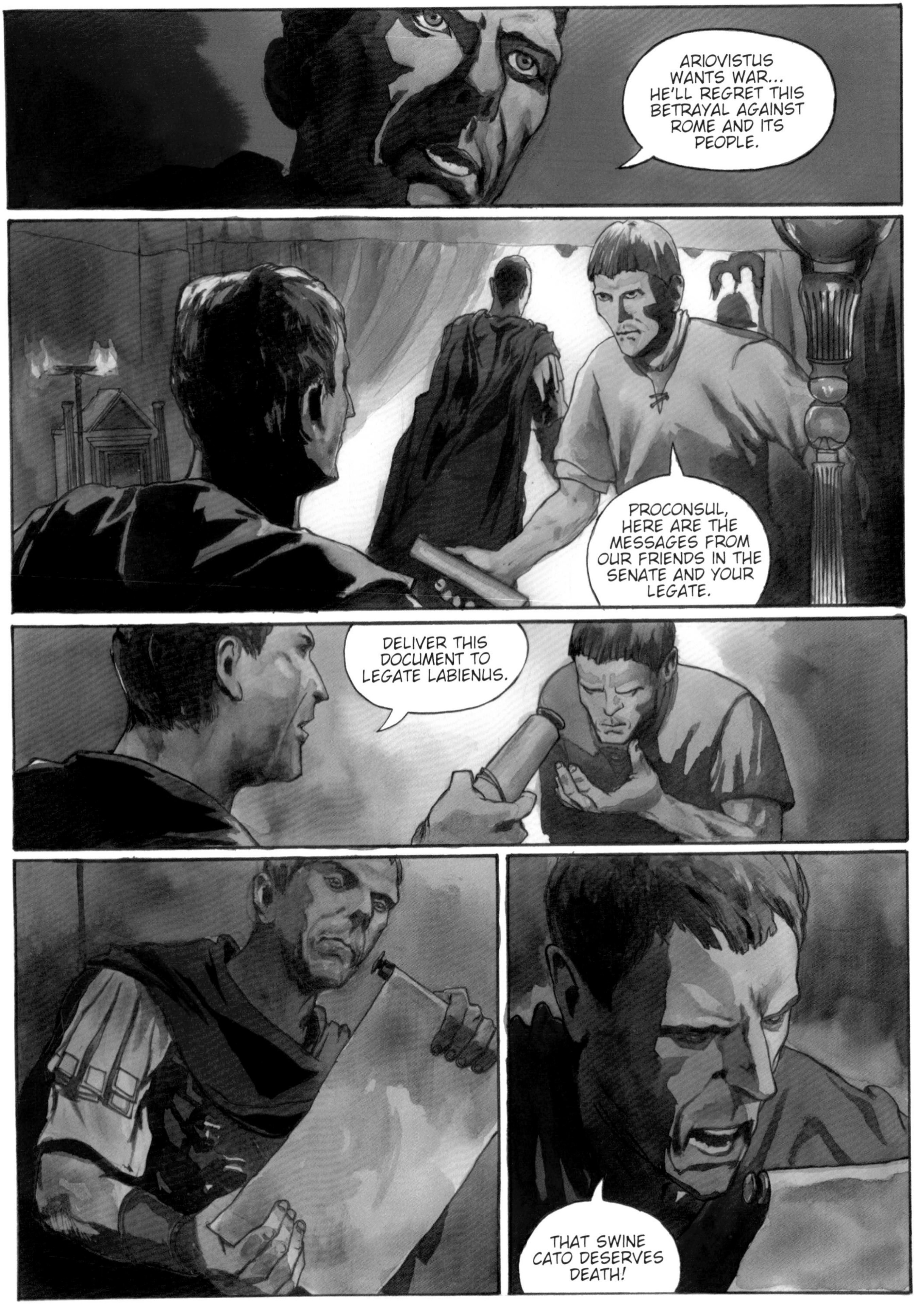
ARIOVISTUS WANTS WAR... HE'LL REGRET THIS BETRAYAL AGAINST ROME AND ITS PEOPLE.
PROCONSUL, HERE ARE THE MESSAGES FROM OUR FRIENDS IN THE SENATE AND YOUR LEGATE.
DELIVER THIS DOCUMENT TO LEGATE LABIENUS.
THAT SWINE CATO DESERVES DEATH!

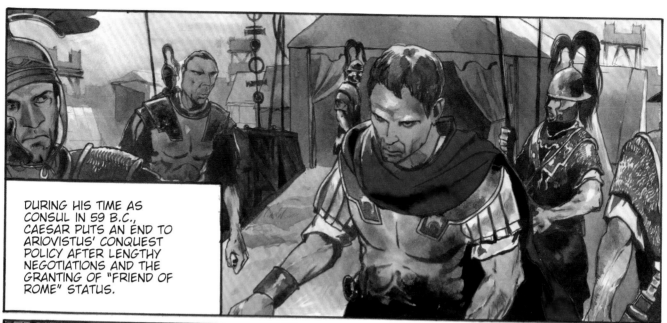

DURING HIS TIME AS CONSUL IN 59 B.C., CAESAR PUTS AN END TO ARIOVISTUS' CONQUEST POLICY AFTER LENGTHY NEGOTIATIONS AND THE GRANTING OF "FRIEND OF ROME" STATUS.

GREETINGS, CAESAR! MY WARRIORS WILL JOIN YOU IN THIS WAR AGAINST THE GERMAN INVADERS!

THE ROMAN EMBASSY FAILS. ARIOVISTUS CATEGORICALLY REFUSES THEIR REQUESTS AND EVEN ASSERTS HIS RIGHT TO CONTROL THE LANDS HE HAS CONQUERED. IN RETURN, HE RECEIVES AN ULTIMATUM. CAESAR WISHES TO PUSH HIS ENEMY INTO A DECLARATION OF WAR.

ROME COULD ALWAYS COUNT ON THE LOYALTY OF YOUR PEOPLE. YOU ARE OUR FRIENDS. WE WOULD NEVER ABANDON YOU AGAINST THIS THREAT.

YOUR TROOPS WILL FALL UNDER THE COMMAND OF LABIENUS.

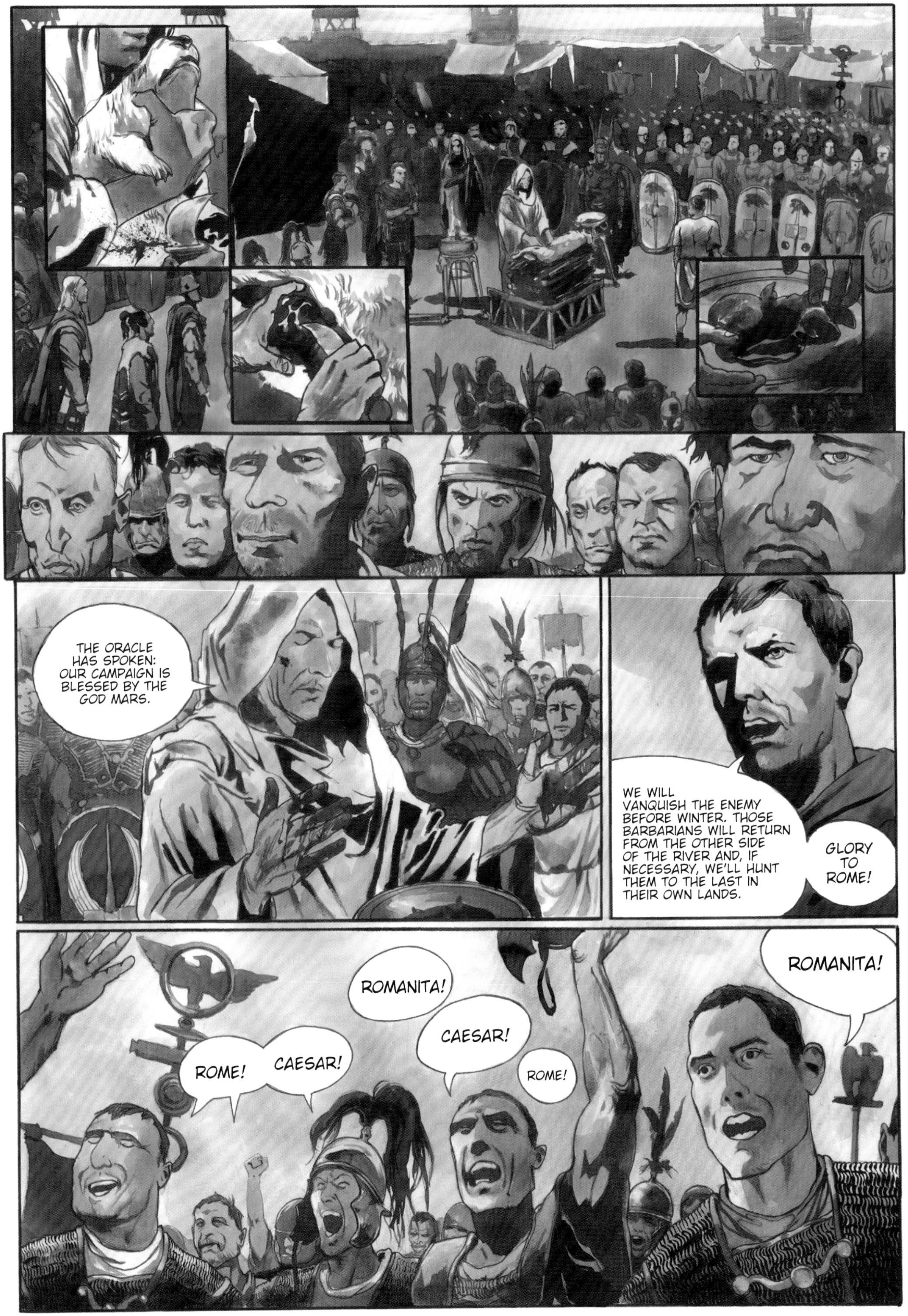
THE ORACLE HAS SPOKEN: OUR CAMPAIGN IS BLESSED BY THE GOD MARS.
WE WILL VANQUISH THE ENEMY BEFORE WINTER. THOSE BARBARIANS WILL RETURN FROM THE OTHER SIDE OF THE RIVER AND, IF NECESSARY, WE'LL HUNT THEM TO THE LAST IN THEIR OWN LANDS.
GLORY TO ROME!
ROMANITA!
ROMANITA!
CAESAR!
ROME!
CAESAR!
ROME!

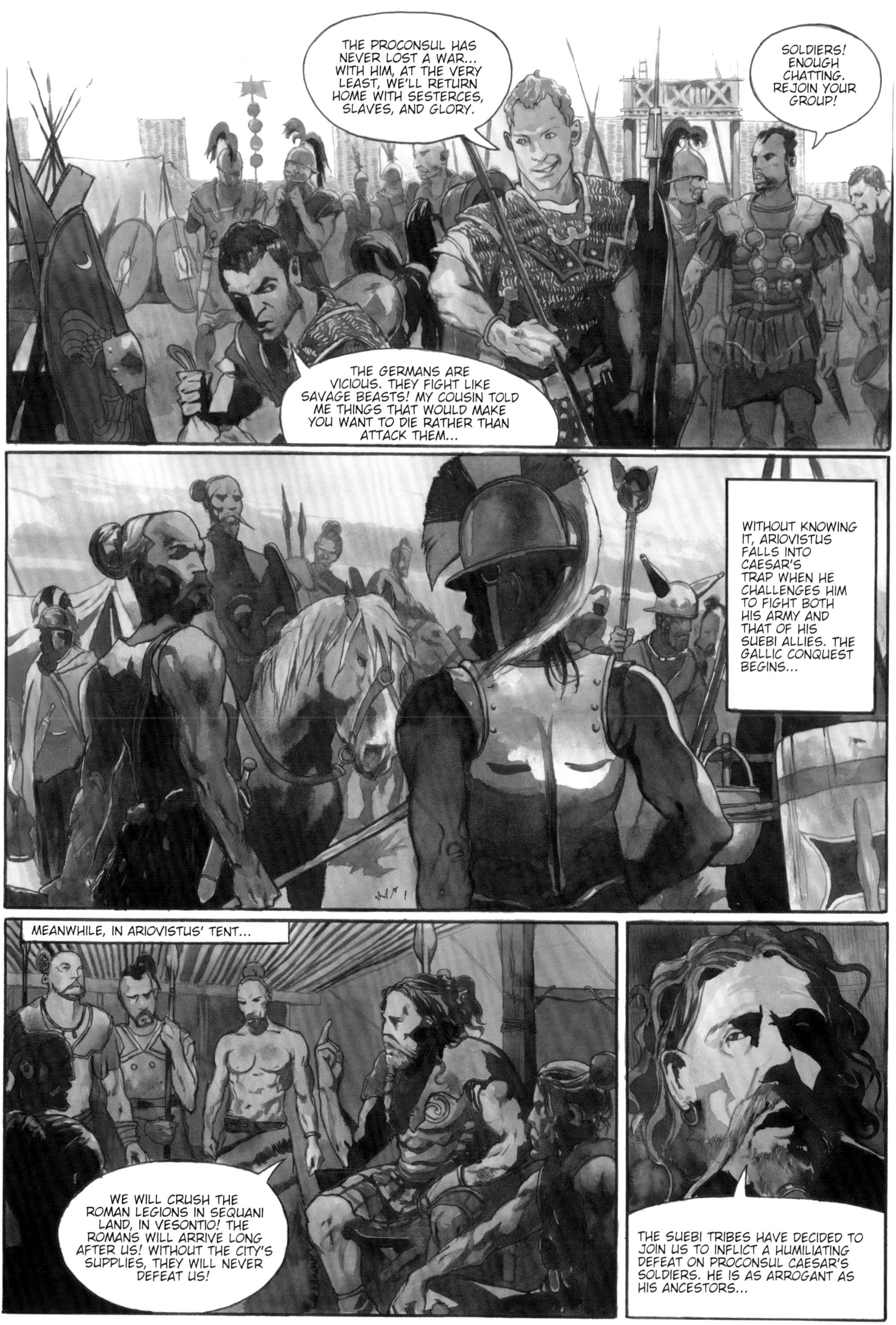
THE PROCONSUL HAS NEVER LOST A WAR... WITH HIM, AT THE VERY LEAST, WE'LL RETURN HOME WITH SESTERCES, SLAVES, AND GLORY.
SOLDIERS! ENOUGH CHATTING. REJOIN YOUR GROUP!
THE GERMANS ARE VICIOUS. THEY FIGHT LIKE SAVAGE BEASTS! MY COUSIN TOLD ME THINGS THAT WOULD MAKE YOU WANT TO DIE RATHER THAN ATTACK THEM...
WITHOUT KNOWING IT, ARIOVISTUS FALLS INTO CAESAR'S TRAP WHEN HE CHALLENGES HIM TO FIGHT BOTH HIS ARMY AND THAT OF HIS SUEBI ALLIES. THE GALLIC CONQUEST BEGINS...
MEANWHILE, IN ARIOVISTUS' TENT...
WE WILL CRUSH THE ROMAN LEGIONS IN SEQUANI LAND, IN VESONTIO! THE ROMANS WILL ARRIVE LONG AFTER US! WITHOUT THE CITY'S SUPPLIES, THEY WILL NEVER DEFEAT US!
THE SUEBI TRIBES HAVE DECIDED TO JOIN US TO INFLICT A HUMILIATING DEFEAT ON PROCONSUL CAESAR'S SOLDIERS. HE IS AS ARROGANT AS HIS ANCESTORS...

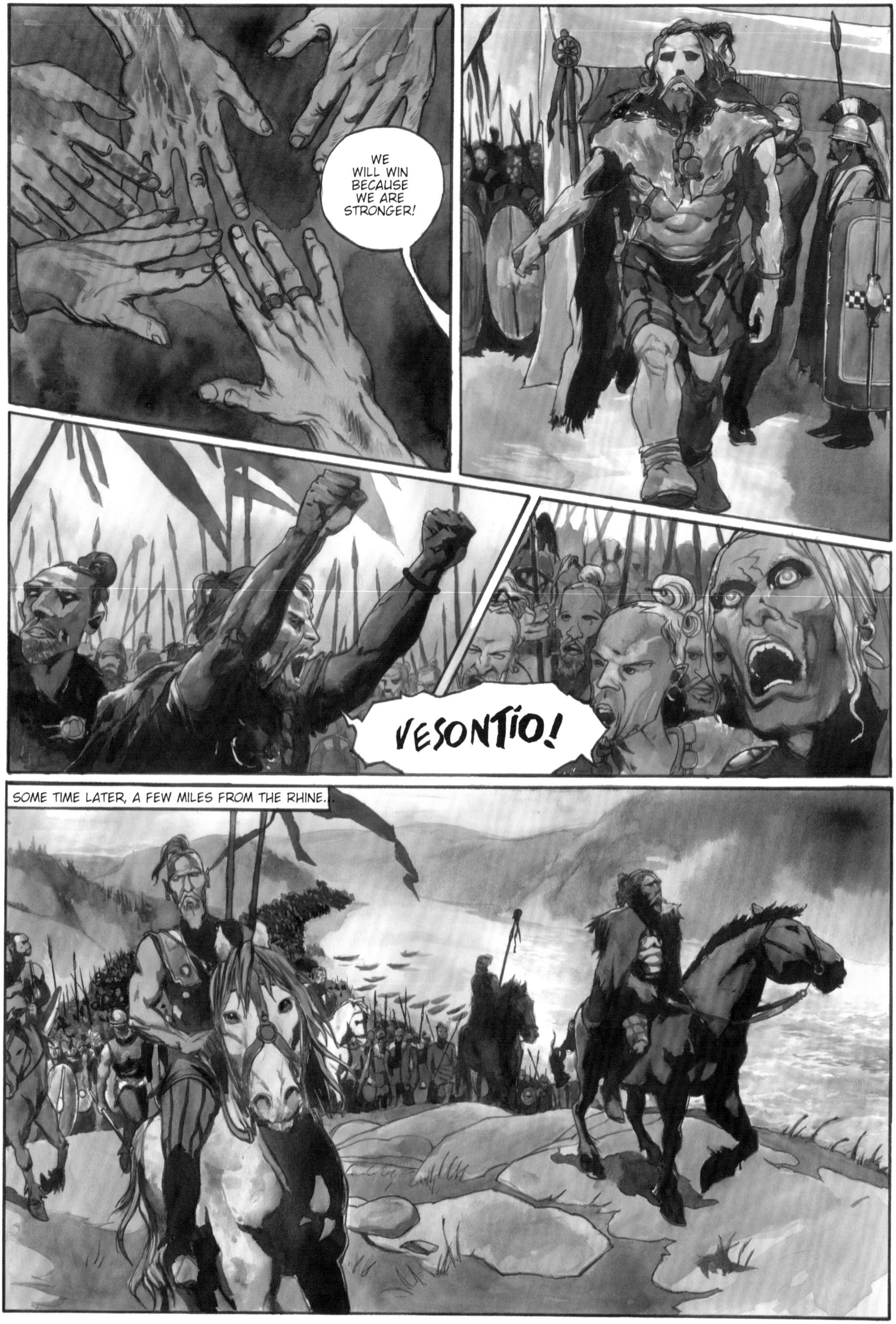
WE WILL WIN BECAUSE WE ARE STRONGER!
VESONTIO!
SOME TIME LATER, A FEW MILES FROM THE RHINE...

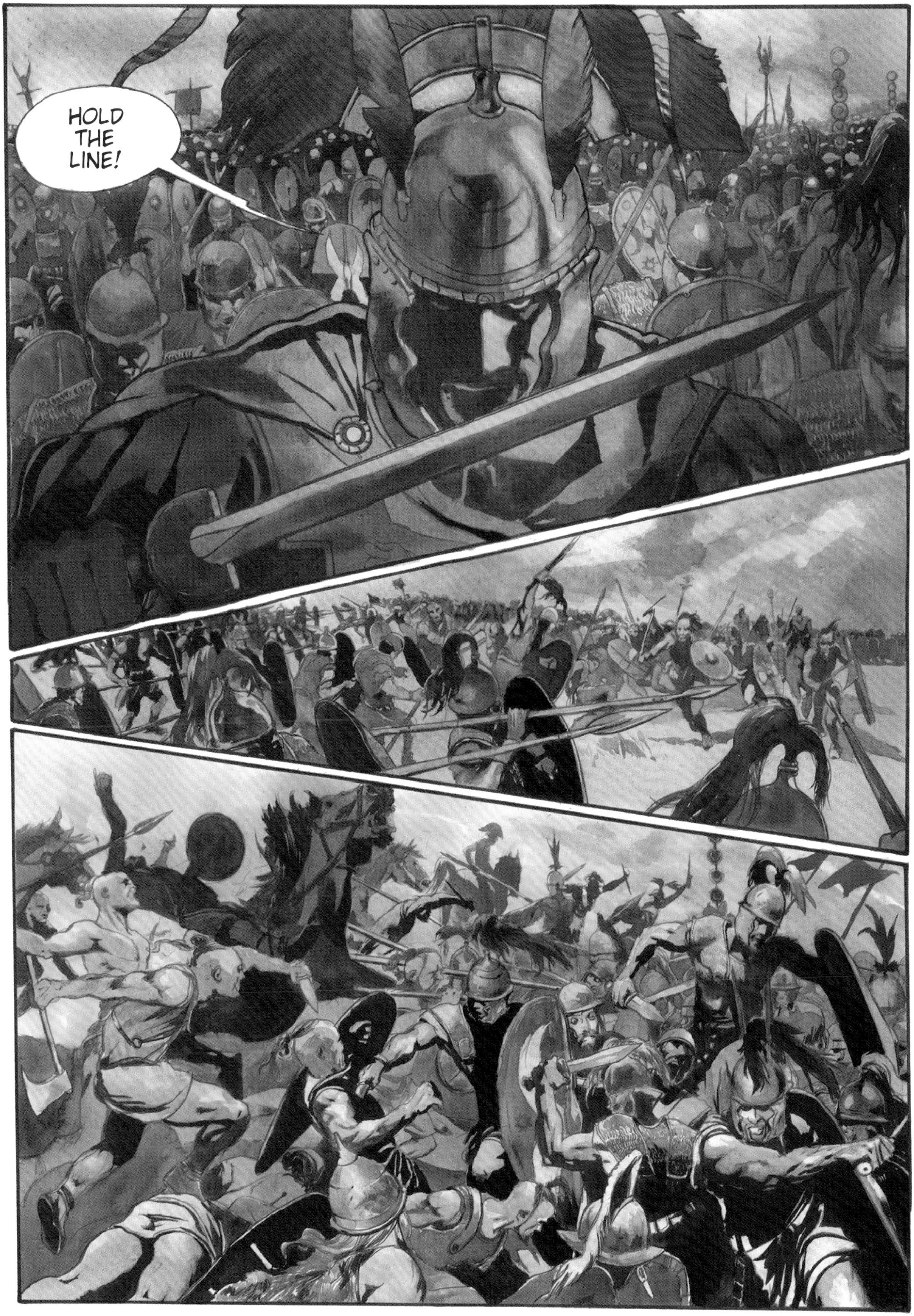
HOLD THE LINE!

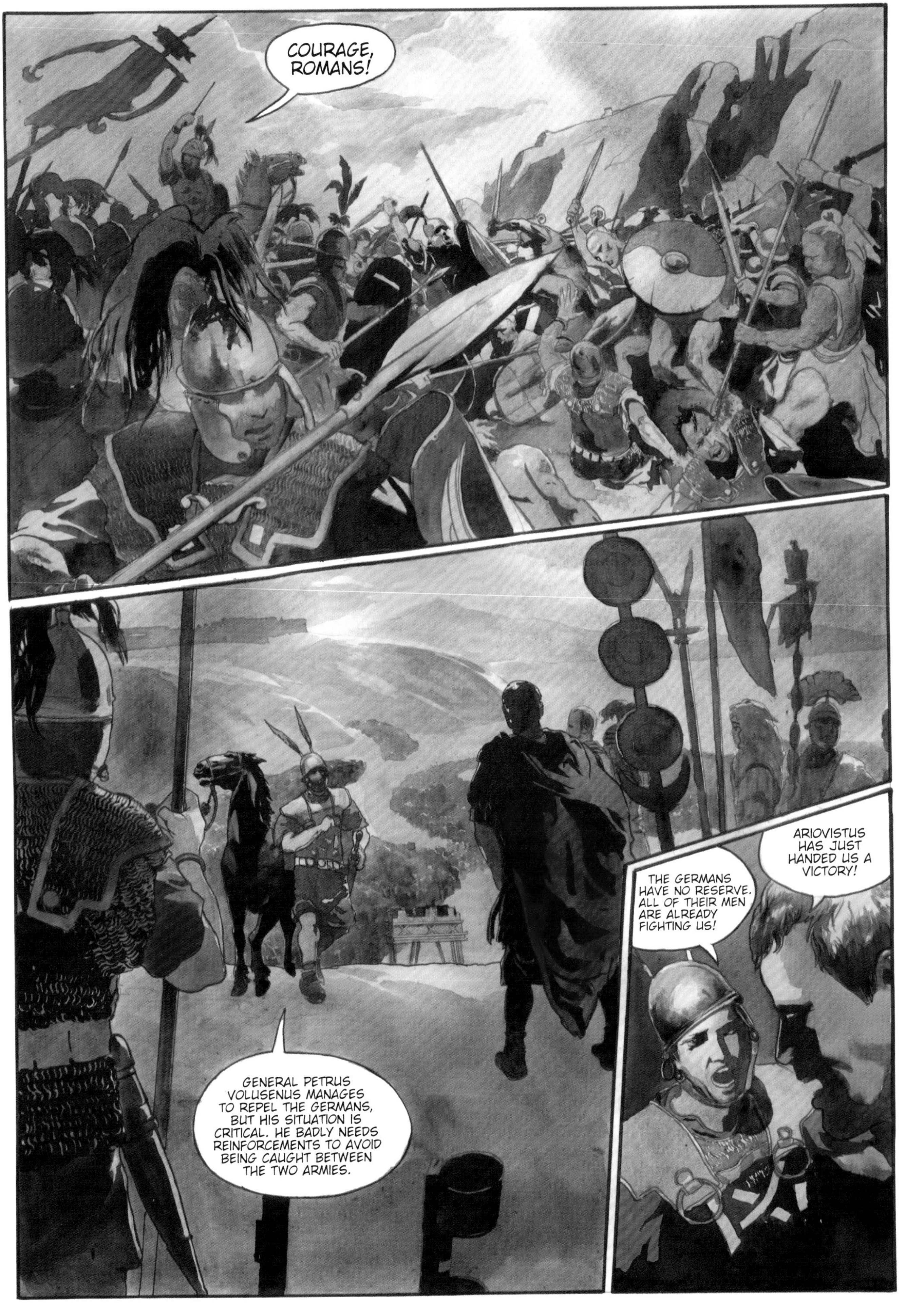
COURAGE, ROMANS!
GENERAL PETRUS VOLUSENUS MANAGES TO REPEL THE GERMANS, BUT HIS SITUATION IS CRITICAL. HE BADLY NEEDS REINFORCEMENTS TO AVOID BEING CAUGHT BETWEEN THE TWO ARMIES.
ARIOVISTUS HAS JUST HANDED US A VICTORY!
THE GERMANS HAVE NO RESERVE. ALL OF THEIR MEN ARE ALREADY FIGHTING US!

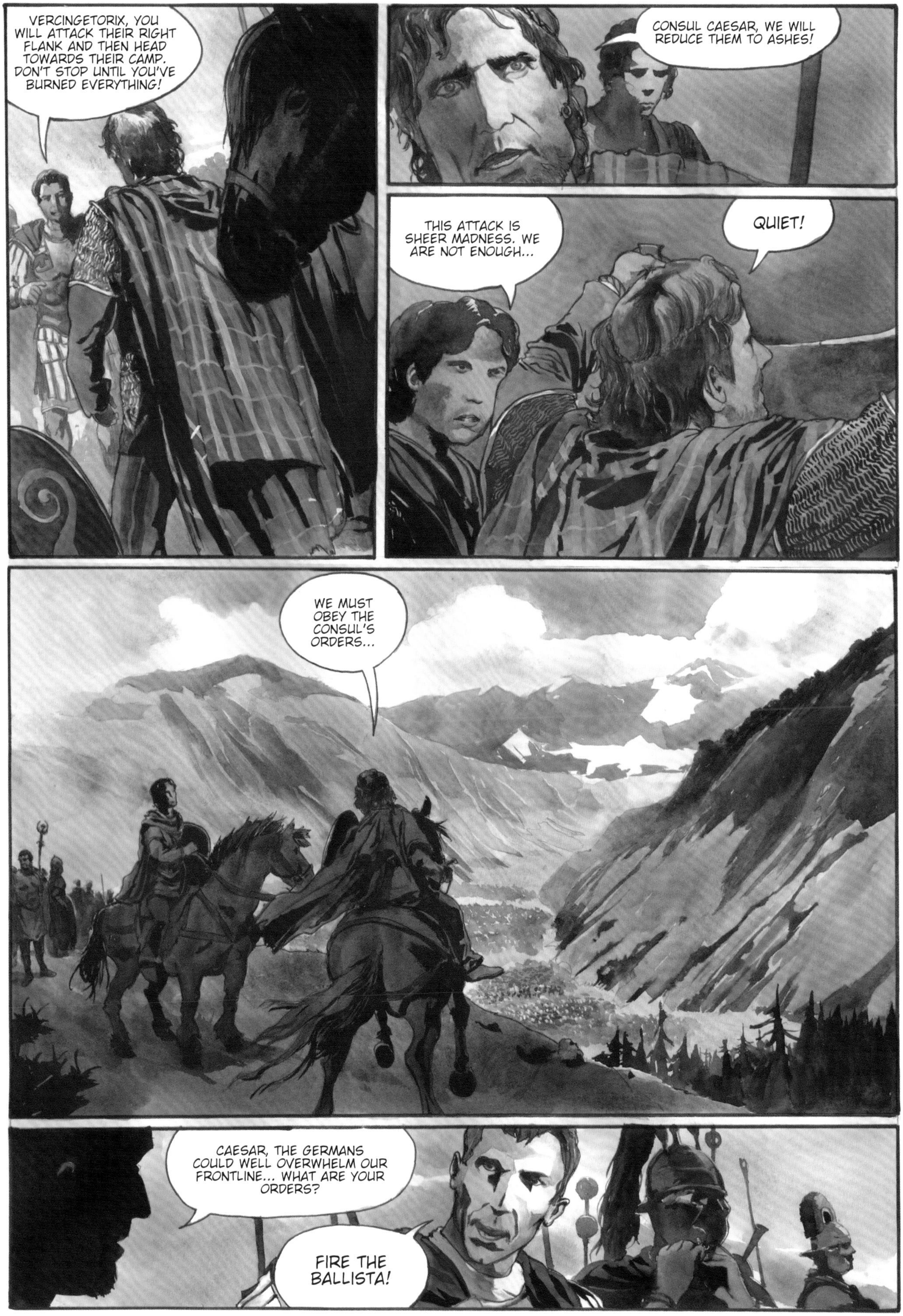
VERCINGETORIX, YOU WILL ATTACK THEIR RIGHT FLANK AND THEN HEAD TOWARDS THEIR CAMP. DON'T STOP UNTIL YOU'VE BURNED EVERYTHING!
CONSUL CAESAR, WE WILL REDUCE THEM TO ASHES!
THIS ATTACK IS SHEER MADNESS. WE ARE NOT ENOUGH...
QUIET!
WE MUST OBEY THE CONSUL'S ORDERS...
CAESAR, THE GERMANS COULD WELL OVERWHELM OUR FRONTLINE... WHAT ARE YOUR ORDERS?
FIRE THE BALLISTA!

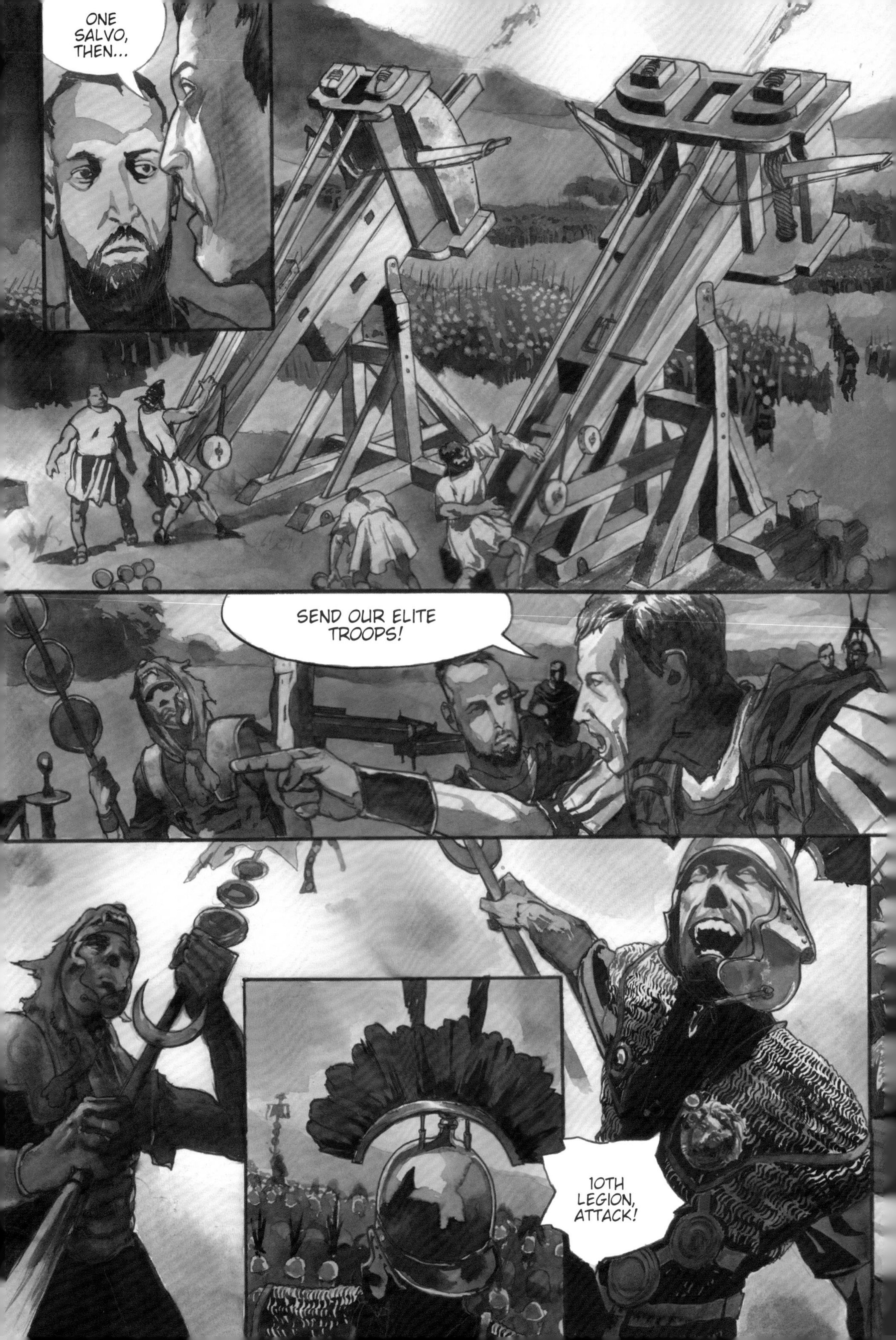
ONE SALVO, THEN...
SEND OUR ELITE TROOPS!
10TH LEGION, ATTACK!

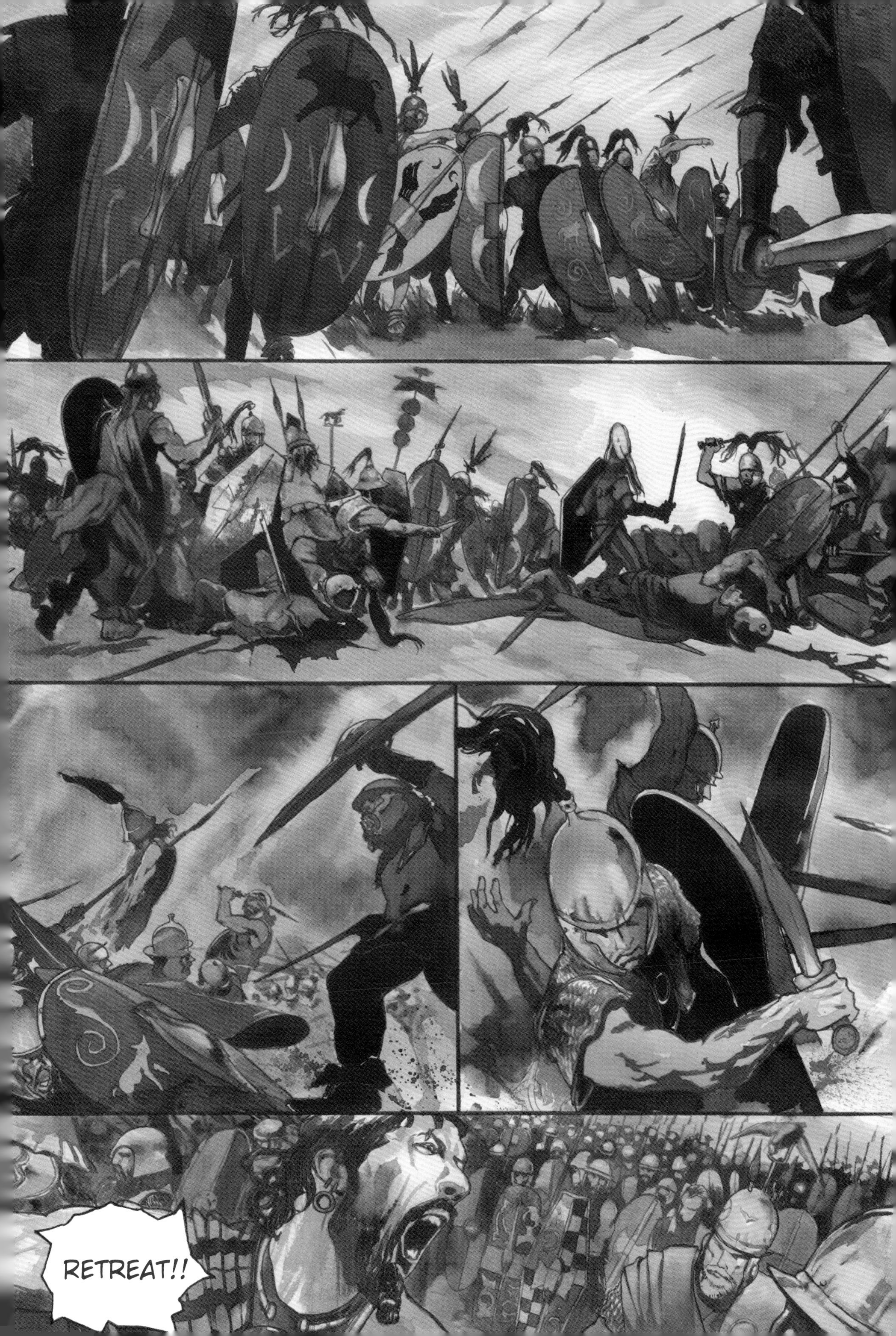
RETREAT!!

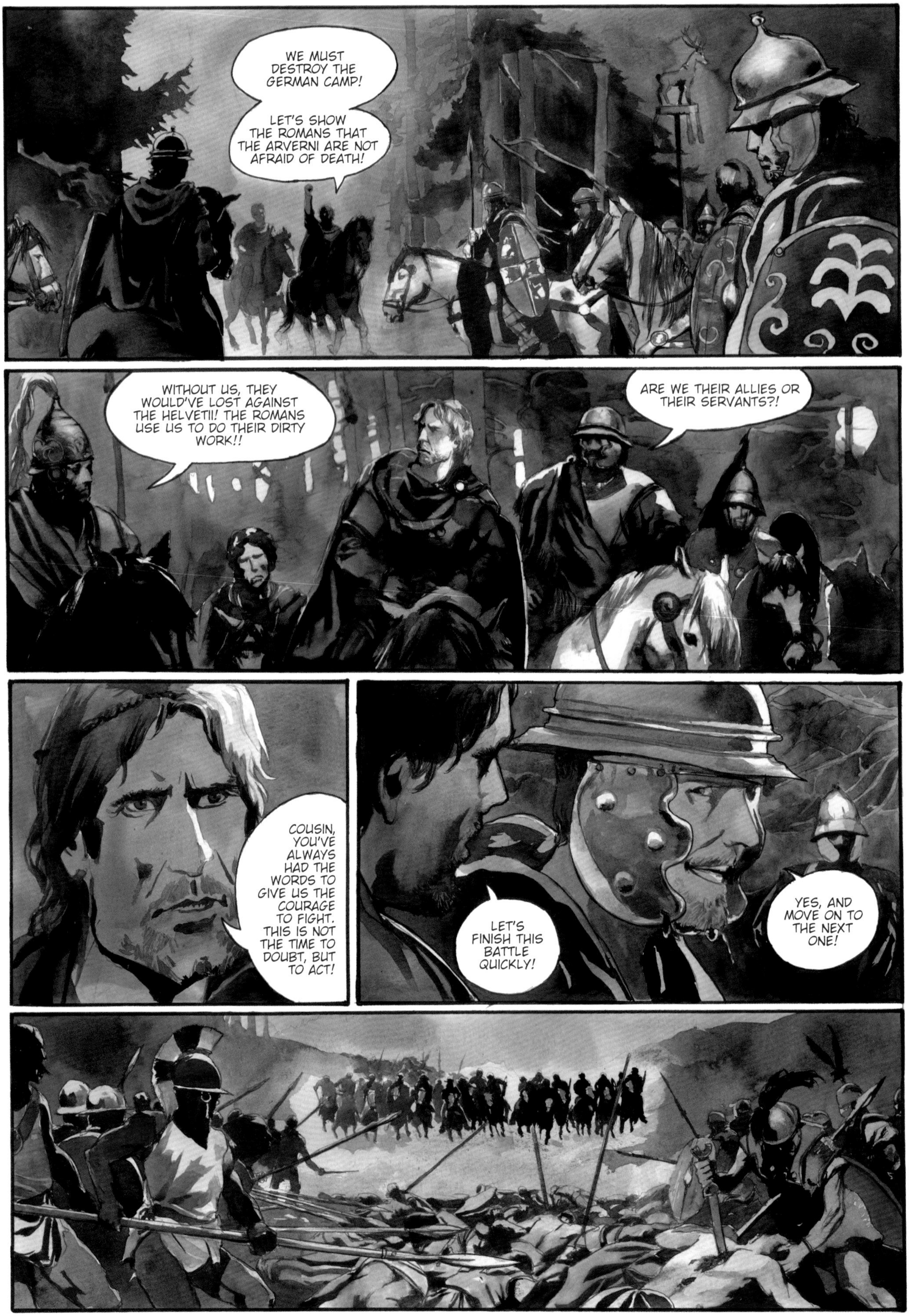
WE MUST DESTROY THE GERMAN CAMP!
LET'S SHOW THE ROMANS THAT THE ARVERNI ARE NOT AFRAID OF DEATH!
WITHOUT US, THEY WOULD'VE LOST AGAINST THE HELVETII! THE ROMANS USE US TO DO THEIR DIRTY WORK!!
ARE WE THEIR ALLIES OR THEIR SERVANTS?!
COUSIN, YOU'VE ALWAYS HAD THE WORDS TO GIVE US THE COURAGE TO FIGHT. THIS IS NOT THE TIME TO DOUBT, BUT TO ACT!
LET'S FINISH THIS BATTLE QUICKLY!
YES, AND MOVE ON TO THE NEXT ONE!

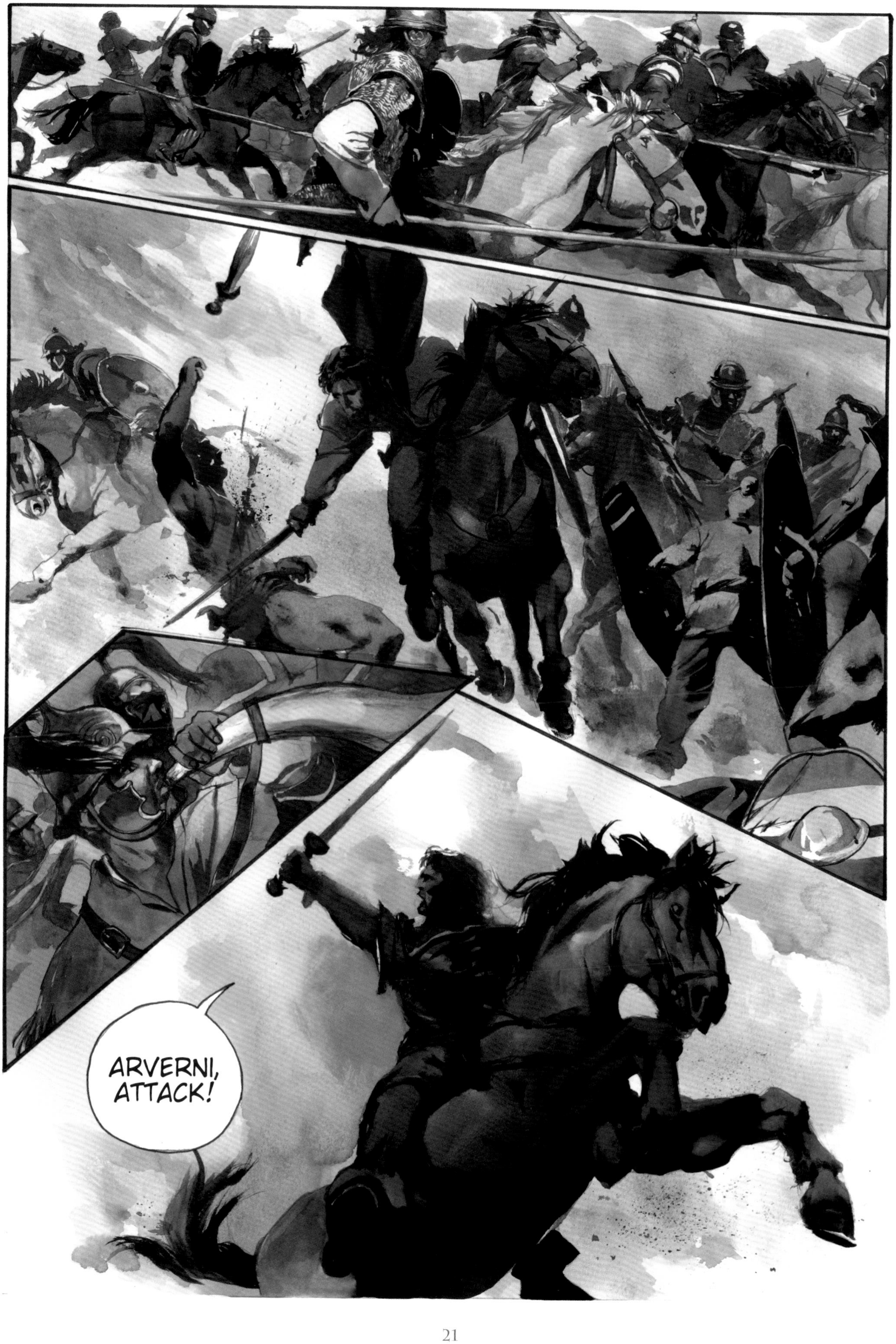
ARVERNI, ATTACK!

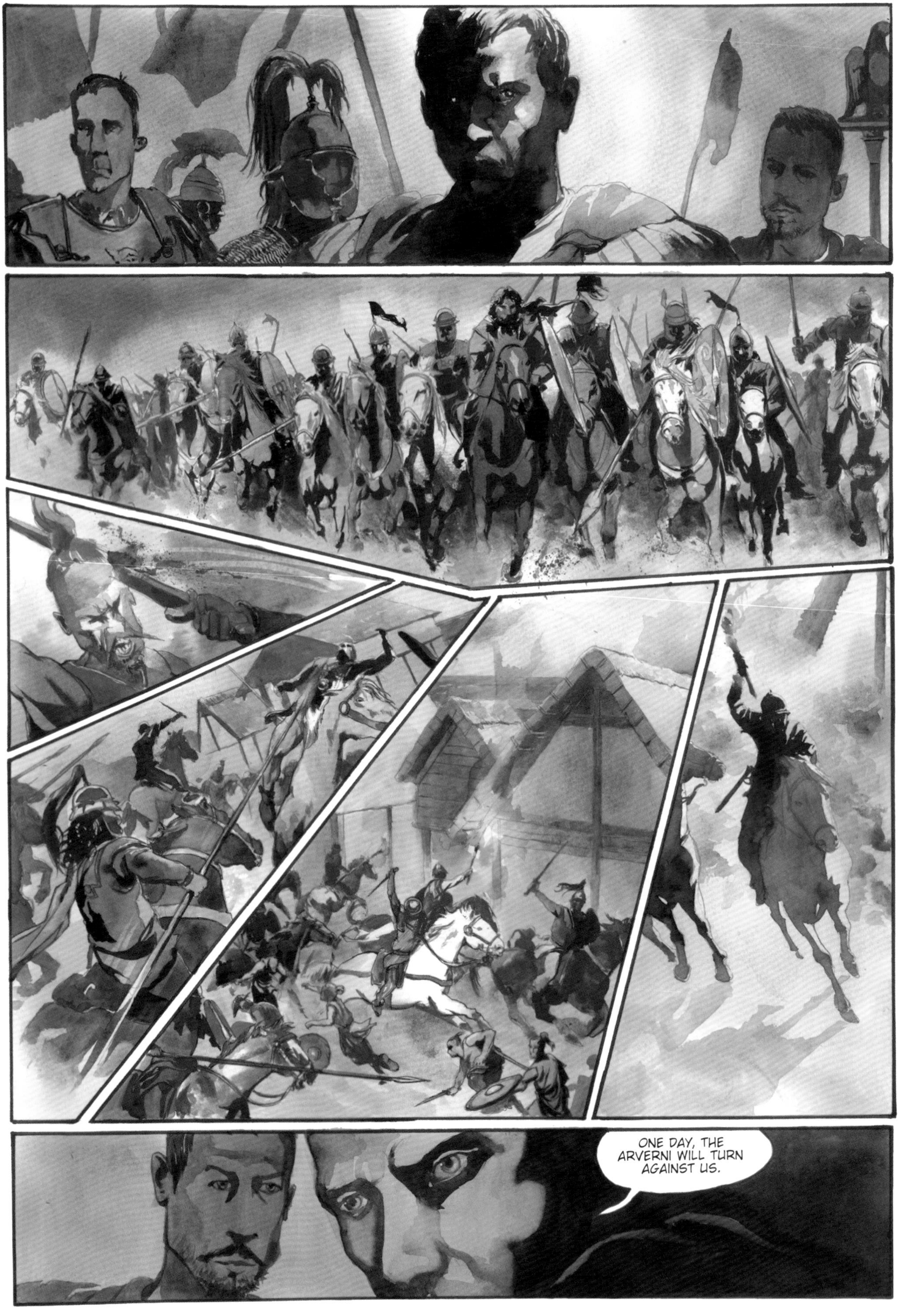
ONE DAY, THE ARVERNI WILL TURN AGAINST US.

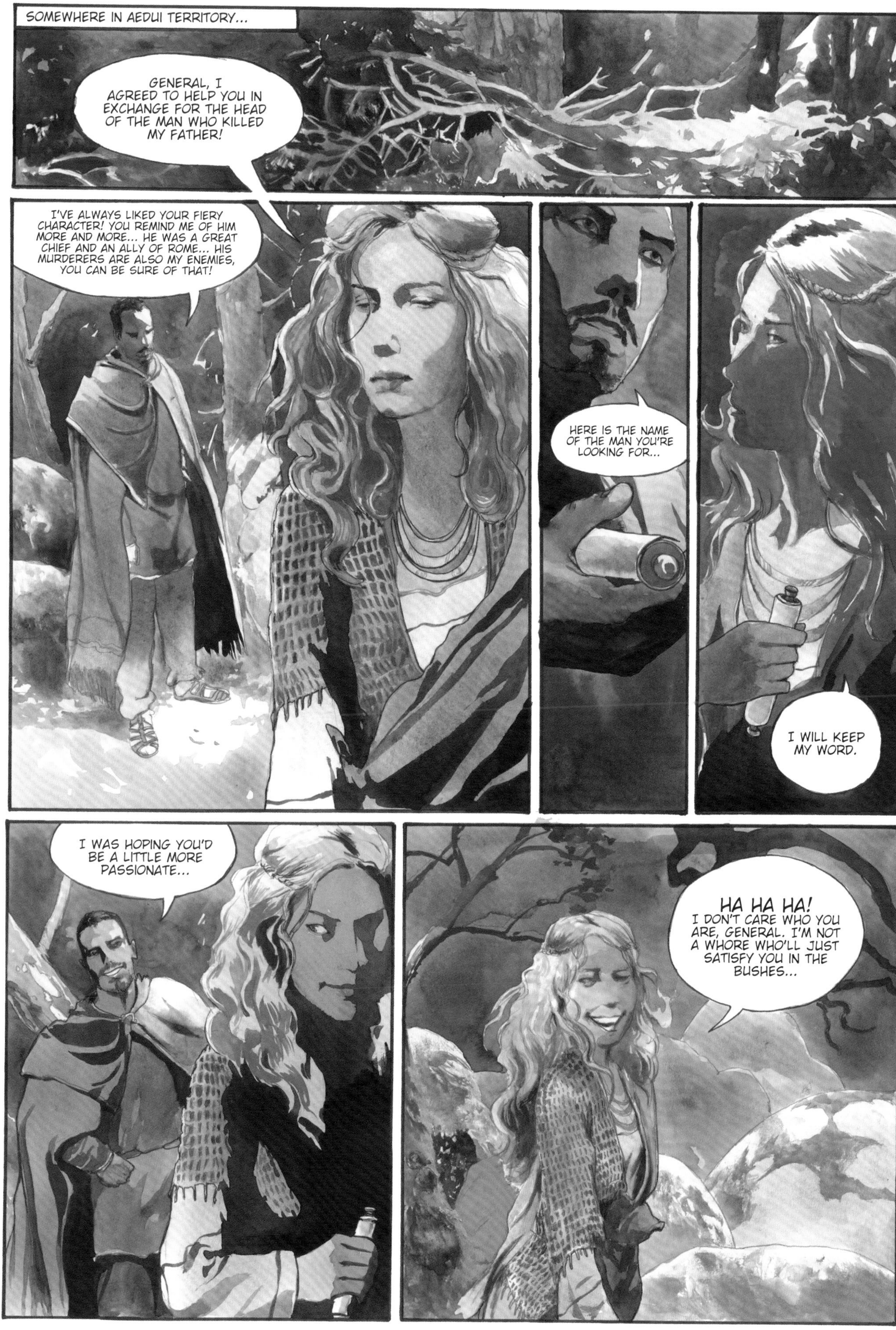
SOMEWHERE IN AEDUI TERRITORY...
GENERAL, I AGREED TO HELP YOU IN EXCHANGE FOR THE HEAD OF THE MAN WHO KILLED MY FATHER!
I'VE ALWAYS LIKED YOUR FIERY CHARACTER! YOU REMIND ME OF HIM MORE AND MORE... HE WAS A GREAT CHIEF AND AN ALLY OF ROME... HIS MURDERERS ARE ALSO MY ENEMIES, YOU CAN BE SURE OF THAT!
HERE IS THE NAME OF THE MAN YOU'RE LOOKING FOR...
I WILL KEEP MY WORD.
I WAS HOPING YOU'D BE A LITTLE MORE PASSIONATE...
HA HA HA! I DON'T CARE WHO YOU ARE, GENERAL. I'M NOT A WHORE WHO'LL JUST SATISFY YOU IN THE BUSHES...

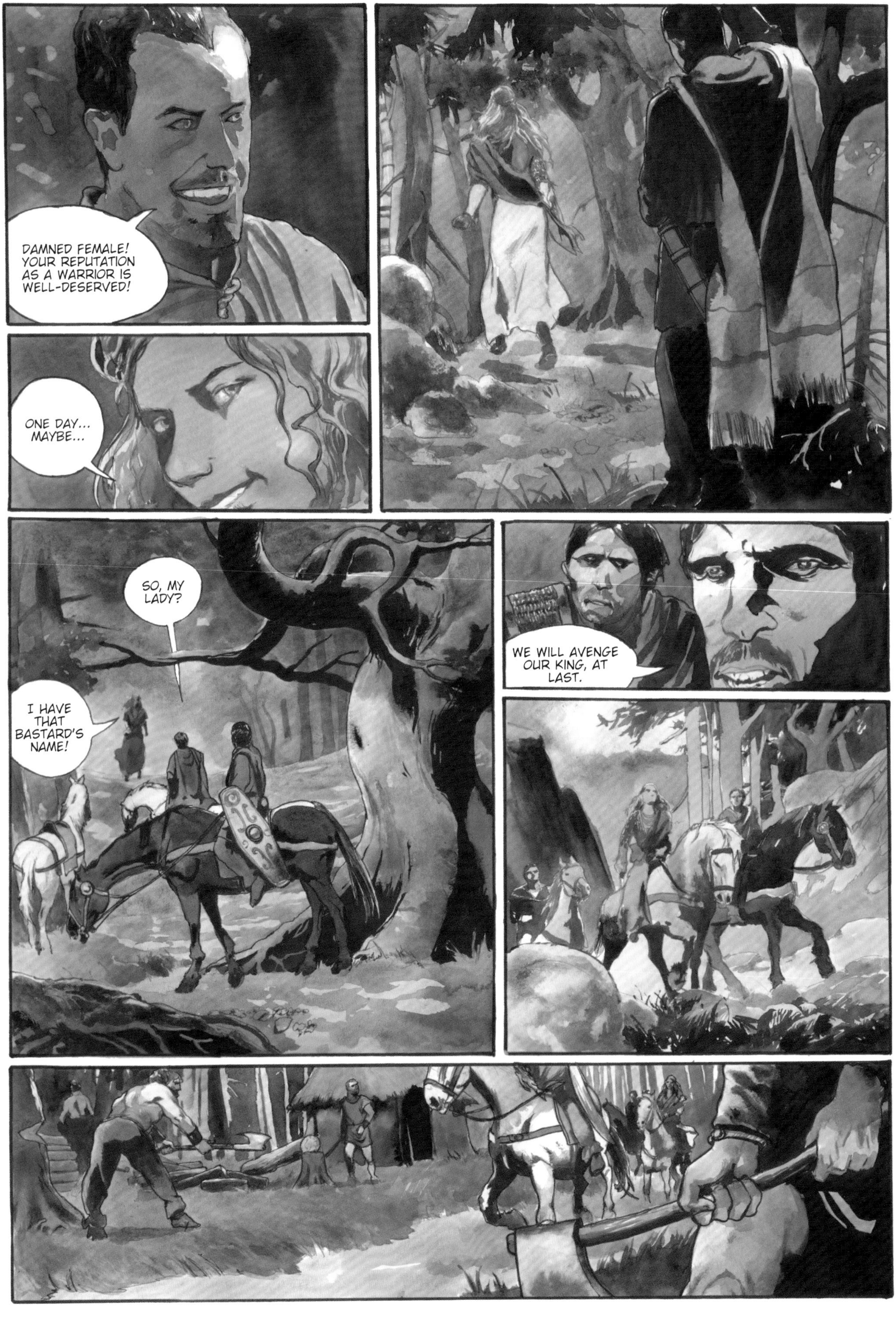
DAMNED FEMALE! YOUR REPUTATION AS A WARRIOR IS WELL-DESERVED!
ONE DAY... MAYBE...
SO, MY LADY?
I HAVE THAT BASTARD'S NAME!
WE WILL AVENGE OUR KING, AT LAST.

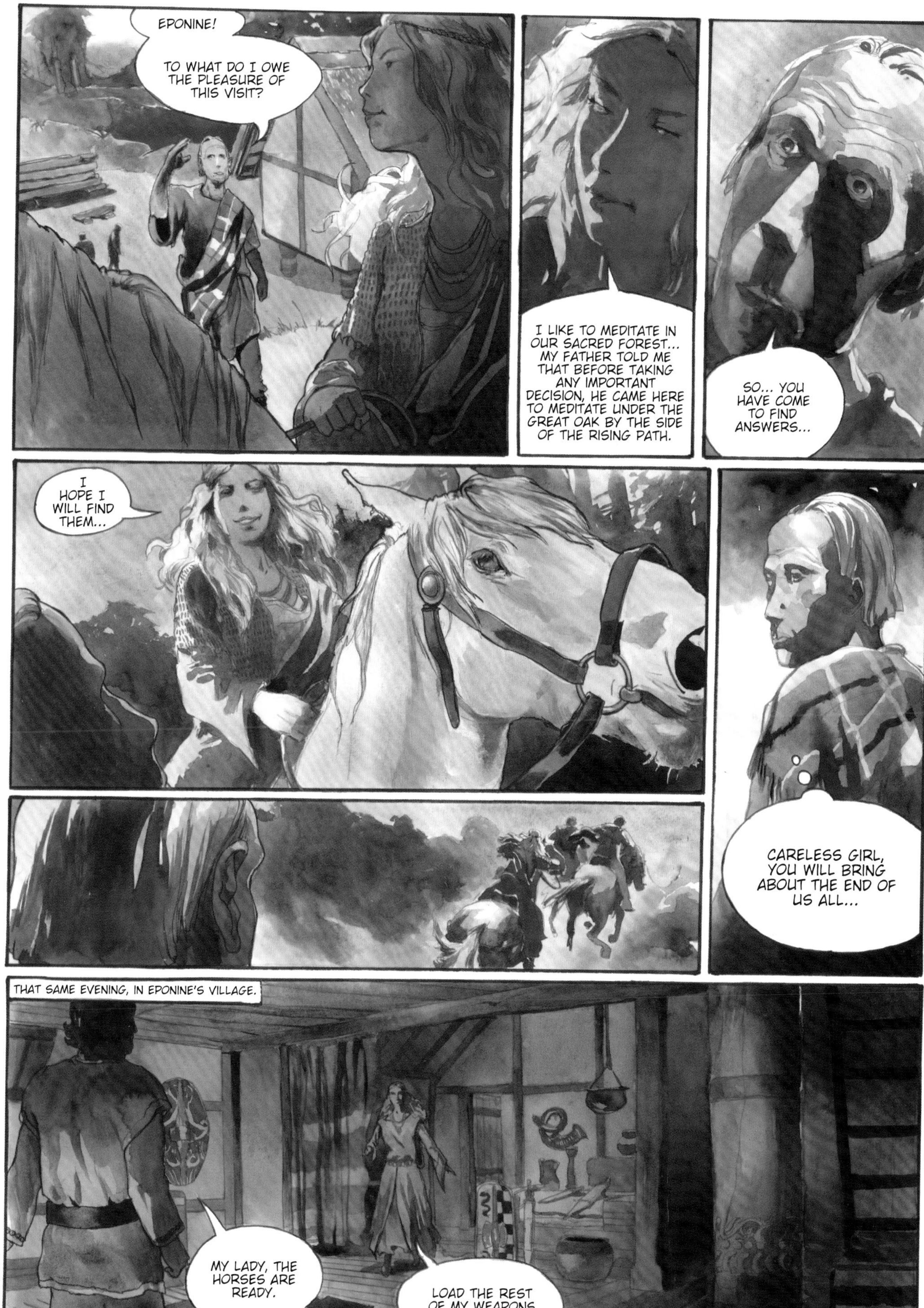
EPONINE!
TO WHAT DO I OWE THE PLEASURE OF THIS VISIT?
I LIKE TO MEDITATE IN OUR SACRED FOREST... MY FATHER TOLD ME THAT BEFORE TAKING ANY IMPORTANT DECISION, HE CAME HERE TO MEDITATE UNDER THE GREAT OAK BY THE SIDE OF THE RISING PATH.
SO... YOU HAVE COME TO FIND ANSWERS...
I HOPE I WILL FIND THEM...
CARELESS GIRL, YOU WILL BRING ABOUT THE END OF US ALL...
THAT SAME EVENING, IN EPONINE'S VILLAGE.
MY LADY, THE HORSES ARE READY.
LOAD THE REST OF MY WEAPONS ON THE MULE!

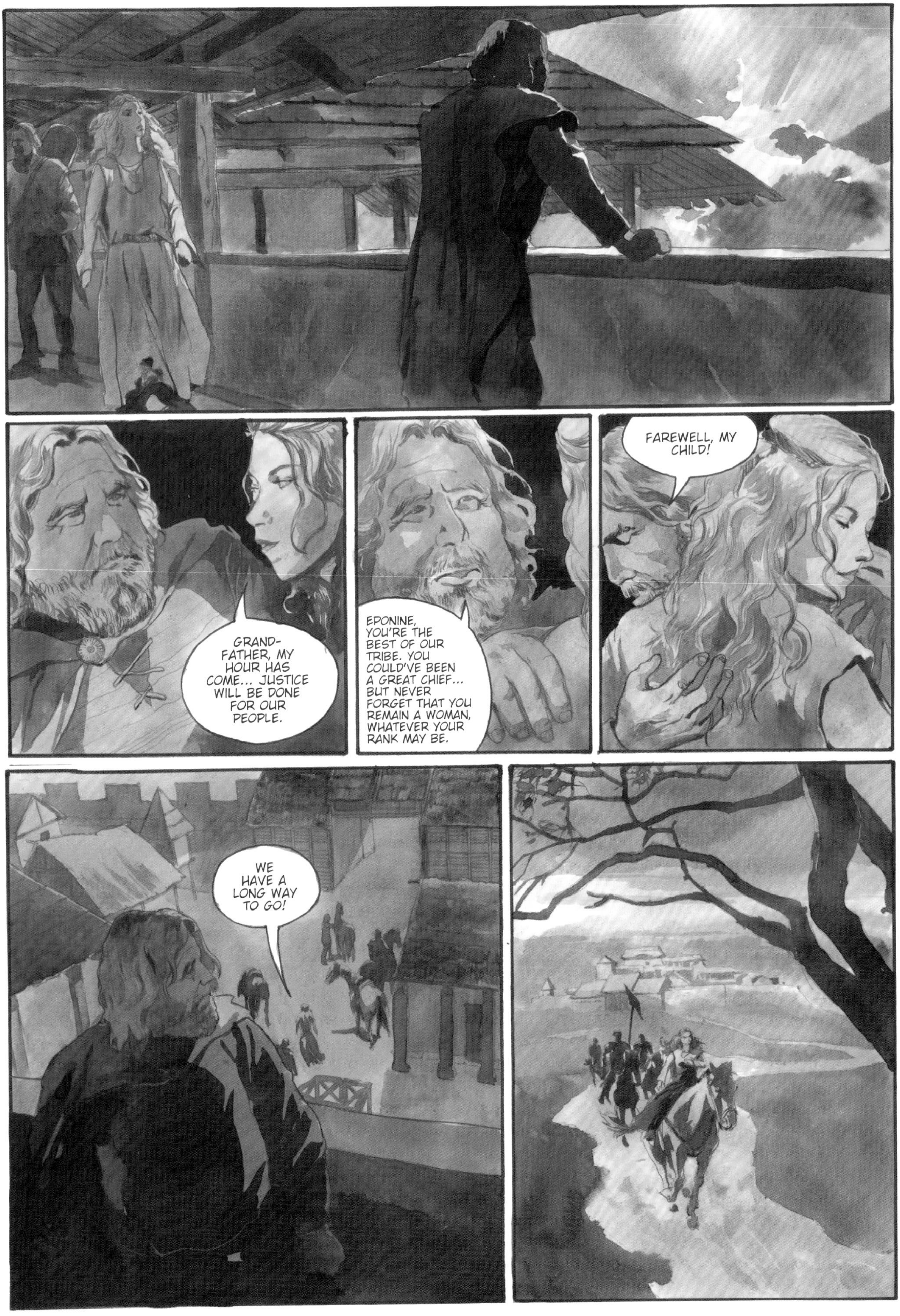
GRAND-FATHER, MY HOUR HAS COME... JUSTICE WILL BE DONE FOR OUR PEOPLE.
EPONINE, YOU'RE THE BEST OF OUR TRIBE. YOU COULD'VE BEEN A GREAT CHIEF... BUT NEVER FORGET THAT YOU REMAIN A WOMAN, WHATEVER YOUR RANK MAY BE.
FAREWELL, MY CHILD!
WE HAVE A LONG WAY TO GO!

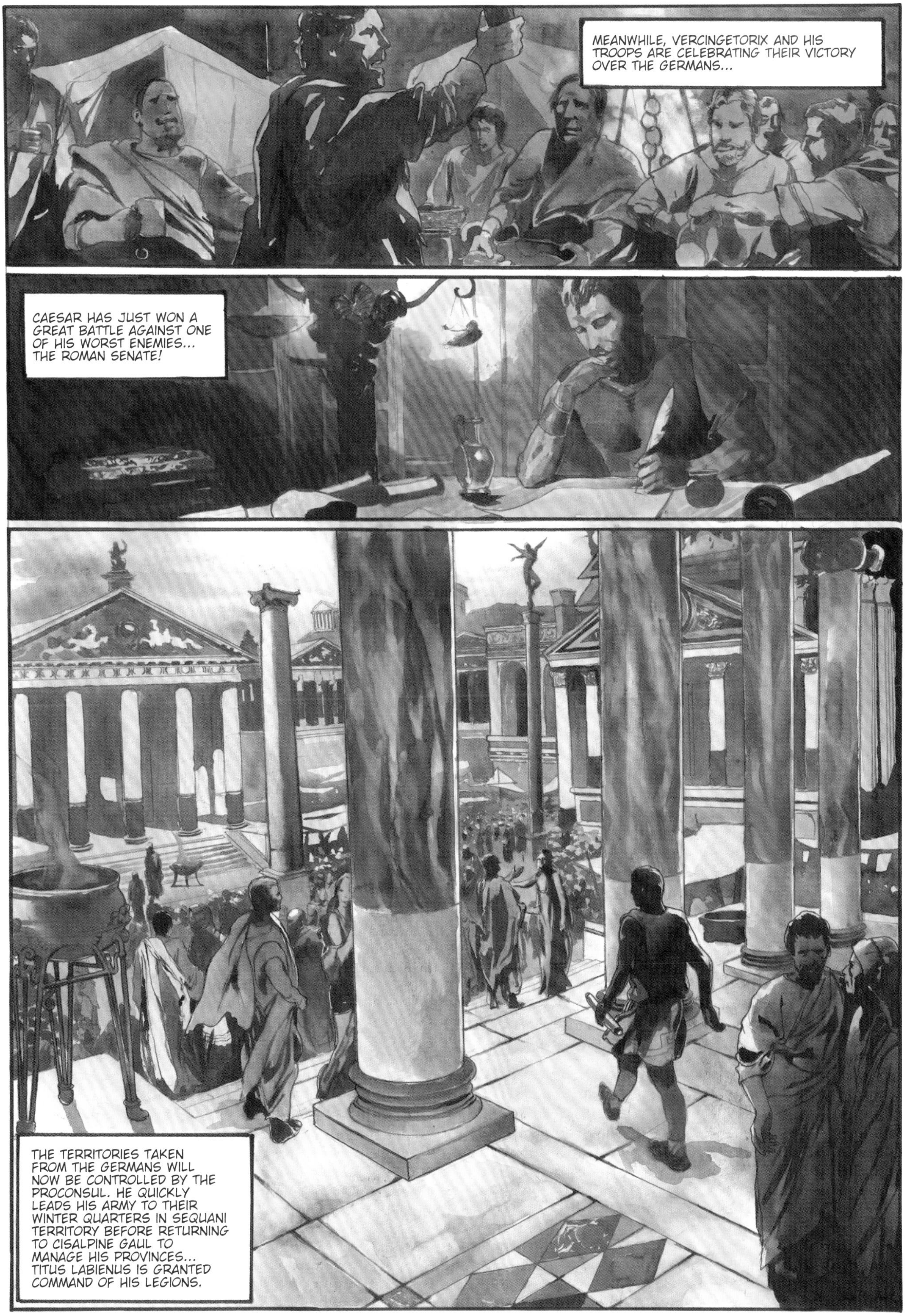
MEANWHILE, VERCINGETORIX AND HIS TROOPS ARE CELEBRATING THEIR VICTORY OVER THE GERMANS...
CAESAR HAS JUST WON A GREAT BATTLE AGAINST ONE OF HIS WORST ENEMIES... THE ROMAN SENATE!
THE TERRITORIES TAKEN FROM THE GERMANS WILL NOW BE CONTROLLED BY THE PROCONSUL. HE QUICKLY LEADS HIS ARMY TO THEIR WINTER QUARTERS IN SEQUANI TERRITORY BEFORE RETURNING TO CISALPINE GAUL TO MANAGE HIS PROVINCES... TITUS LABIENUS IS GRANTED COMMAND OF HIS LEGIONS.

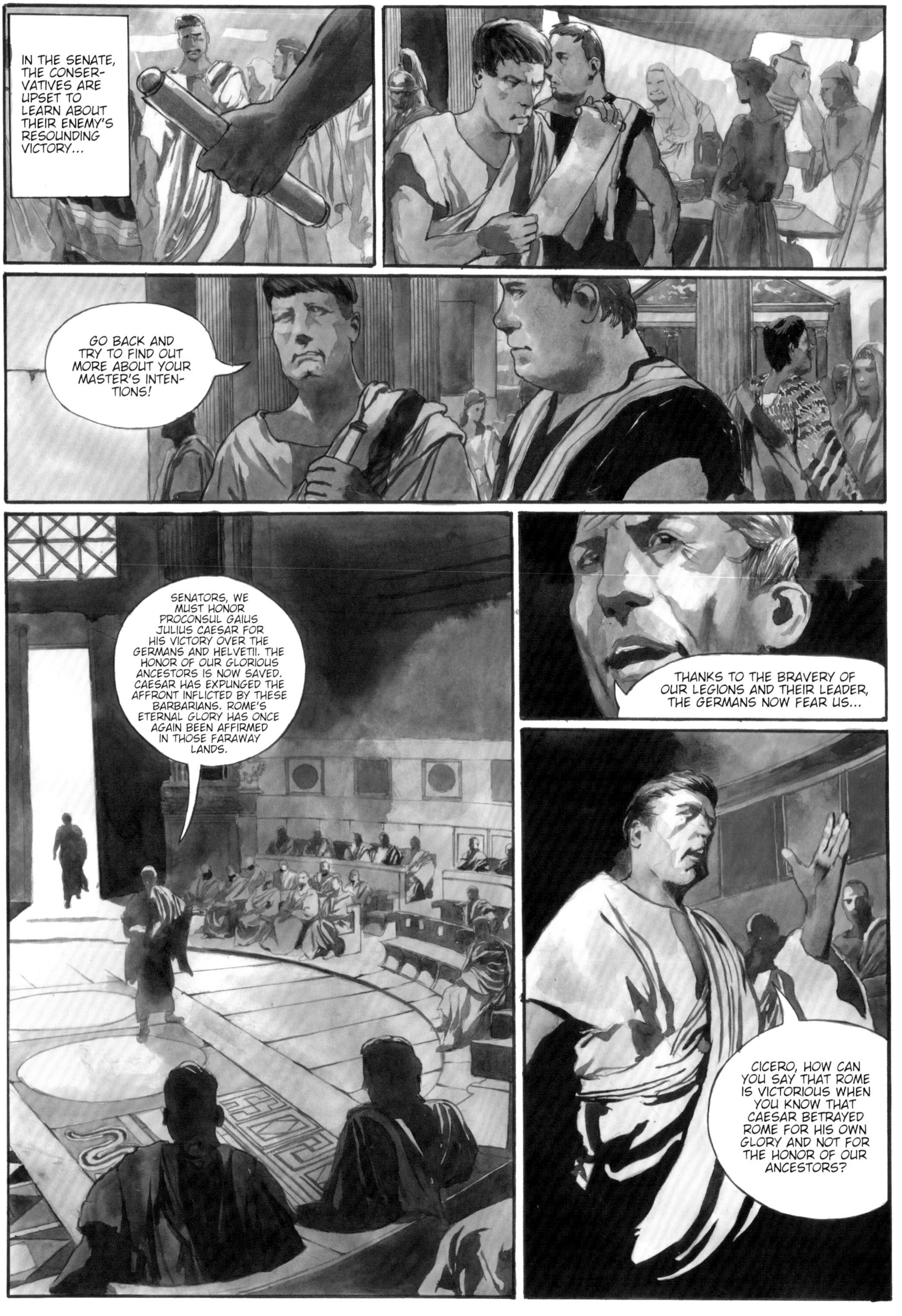
IN THE SENATE, THE CONSERVATIVES ARE UPSET TO LEARN ABOUT THEIR ENEMY'S RESOUNDING VICTORY...
GO BACK AND TRY TO FIND OUT MORE ABOUT YOUR MASTER'S INTENTIONS!
SENATORS, WE MUST HONOR PROCONSUL GAIUS JULIUS CAESAR FOR HIS VICTORY OVER THE GERMANS AND HELVETII. THE HONOR OF OUR GLORIOUS ANCESTORS IS NOW SAVED. CAESAR HAS EXPUNGED THE AFFRONT INFLICTED BY THESE BARBARIANS. ROME'S ETERNAL GLORY HAS ONCE AGAIN BEEN AFFIRMED IN THOSE FARAWAY LANDS.
THANKS TO THE BRAVERY OF OUR LEGIONS AND THEIR LEADER, THE GERMANS NOW FEAR US...
CICERO, HOW CAN YOU SAY THAT ROME IS VICTORIOUS WHEN YOU KNOW THAT CAESAR BETRAYED ROME FOR HIS OWN GLORY AND NOT FOR THE HONOR OF OUR ANCESTORS?

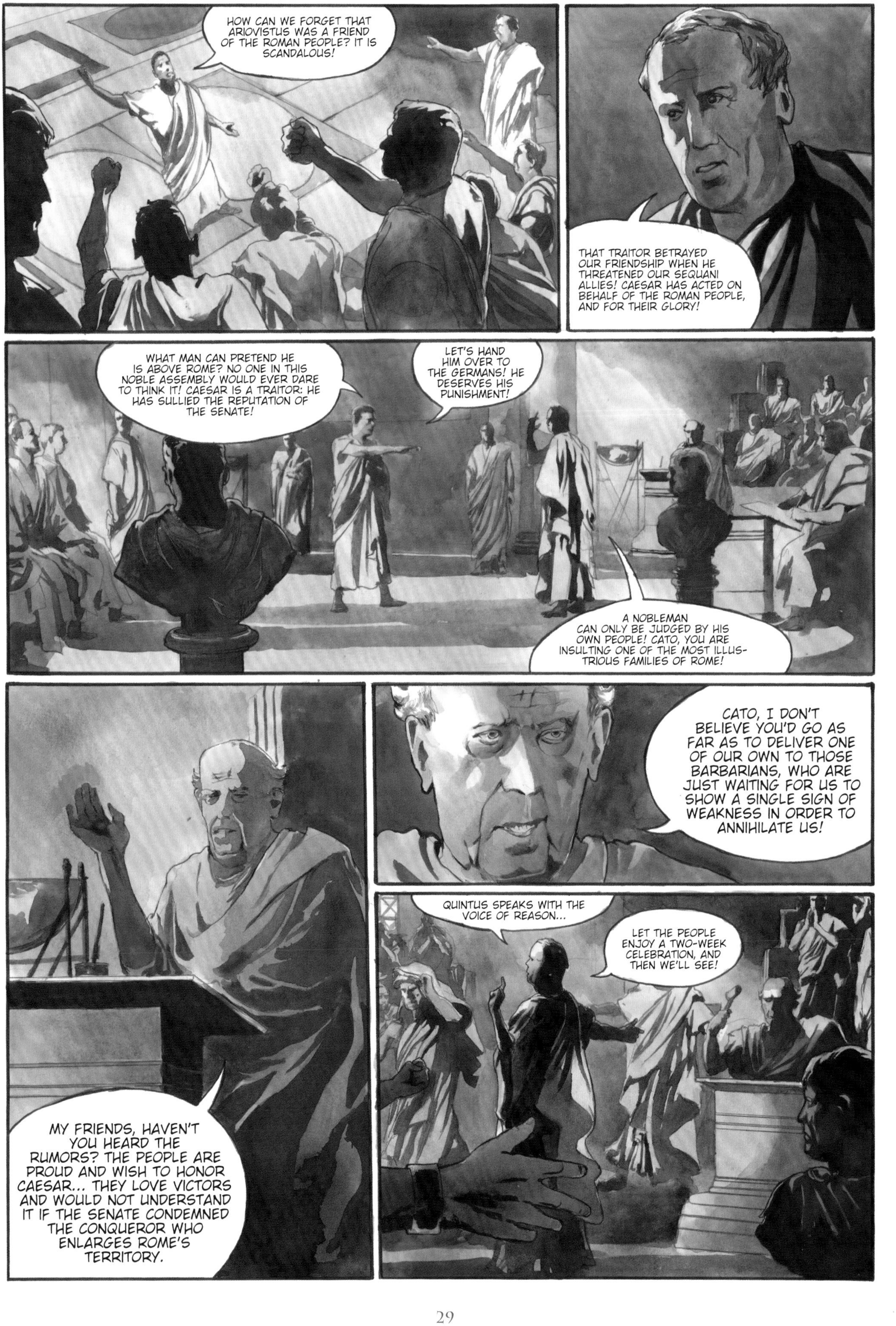
HOW CAN WE FORGET THAT ARIOVISTUS WAS A FRIEND OF THE ROMAN PEOPLE? IT IS SCANDALOUS!
THAT TRAITOR BETRAYED OUR FRIENDSHIP WHEN HE THREATENED OUR SEQUANI ALLIES! CAESAR HAS ACTED ON BEHALF OF THE ROMAN PEOPLE, AND FOR THEIR GLORY!
WHAT MAN CAN PRETEND HE IS ABOVE ROME? NO ONE IN THIS NOBLE ASSEMBLY WOULD EVER DARE TO THINK IT! CAESAR IS A TRAITOR: HE HAS SULLIED THE REPUTATION OF THE SENATE!
LET'S HAND HIM OVER TO THE GERMANS! HE DESERVES HIS PUNISHMENT!
A NOBLEMAN CAN ONLY BE JUDGED BY HIS OWN PEOPLE! CATO, YOU ARE INSULTING ONE OF THE MOST ILLUS-TRIOUS FAMILIES OF ROME!
MY FRIENDS, HAVEN'T YOU HEARD THE RUMORS? THE PEOPLE ARE PROUD AND WISH TO HONOR CAESAR... THEY LOVE VICTORS AND WOULD NOT UNDERSTAND IT IF THE SENATE CONDEMNED THE CONQUEROR WHO ENLARGES ROME'S TERRITORY.
CATO, I DON'T BELIEVE YOU'D GO AS FAR AS TO DELIVER ONE OF OUR OWN TO THOSE BARBARIANS, WHO ARE JUST WAITING FOR US TO SHOW A SINGLE SIGN OF WEAKNESS IN ORDER TO ANNIHILATE US!
QUINTUS SPEAKS WITH THE VOICE OF REASON...
LET THE PEOPLE ENJOY A TWO-WEEK CELEBRATION, AND THEN WE'LL SEE!

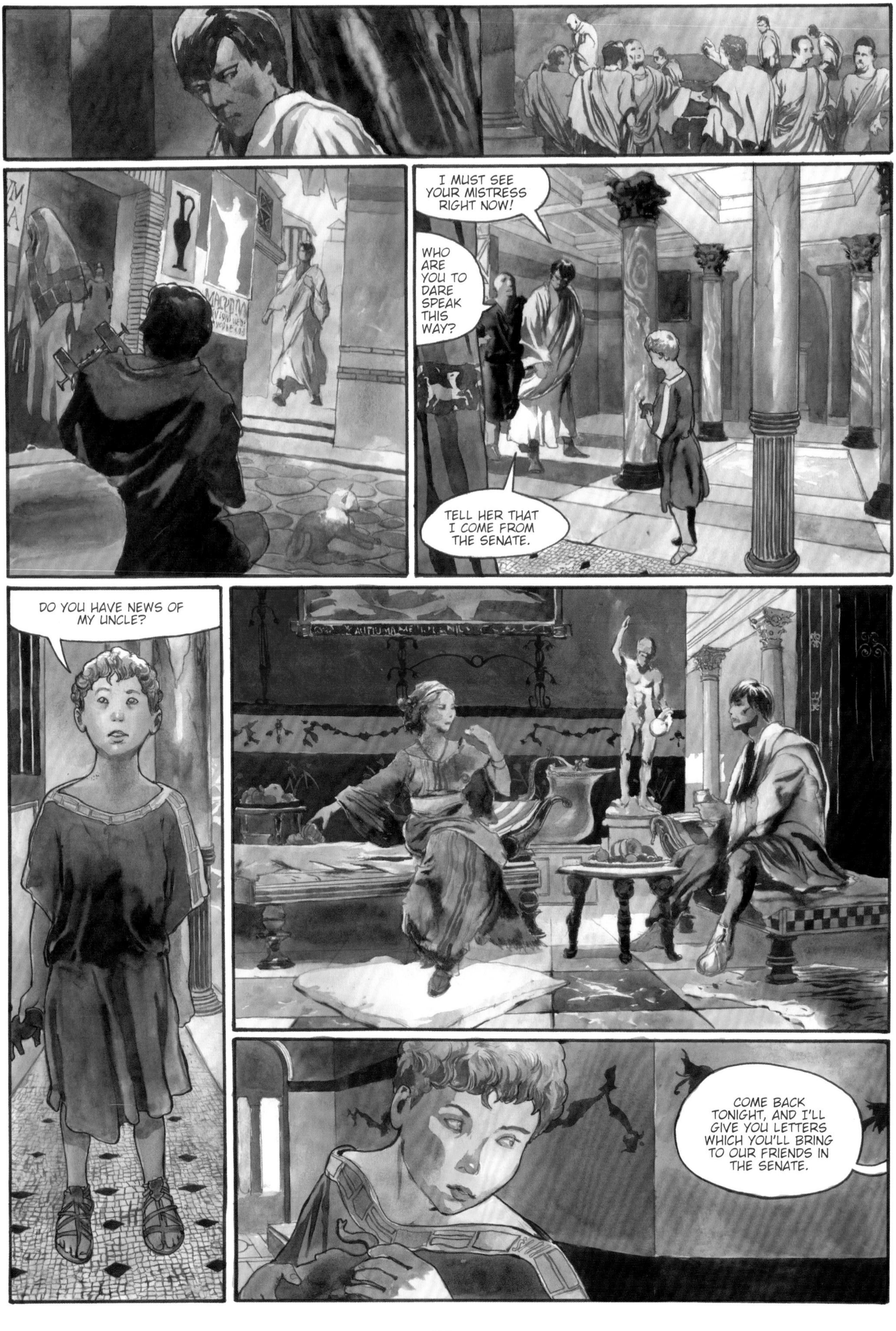
I MUST SEE YOUR MISTRESS RIGHT NOW!
WHO ARE YOU TO DARE SPEAK THIS WAY?
TELL HER THAT I COME FROM THE SENATE.
DO YOU HAVE NEWS OF MY UNCLE?
COME BACK TONIGHT, AND I'LL GIVE YOU LETTERS WHICH YOU'LL BRING TO OUR FRIENDS IN THE SENATE.

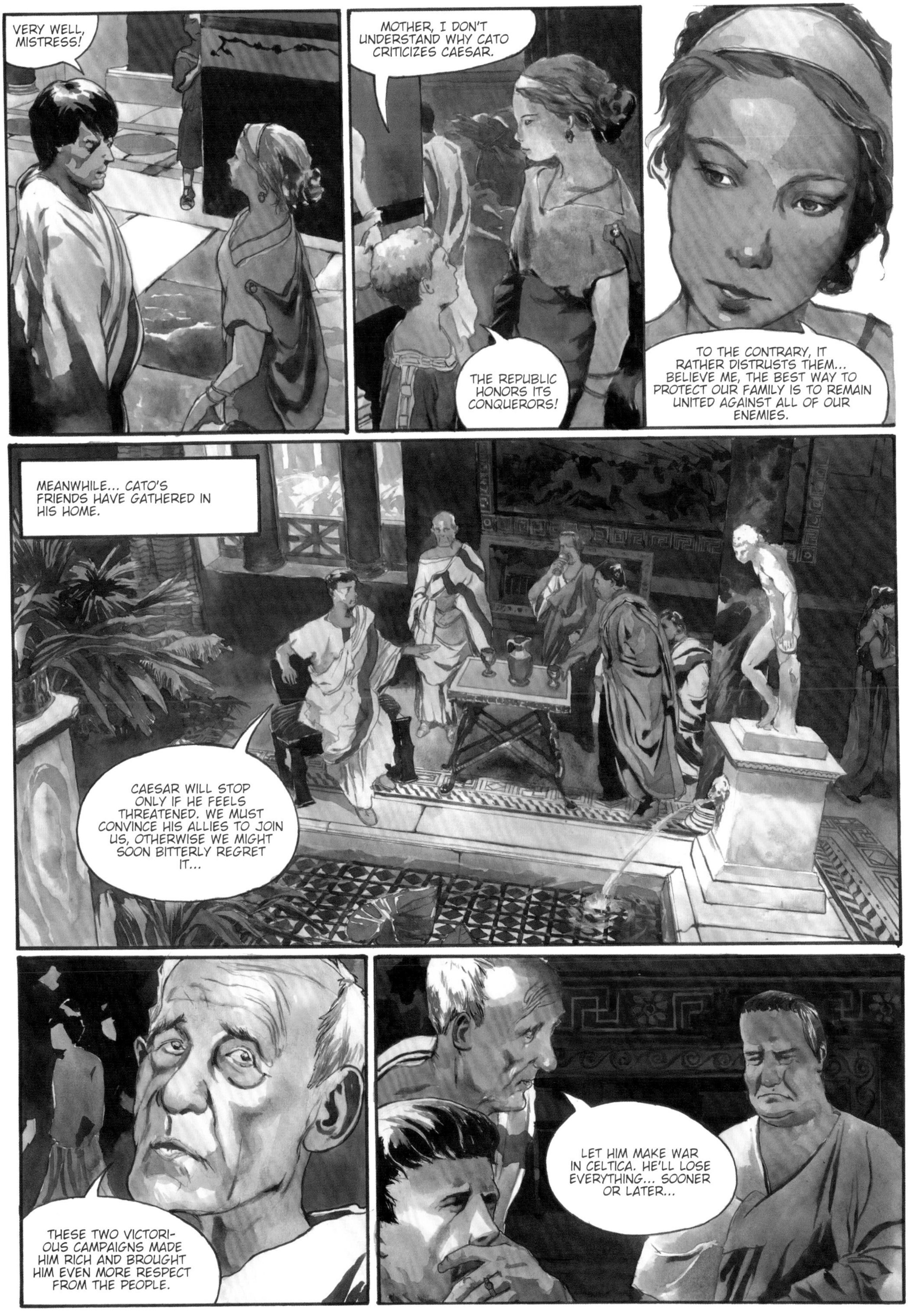
VERY WELL, MISTRESS!
MOTHER, I DON'T UNDERSTAND WHY CATO CRITICIZES CAESAR.
THE REPUBLIC HONORS ITS CONQUERORS!
TO THE CONTRARY, IT RATHER DISTRUSTS THEM... BELIEVE ME, THE BEST WAY TO PROTECT OUR FAMILY IS TO REMAIN UNITED AGAINST ALL OF OUR ENEMIES.
MEANWHILE... CATO'S FRIENDS HAVE GATHERED IN HIS HOME.
CAESAR WILL STOP ONLY IF HE FEELS THREATENED. WE MUST CONVINCE HIS ALLIES TO JOIN US, OTHERWISE WE MIGHT SOON BITTERLY REGRET IT...
THESE TWO VICTORIOUS CAMPAIGNS MADE HIM RICH AND BROUGHT HIM EVEN MORE RESPECT FROM THE PEOPLE.
LET HIM MAKE WAR IN CELTICA. HE'LL LOSE EVERYTHING... SOONER OR LATER...

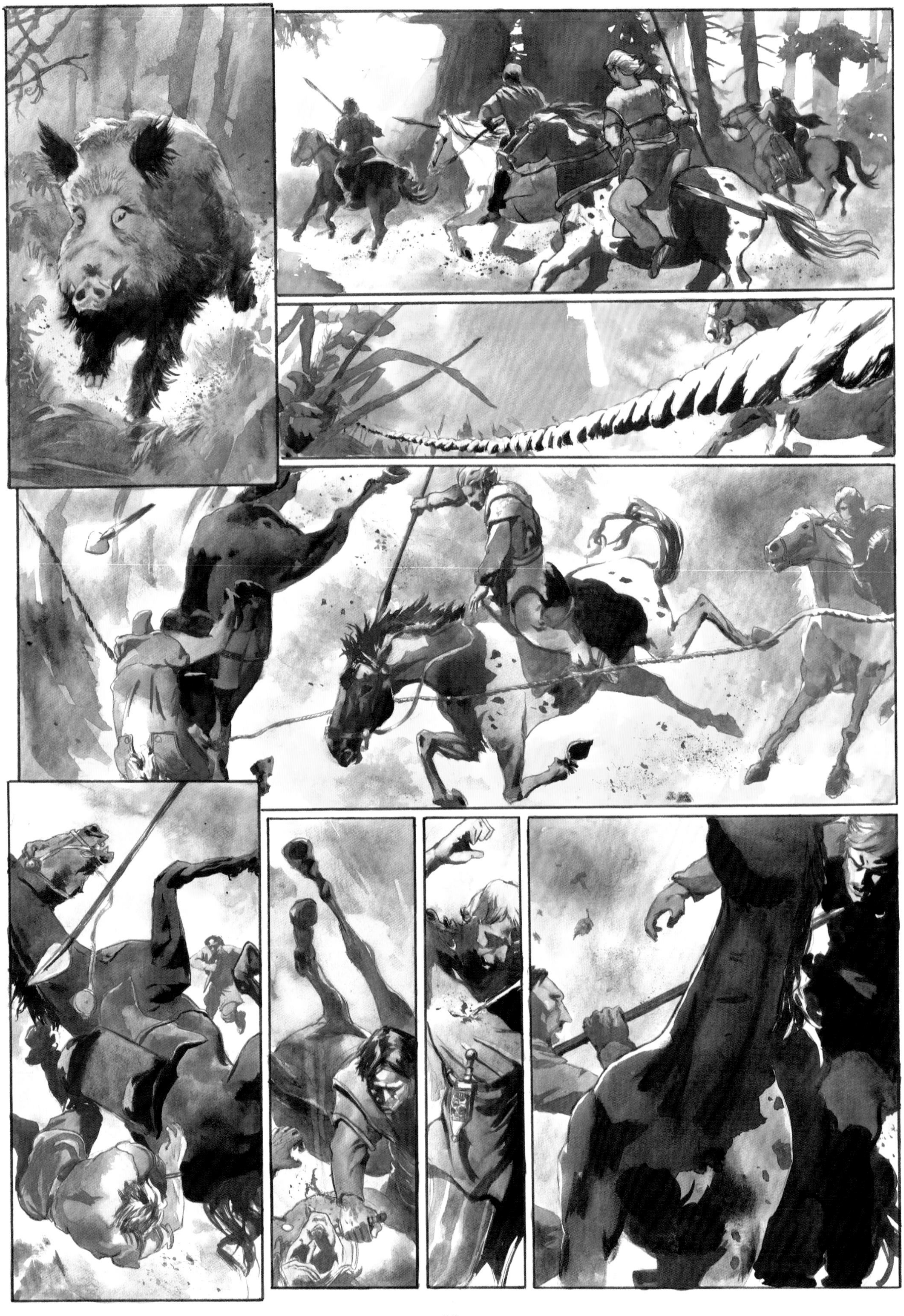

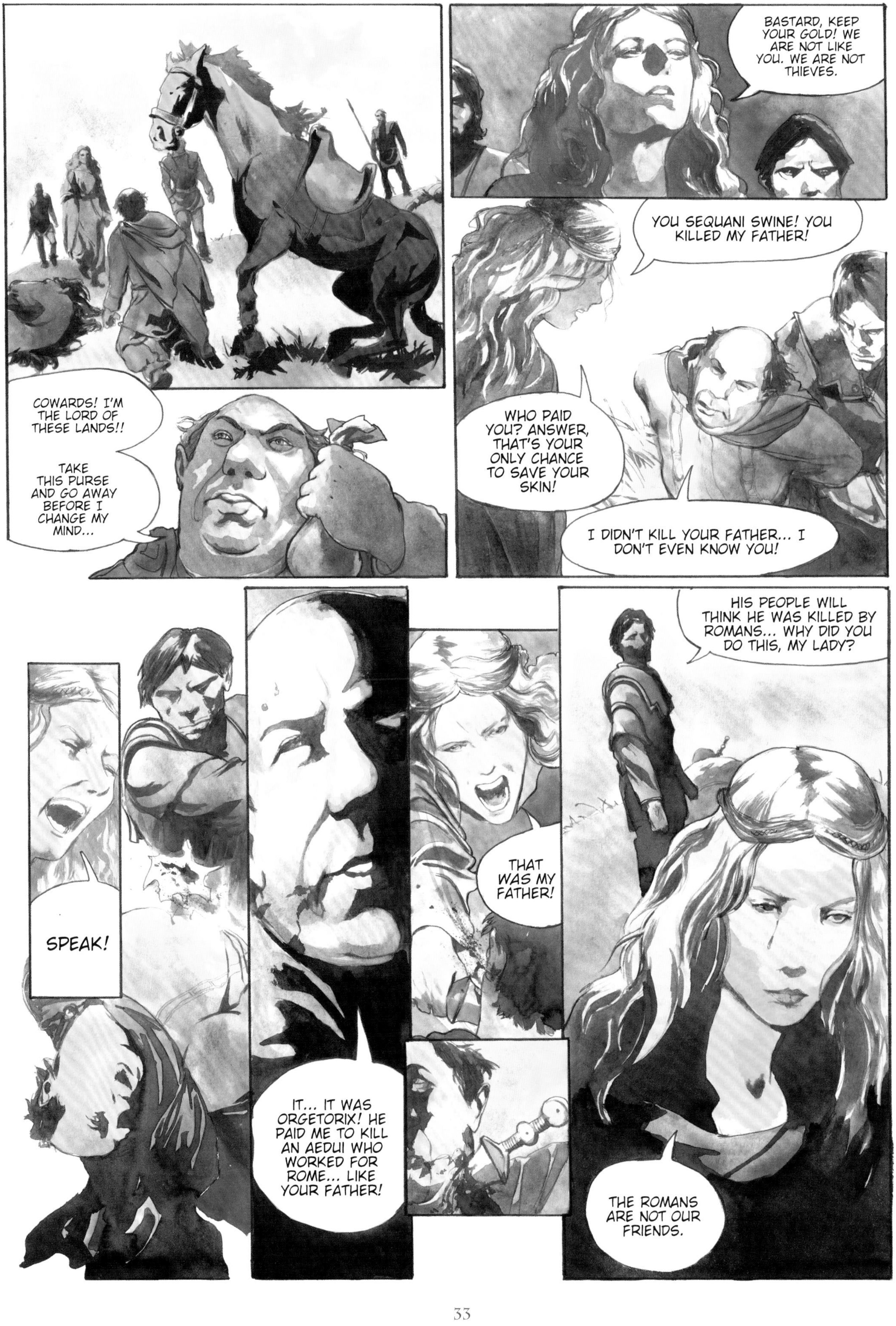
BASTARD, KEEP YOUR GOLD! WE ARE NOT LIKE YOU. WE ARE NOT THIEVES.
COWARDS! I'M THE LORD OF THESE LANDS!!
TAKE THIS PURSE AND GO AWAY BEFORE I CHANGE MY MIND...
YOU SEQUANI SWINE! YOU KILLED MY FATHER!
WHO PAID YOU? ANSWER, THAT'S YOUR ONLY CHANCE TO SAVE YOUR SKIN!
I DIDN'T KILL YOUR FATHER... I DON'T EVEN KNOW YOU!
SPEAK!
IT... IT WAS ORGETORIX! HE PAID ME TO KILL AN AEDUI WHO WORKED FOR ROME... LIKE YOUR FATHER!
THAT WAS MY FATHER!
HIS PEOPLE WILL THINK HE WAS KILLED BY ROMANS... WHY DID YOU DO THIS, MY LADY?
THE ROMANS ARE NOT OUR FRIENDS.

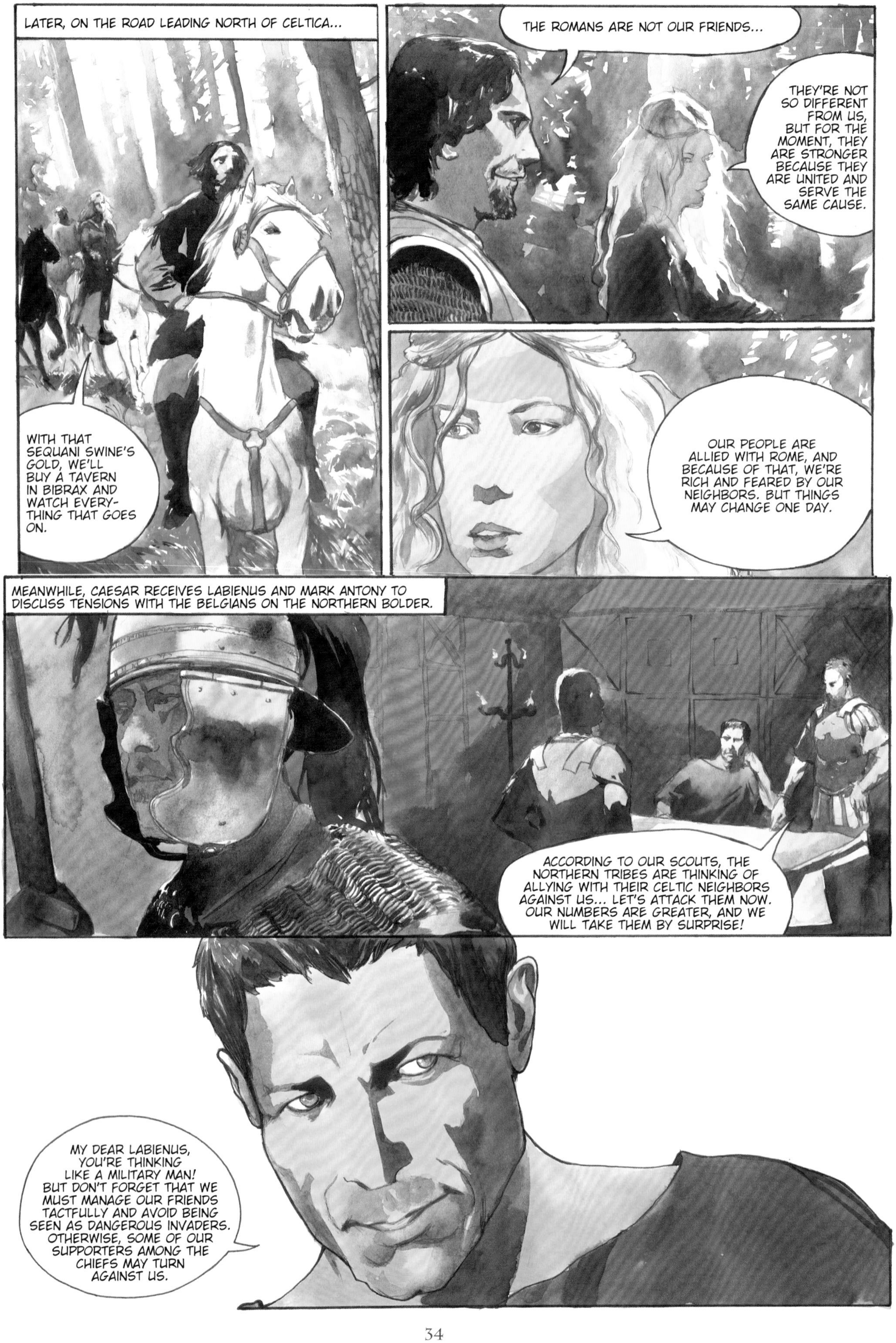
LATER, ON THE ROAD LEADING NORTH OF CELTICA...
WITH THAT SEQUANI SWINE'S GOLD, WE'LL BUY A TAVERN IN BIBRAX AND WATCH EVERYTHING THAT GOES ON.
THE ROMANS ARE NOT OUR FRIENDS...
THEY'RE NOT SO DIFFERENT FROM US, BUT FOR THE MOMENT, THEY ARE STRONGER BECAUSE THEY ARE UNITED AND SERVE THE SAME CAUSE.
OUR PEOPLE ARE ALLIED WITH ROME, AND BECAUSE OF THAT, WE'RE RICH AND FEARED BY OUR NEIGHBORS. BUT THINGS MAY CHANGE ONE DAY.
MEANWHILE, CAESAR RECEIVES LABIENUS AND MARK ANTONY TO DISCUSS TENSIONS WITH THE BELGIANS ON THE NORTHERN BOLDER.
ACCORDING TO OUR SCOUTS, THE NORTHERN TRIBES ARE THINKING OF ALLYING WITH THEIR CELTIC NEIGHBORS AGAINST US... LET'S ATTACK THEM NOW. OUR NUMBERS ARE GREATER, AND WE WILL TAKE THEM BY SURPRISE!
MY DEAR LABIENUS, YOU'RE THINKING LIKE A MILITARY MAN! BUT DON'T FORGET THAT WE MUST MANAGE OUR FRIENDS TACTFULLY AND AVOID BEING SEEN AS DANGEROUS INVADERS. OTHERWISE, SOME OF OUR SUPPORTERS AMONG THE CHIEFS MAY TURN AGAINST US.

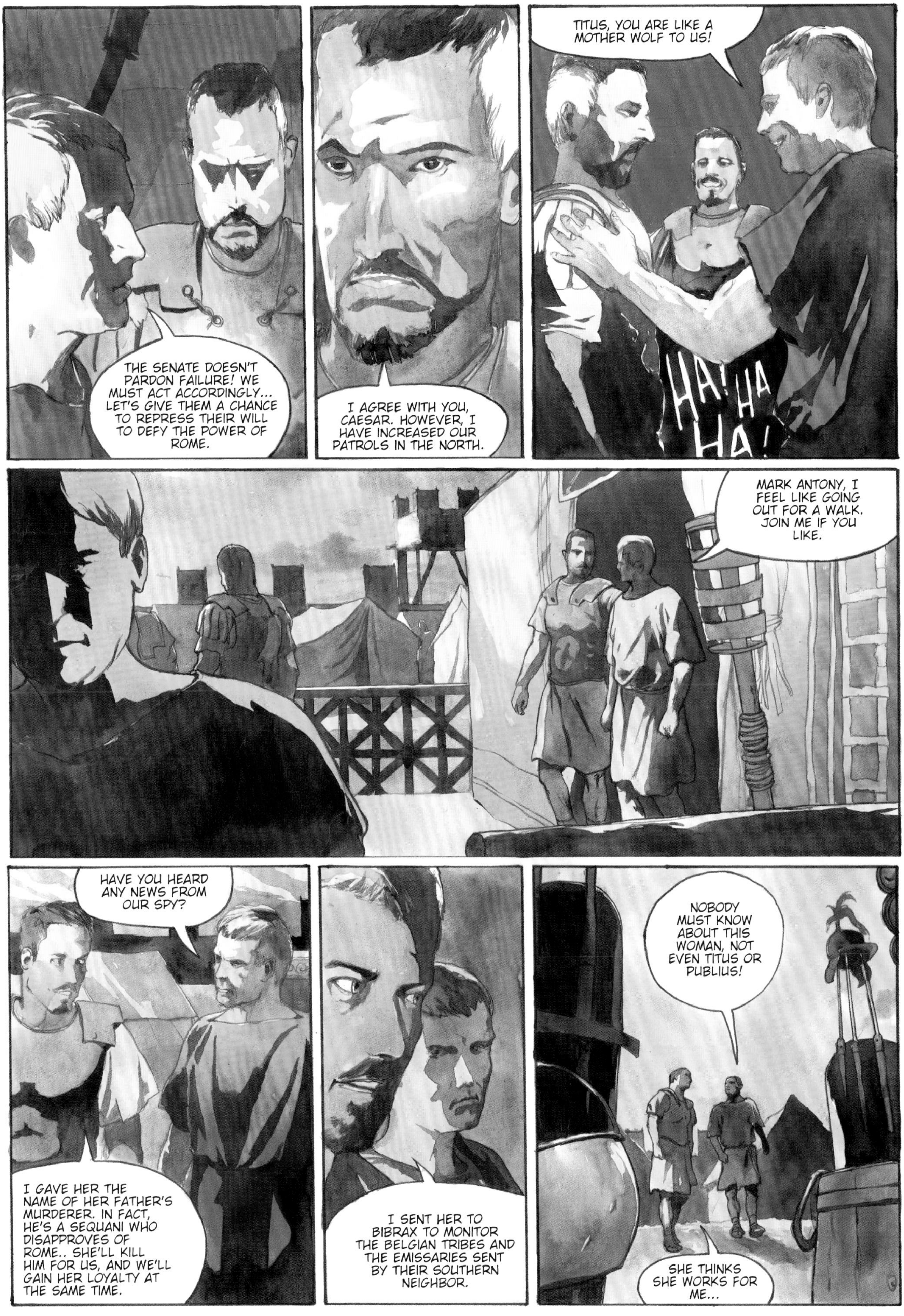
THE SENATE DOESN'T PARDON FAILURE! WE MUST ACT ACCORDINGLY... LET'S GIVE THEM A CHANCE TO REPRESS THEIR WILL TO DEFY THE POWER OF ROME.
I AGREE WITH YOU, CAESAR. HOWEVER, I HAVE INCREASED OUR PATROLS IN THE NORTH.
TITUS, YOU ARE LIKE A MOTHER WOLF TO US!
HA! HA HA! HA!
MARK ANTONY, I FEEL LIKE GOING OUT FOR A WALK. JOIN ME IF YOU LIKE.
HAVE YOU HEARD ANY NEWS FROM OUR SPY?
I GAVE HER THE NAME OF HER FATHER'S MURDERER. IN FACT, HE'S A SEQUANI WHO DISAPPROVES OF ROME.. SHE'LL KILL HIM FOR US, AND WE'LL GAIN HER LOYALTY AT THE SAME TIME.
I SENT HER TO BIBRAX TO MONITOR THE BELGIAN TRIBES AND THE EMISSARIES SENT BY THEIR SOUTHERN NEIGHBOR.
NOBODY MUST KNOW ABOUT THIS WOMAN, NOT EVEN TITUS OR PUBLIUS!
SHE THINKS SHE WORKS FOR ME...

TWO WEEKS LATER... AT CAESAR'S CAMP IN CISALPINE GAUL. MARK ANTONY RECEIVES REGULAR REPORTS FROM EPONINE...

HIS SPY HAS BOUGHT AN INN IN BIBRAX AND SETTLED THERE WITH HER MEN.

CAESAR! I'VE JUST RECEIVED...

LABIENUS HAS INFORMED ME THAT SEVERAL BELGIAN TRIBES HAVE BECOME ALLIED. ACCORDING TO HIM, THEY INTEND TO ATTACK US IN SEQUANI TERRITORY.

TITUS SPEAKS THE TRUTH! GALBA, THE SUESSIONE KING, IS RAISING AN ARMY AGAINST US.

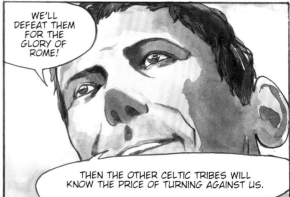

WE'LL DEFEAT THEM FOR THE GLORY OF ROME!

THEN THE OTHER CELTIC TRIBES WILL KNOW THE PRICE OF TURNING AGAINST US.

WHAT HAVE YOU DECIDED?

I'VE ALREADY ORDERED THE THIRTEENTH AND FOURTEENTH LEGIONS TO GO TO VESONTIO. WE'LL FIGHT THEM FURTHER NORTH ON THE BANKS OF THE AXONA RIVER TO PREVENT THEM FROM ENTERING OUR ALLIED TERRITORIES.

IN THE SPRING OF 57 B.C. CAESAR'S LEGIONS MARCH ON THE SEQUANI CAPITAL. GALBA HAS MANAGED TO UNITE PART OF THE GERMANS AND THE BELLOVACI AS WELL AS THE NERVII, THE MORINI, THE ATUATUCI, THE ATREBATES, THE AMBIANI, THE CALETI, THE VELIOCASSES, THE VIROMANDUI, AND THE MENAPII. AN EXTREMELY POWERFUL COALITION.

FIFTEEN DAYS OF FORCED MARCHING ALLOW CAESAR AND HIS TWO LEGIONS TO CATCH UP WITH BELGIAN FORCES HOSTILE TO ROME.

36

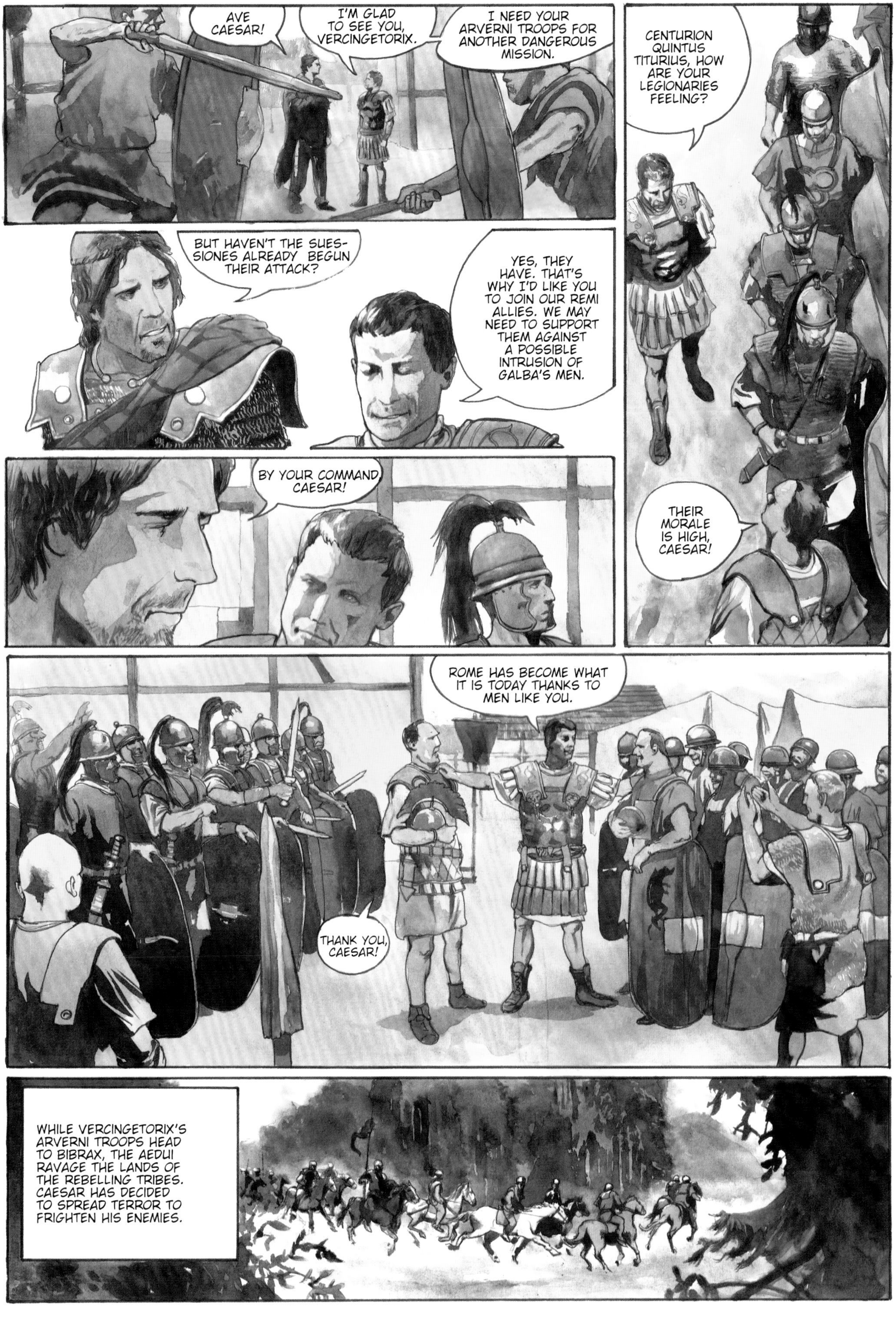
AVE CAESAR!
I'M GLAD TO SEE YOU, VERCINGETORIX.
I NEED YOUR ARVERNI TROOPS FOR ANOTHER DANGEROUS MISSION.
BUT HAVEN'T THE SUESSIONES ALREADY BEGUN THEIR ATTACK?
YES, THEY HAVE. THAT'S WHY I'D LIKE YOU TO JOIN OUR REMI ALLIES. WE MAY NEED TO SUPPORT THEM AGAINST A POSSIBLE INTRUSION OF GALBA'S MEN.
BY YOUR COMMAND, CAESAR!
CENTURION QUINTUS TITURIUS, HOW ARE YOUR LEGIONARIES FEELING?
THEIR MORALE IS HIGH, CAESAR!
ROME HAS BECOME WHAT IT IS TODAY THANKS TO MEN LIKE YOU.
THANK YOU, CAESAR!
WHILE VERCINGETORIX'S ARVERNI TROOPS HEAD TO BIBRAX, THE AEDUI RAVAGE THE LANDS OF THE REBELLING TRIBES. CAESAR HAS DECIDED TO SPREAD TERROR TO FRIGHTEN HIS ENEMIES.

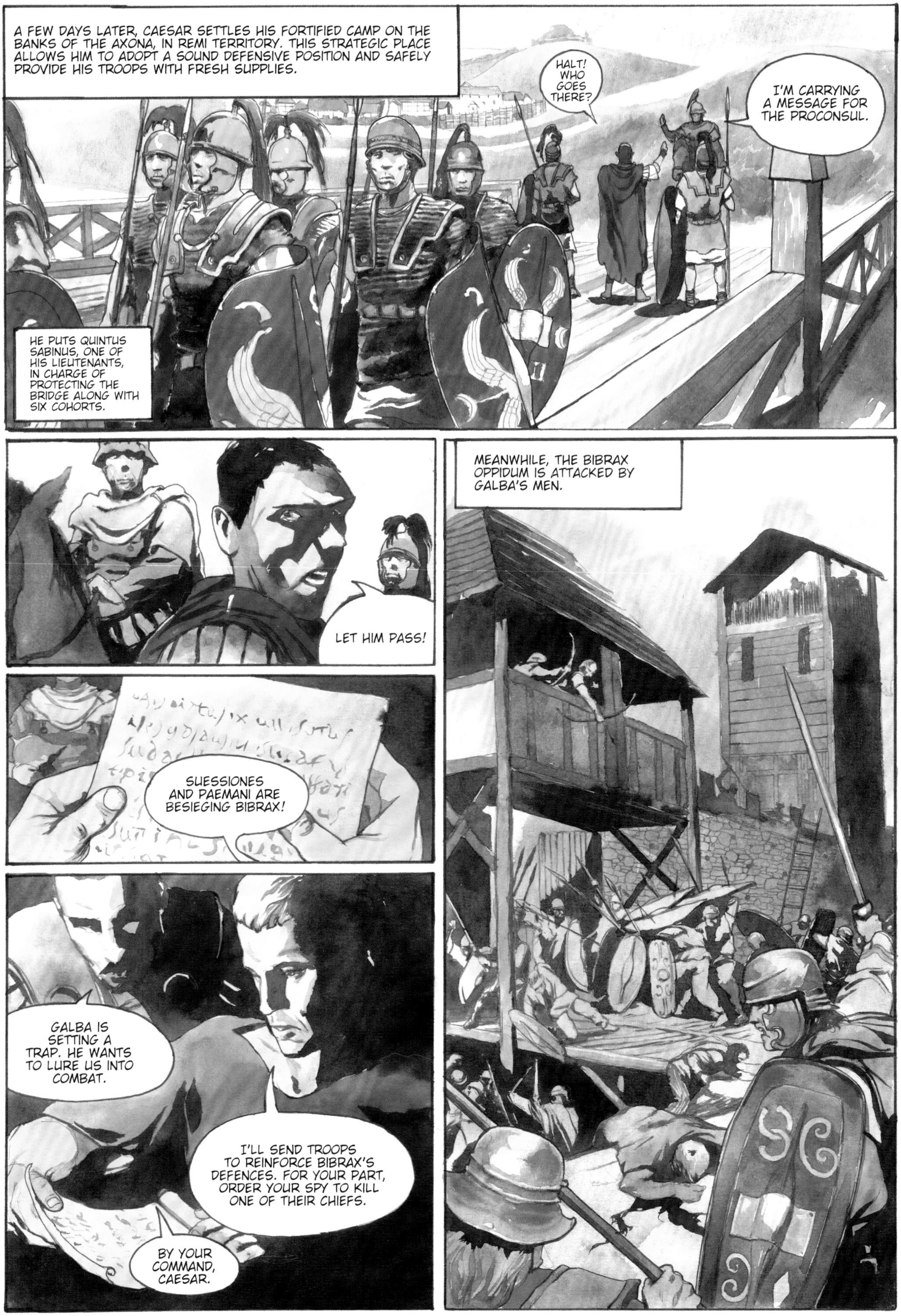
A FEW DAYS LATER, CAESAR SETTLES HIS FORTIFIED CAMP ON THE BANKS OF THE AXONA, IN REMI TERRITORY. THIS STRATEGIC PLACE ALLOWS HIM TO ADOPT A SOUND DEFENSIVE POSITION AND SAFELY PROVIDE HIS TROOPS WITH FRESH SUPPLIES.
HALT! WHO GOES THERE?
I'M CARRYING A MESSAGE FOR THE PROCONSUL.
HE PUTS QUINTUS SABINUS, ONE OF HIS LIEUTENANTS, IN CHARGE OF PROTECTING THE BRIDGE ALONG WITH SIX COHORTS.
LET HIM PASS!
SUESSIONES AND PAEMANI ARE BESIEGING BIBRAX!
GALBA IS SETTING A TRAP. HE WANTS TO LURE US INTO COMBAT.
I'LL SEND TROOPS TO REINFORCE BIBRAX'S DEFENCES. FOR YOUR PART, ORDER YOUR SPY TO KILL ONE OF THEIR CHIEFS.
BY YOUR COMMAND, CAESAR.
MEANWHILE, THE BIBRAX OPPIDUM IS ATTACKED BY GALBA'S MEN.

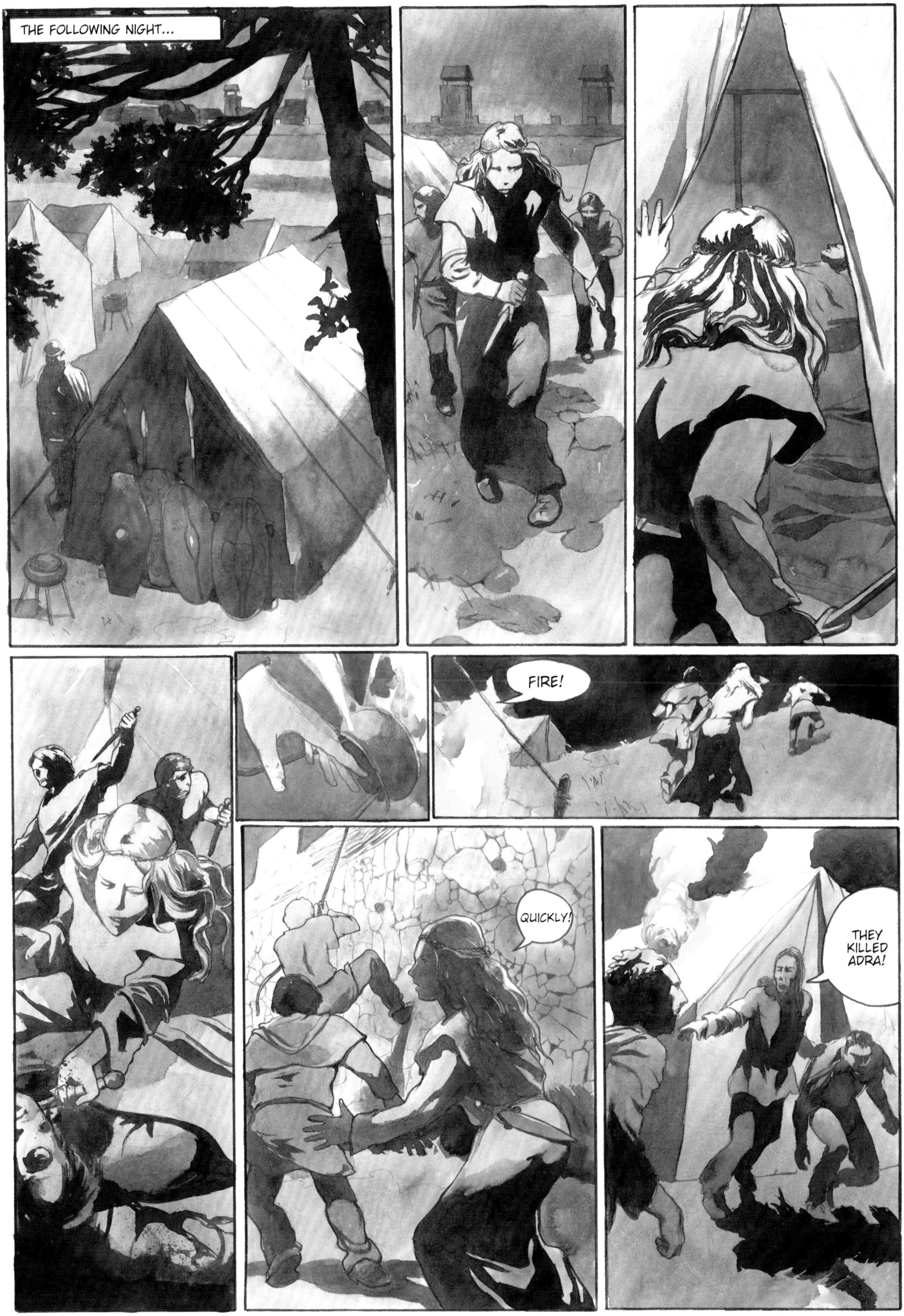
THE FOLLOWING NIGHT...
FIRE!
QUICKLY!
THEY KILLED ADRA!

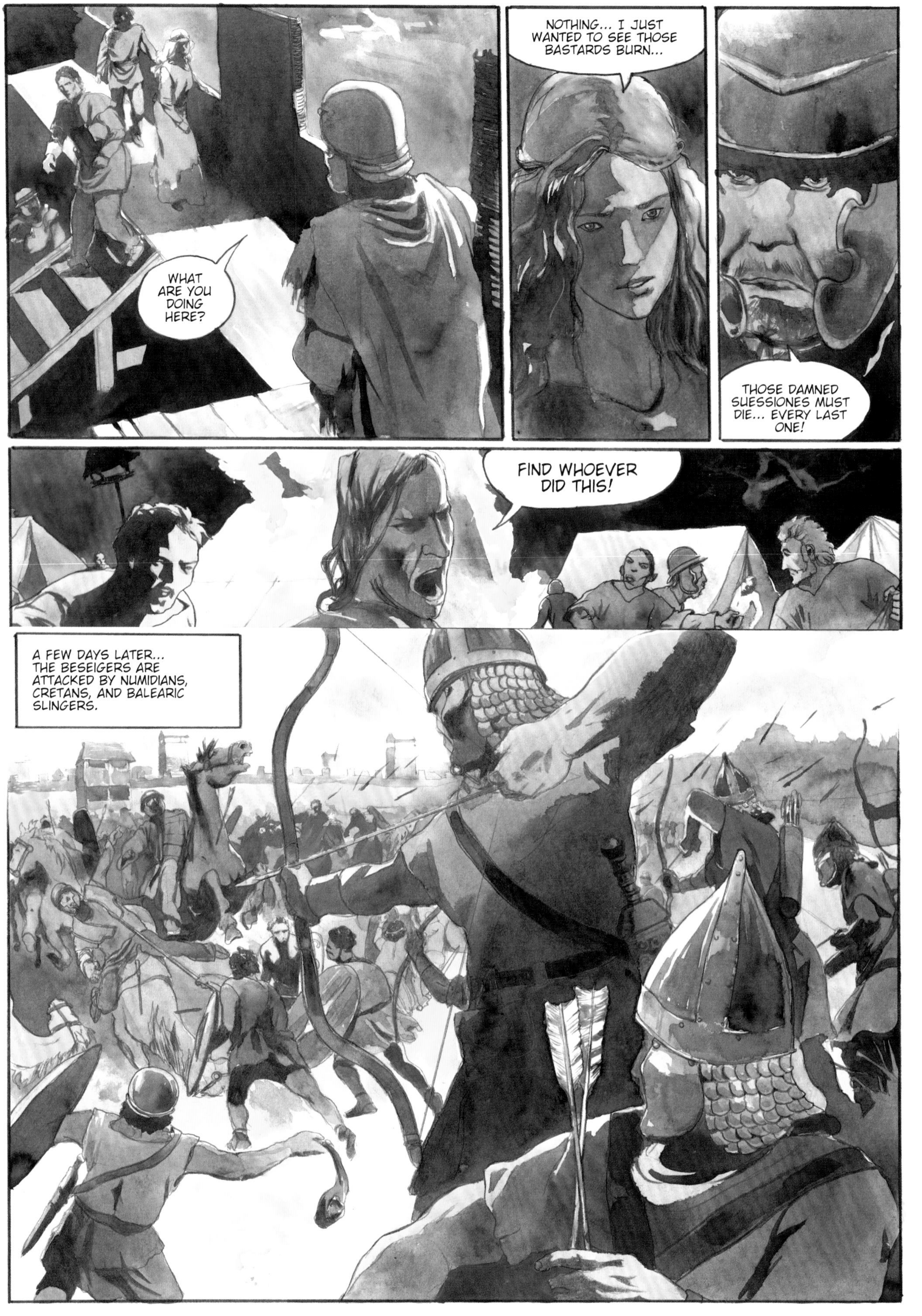
WHAT ARE YOU DOING HERE?
NOTHING... I JUST WANTED TO SEE THOSE BASTARDS BURN...
THOSE DAMNED SUESSIONES MUST DIE... EVERY LAST ONE!
FIND WHOEVER DID THIS!
A FEW DAYS LATER... THE BESEIGERS ARE ATTACKED BY NUMIDIANS, CRETANS, AND BALEARIC SLINGERS.

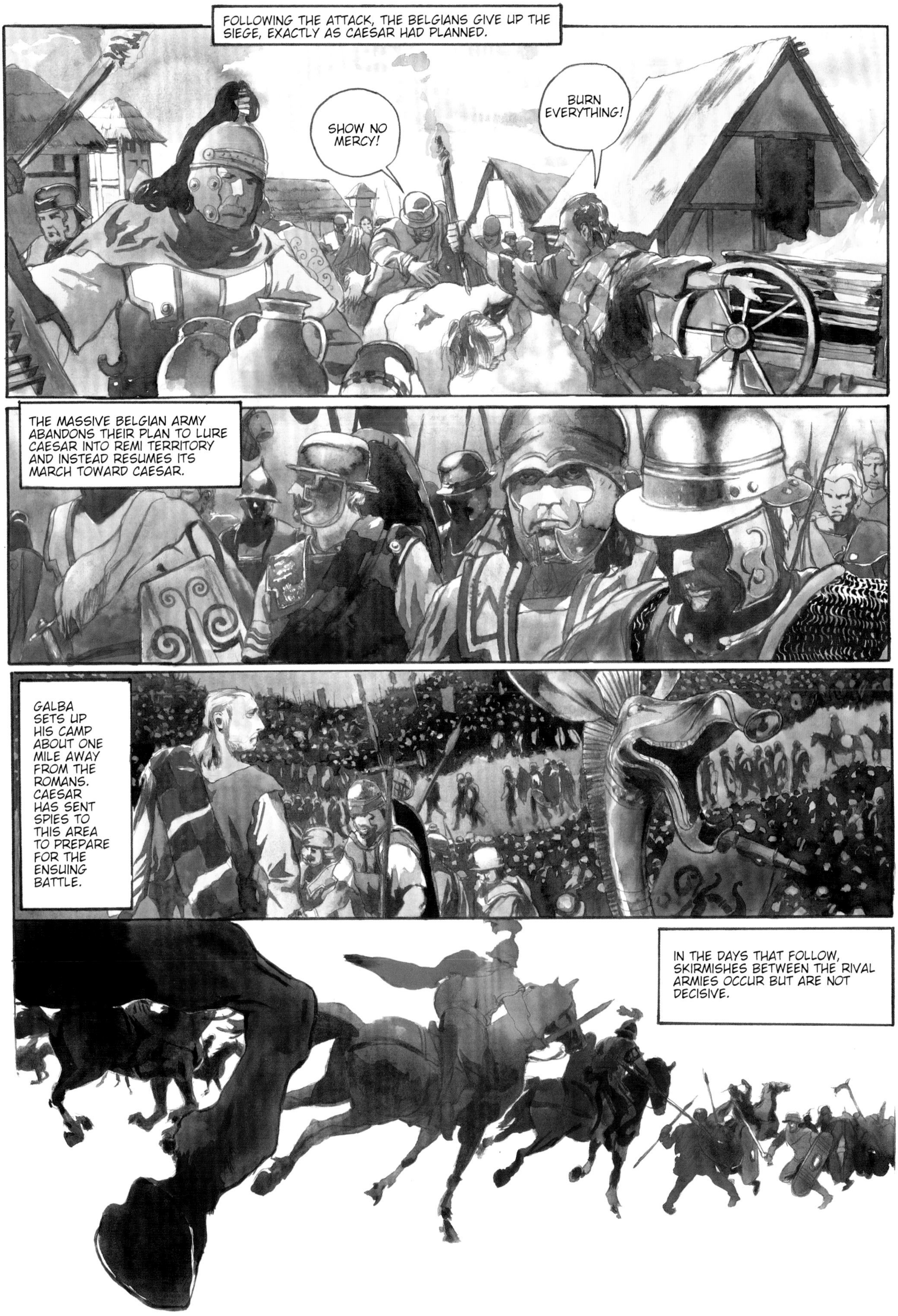
FOLLOWING THE ATTACK, THE BELGIANS GIVE UP THE SIEGE, EXACTLY AS CAESAR HAD PLANNED.
SHOW NO MERCY!
BURN EVERYTHING!
THE MASSIVE BELGIAN ARMY ABANDONS THEIR PLAN TO LURE CAESAR INTO REMI TERRITORY AND INSTEAD RESUMES ITS MARCH TOWARD CAESAR.
GALBA SETS UP HIS CAMP ABOUT ONE MILE AWAY FROM THE ROMANS. CAESAR HAS SENT SPIES TO THIS AREA TO PREPARE FOR THE ENSUING BATTLE.
IN THE DAYS THAT FOLLOW, SKIRMISHES BETWEEN THE RIVAL ARMIES OCCUR BUT ARE NOT DECISIVE.

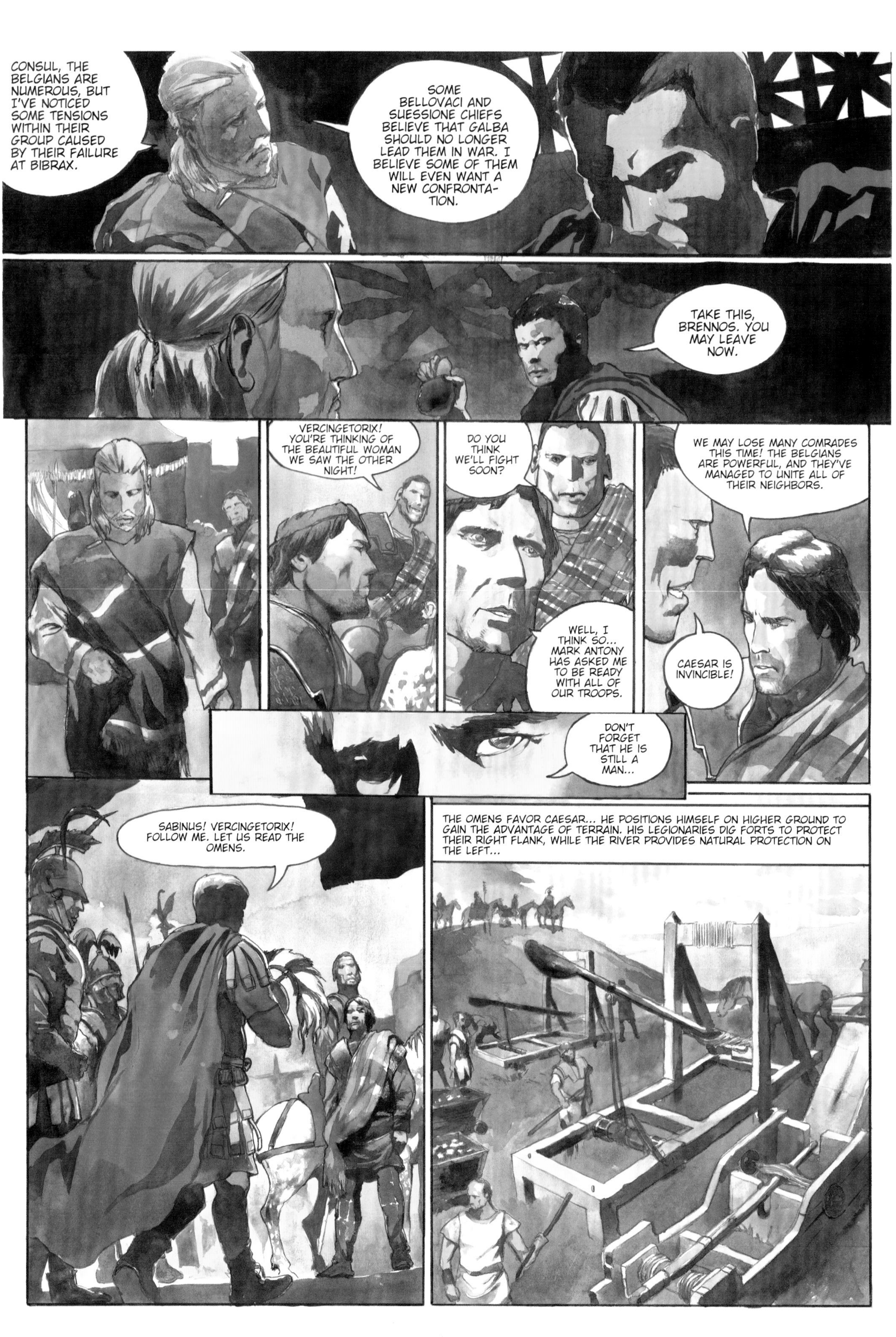
CONSUL, THE BELGIANS ARE NUMEROUS, BUT I'VE NOTICED SOME TENSIONS WITHIN THEIR GROUP CAUSED BY THEIR FAILURE AT BIBRAX.
SOME BELLOVACI AND SUESSIONE CHIEFS BELIEVE THAT GALBA SHOULD NO LONGER LEAD THEM IN WAR. I BELIEVE SOME OF THEM WILL EVEN WANT A NEW CONFRONTA-TION.
TAKE THIS, BRENNOS. YOU MAY LEAVE NOW.
VERCINGETORIX! YOU'RE THINKING OF THE BEAUTIFUL WOMAN WE SAW THE OTHER NIGHT!
DO YOU THINK WE'LL FIGHT SOON?
WELL, I THINK SO... MARK ANTONY HAS ASKED ME TO BE READY WITH ALL OF OUR TROOPS.
WE MAY LOSE MANY COMRADES THIS TIME! THE BELGIANS ARE POWERFUL, AND THEY'VE MANAGED TO UNITE ALL OF THEIR NEIGHBORS.
CAESAR IS INVINCIBLE!
DON'T FORGET THAT HE IS STILL A MAN...
SABINUS! VERCINGETORIX! FOLLOW ME. LET US READ THE OMENS.
THE OMENS FAVOR CAESAR... HE POSITIONS HIMSELF ON HIGHER GROUND TO GAIN THE ADVANTAGE OF TERRAIN. HIS LEGIONARIES DIG FORTS TO PROTECT THEIR RIGHT FLANK, WHILE THE RIVER PROVIDES NATURAL PROTECTION ON THE LEFT...

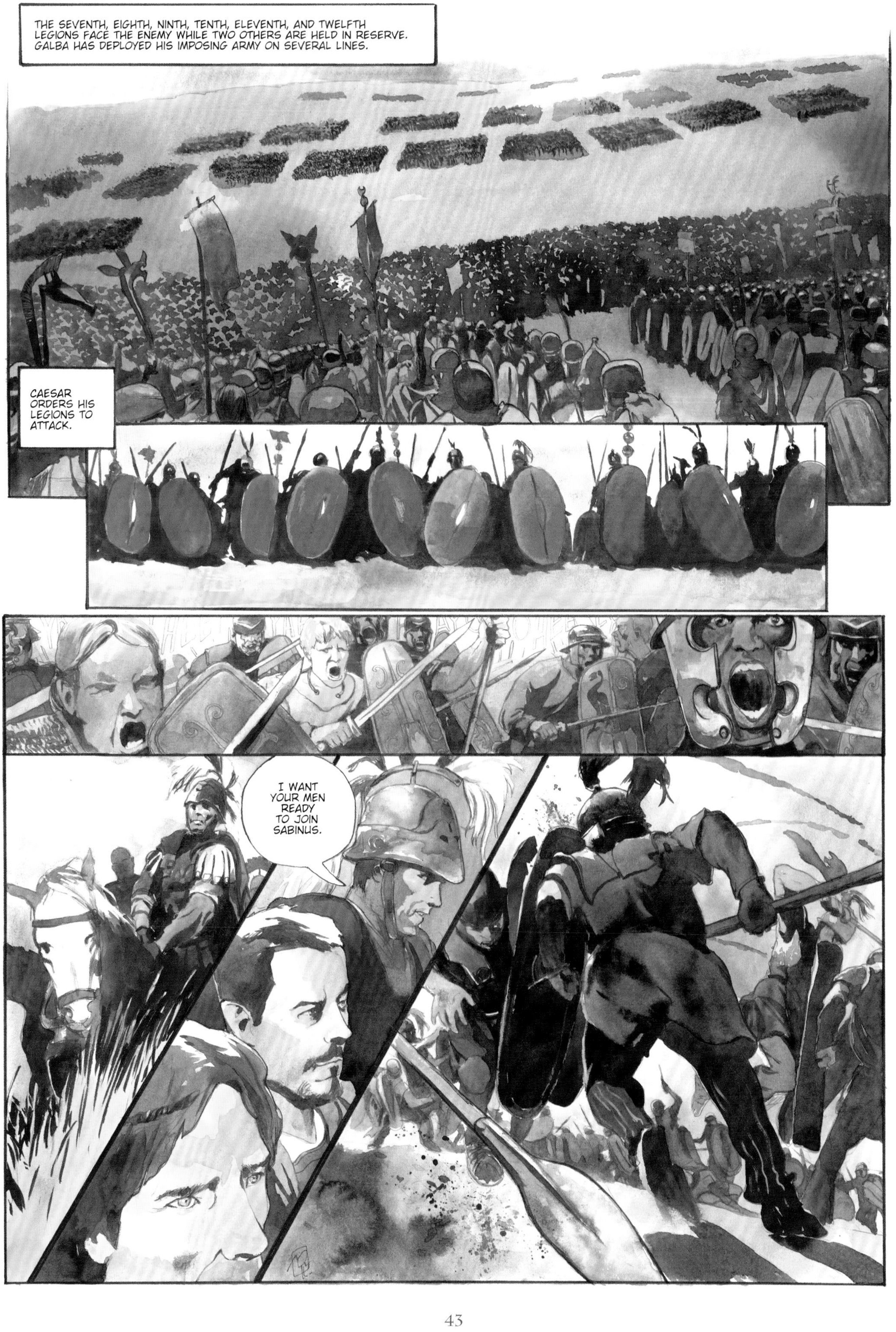
THE SEVENTH, EIGHTH, NINTH, TENTH, ELEVENTH, AND TWELFTH LEGIONS FACE THE ENEMY WHILE TWO OTHERS ARE HELD IN RESERVE. GALBA HAS DEPLOYED HIS IMPOSING ARMY ON SEVERAL LINES.
CAESAR ORDERS HIS LEGIONS TO ATTACK.
I WANT YOUR MEN READY TO JOIN SABINUS.

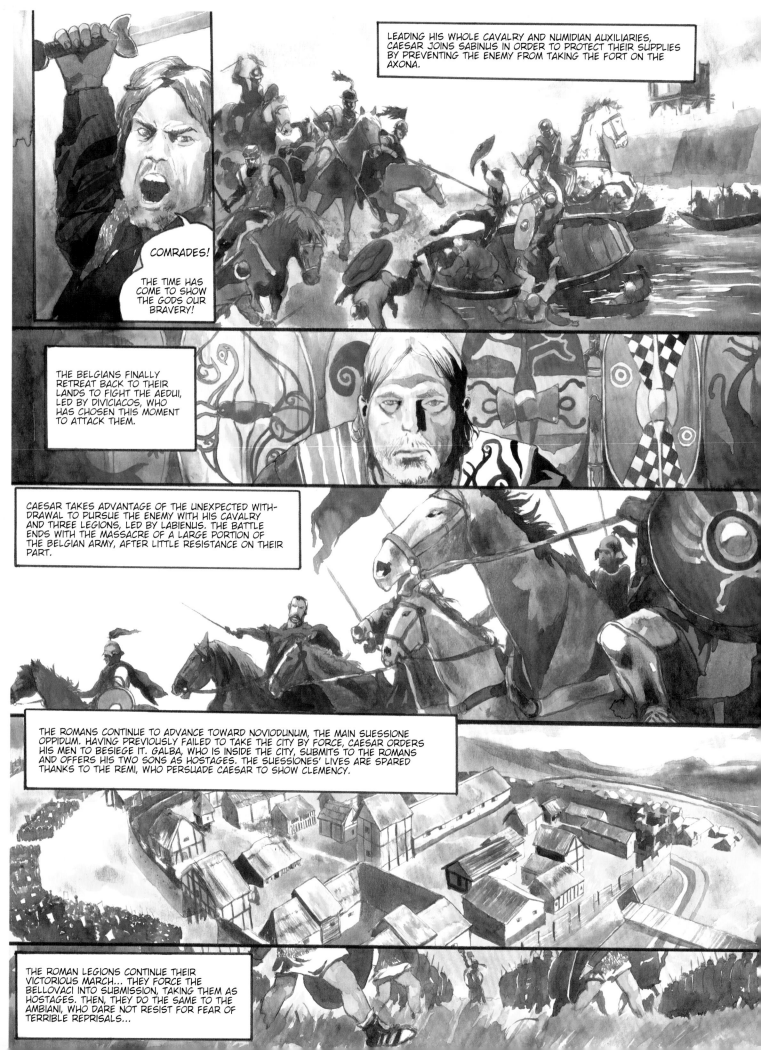

LEADING HIS WHOLE CAVALRY AND NUMIDIAN AUXILIARIES, CAESAR JOINS SABINUS IN ORDER TO PROTECT THEIR SUPPLIES BY PREVENTING THE ENEMY FROM TAKING THE FORT ON THE AXONA.

COMRADES!

THE TIME HAS COME TO SHOW THE GODS OUR BRAVERY!

THE BELGIANS FINALLY RETREAT BACK TO THEIR LANDS TO FIGHT THE AEDUI, LED BY DIVICIACOS, WHO HAS CHOSEN THIS MOMENT TO ATTACK THEM.

CAESAR TAKES ADVANTAGE OF THE UNEXPECTED WITH-DRAWAL TO PURSUE THE ENEMY WITH HIS CAVALRY AND THREE LEGIONS, LED BY LABIENUS. THE BATTLE ENDS WITH THE MASSACRE OF A LARGE PORTION OF THE BELGIAN ARMY, AFTER LITTLE RESISTANCE ON THEIR PART.

THE ROMANS CONTINUE TO ADVANCE TOWARD NOVIODUNUM, THE MAIN SUESSIONE OPPIDUM. HAVING PREVIOUSLY FAILED TO TAKE THE CITY BY FORCE, CAESAR ORDERS HIS MEN TO BESIEGE IT. GALBA, WHO IS INSIDE THE CITY, SUBMITS TO THE ROMANS AND OFFERS HIS TWO SONS AS HOSTAGES. THE SUESSIONES' LIVES ARE SPARED THANKS TO THE REMI, WHO PERSUADE CAESAR TO SHOW CLEMENCY.

THE ROMAN LEGIONS CONTINUE THEIR VICTORIOUS MARCH... THEY FORCE THE BELLOVACI INTO SUBMISSION, TAKING THEM AS HOSTAGES. THEN, THEY DO THE SAME TO THE AMBIANI, WHO DARE NOT RESIST FOR FEAR OF TERRIBLE REPRISALS...

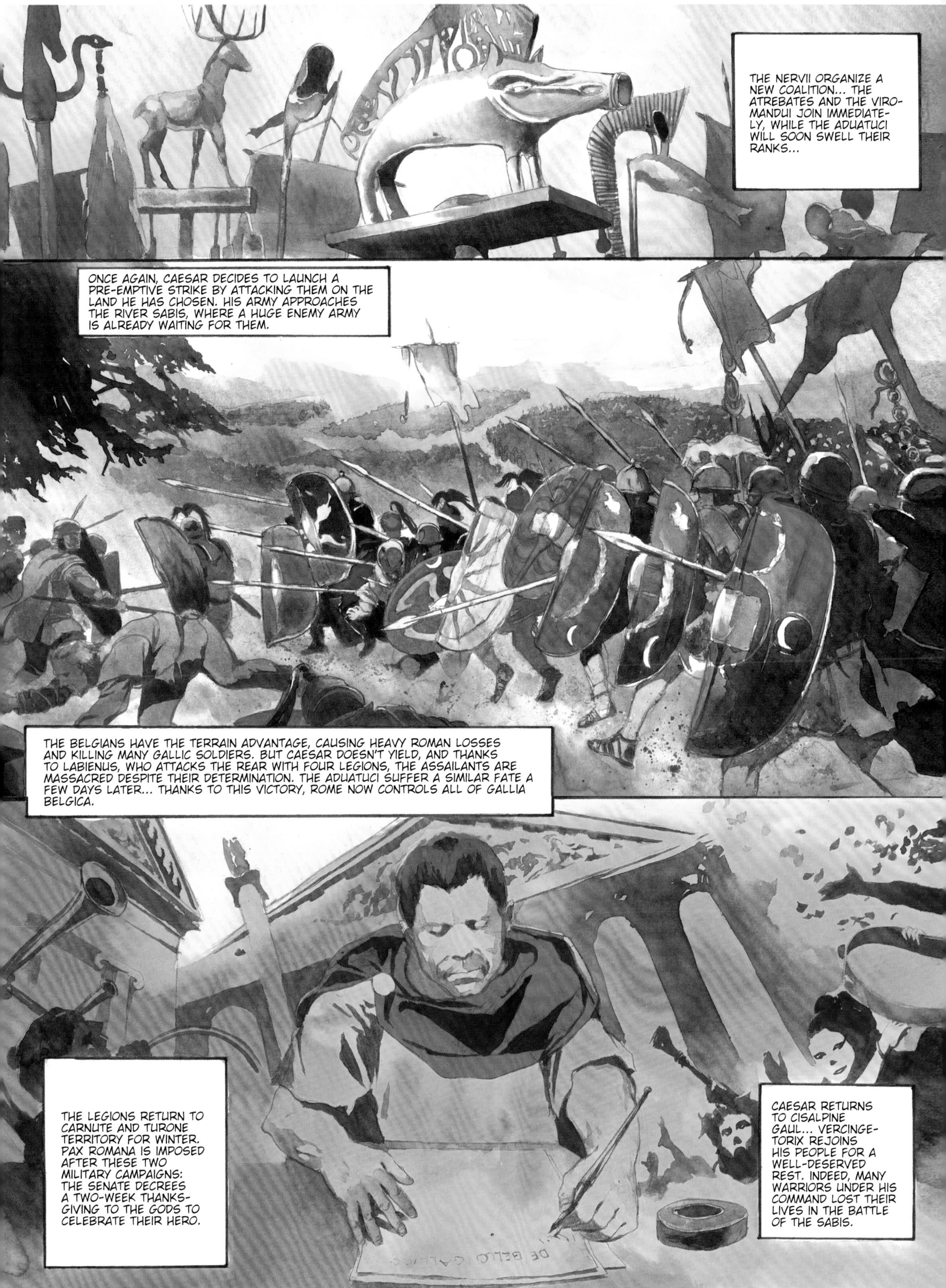
THE NERVII ORGANIZE A NEW COALITION... THE ATREBATES AND THE VIROMANDUI JOIN IMMEDIATELY, WHILE THE ADUATUCI WILL SOON SWELL THEIR RANKS...
ONCE AGAIN, CAESAR DECIDES TO LAUNCH A PRE-EMPTIVE STRIKE BY ATTACKING THEM ON THE LAND HE HAS CHOSEN. HIS ARMY APPROACHES THE RIVER SABIS, WHERE A HUGE ENEMY ARMY IS ALREADY WAITING FOR THEM.
THE BELGIANS HAVE THE TERRAIN ADVANTAGE, CAUSING HEAVY ROMAN LOSSES AND KILLING MANY GALLIC SOLDIERS. BUT CAESAR DOESN'T YIELD, AND THANKS TO LABIENUS, WHO ATTACKS THE REAR WITH FOUR LEGIONS, THE ASSAILANTS ARE MASSACRED DESPITE THEIR DETERMINATION. THE ADUATUCI SUFFER A SIMILAR FATE A FEW DAYS LATER... THANKS TO THIS VICTORY, ROME NOW CONTROLS ALL OF GALLIA BELGICA.
THE LEGIONS RETURN TO CARNUTE AND TURONE TERRITORY FOR WINTER. PAX ROMANA IS IMPOSED AFTER THESE TWO MILITARY CAMPAIGNS: THE SENATE DECREES A TWO-WEEK THANKSGIVING TO THE GODS TO CELEBRATE THEIR HERO.
CAESAR RETURNS TO CISALPINE GAUL... VERCINGETORIX REJOINS HIS PEOPLE FOR A WELL-DESERVED REST. INDEED, MANY WARRIORS UNDER HIS COMMAND LOST THEIR LIVES IN THE BATTLE OF THE SABIS.

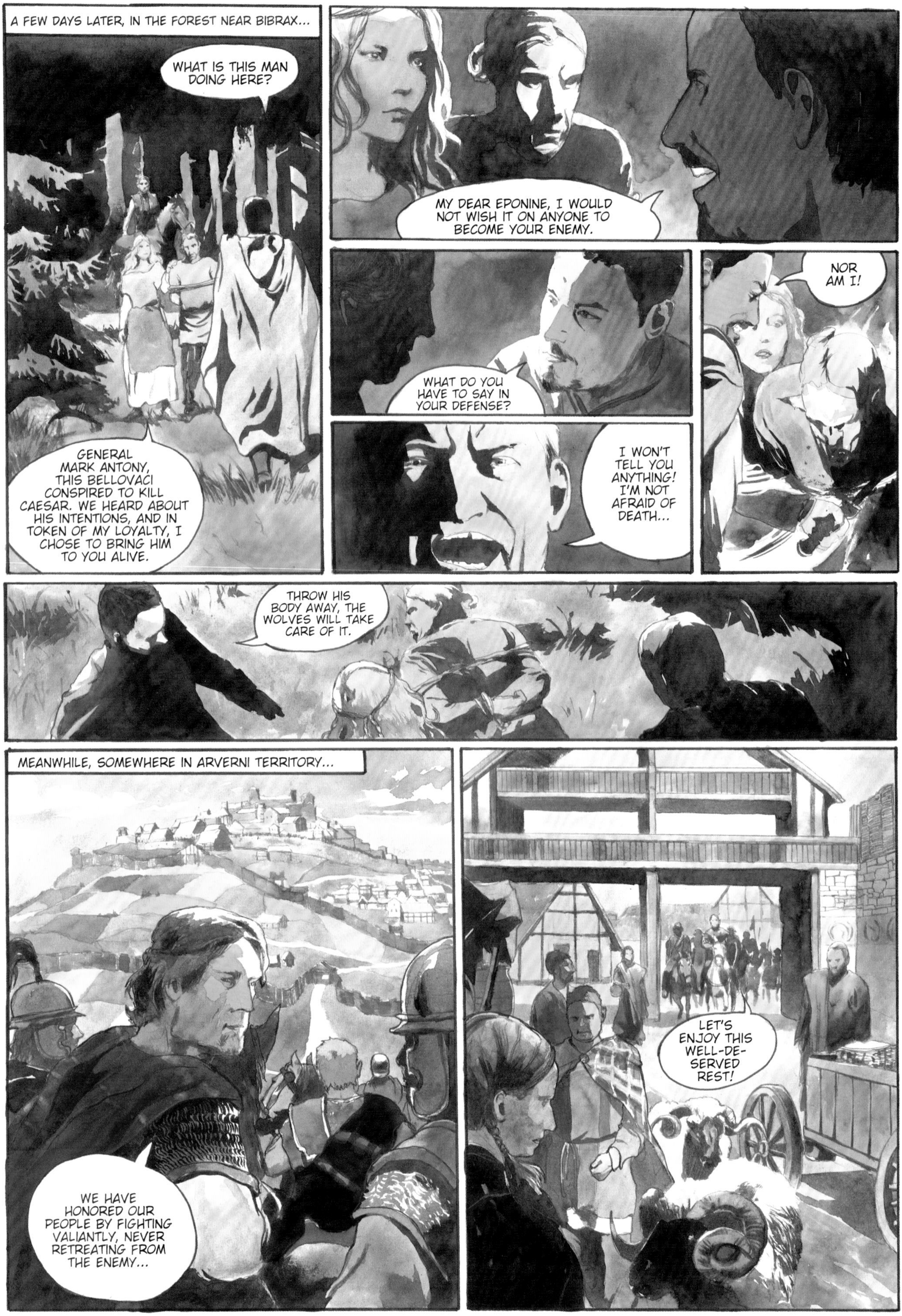
A FEW DAYS LATER, IN THE FOREST NEAR BIBRAX...
WHAT IS THIS MAN DOING HERE?
GENERAL MARK ANTONY, THIS BELLOVACI CONSPIRED TO KILL CAESAR. WE HEARD ABOUT HIS INTENTIONS, AND IN TOKEN OF MY LOYALTY, I CHOSE TO BRING HIM TO YOU ALIVE.
MY DEAR EPONINE, I WOULD NOT WISH IT ON ANYONE TO BECOME YOUR ENEMY.
WHAT DO YOU HAVE TO SAY IN YOUR DEFENSE?
I WON'T TELL YOU ANYTHING! I'M NOT AFRAID OF DEATH...
NOR AM I!
THROW HIS BODY AWAY, THE WOLVES WILL TAKE CARE OF IT.
MEANWHILE, SOMEWHERE IN ARVERNI TERRITORY...
WE HAVE HONORED OUR PEOPLE BY FIGHTING VALIANTLY, NEVER RETREATING FROM THE ENEMY...
LET'S ENJOY THIS WELL-DESERVED REST!

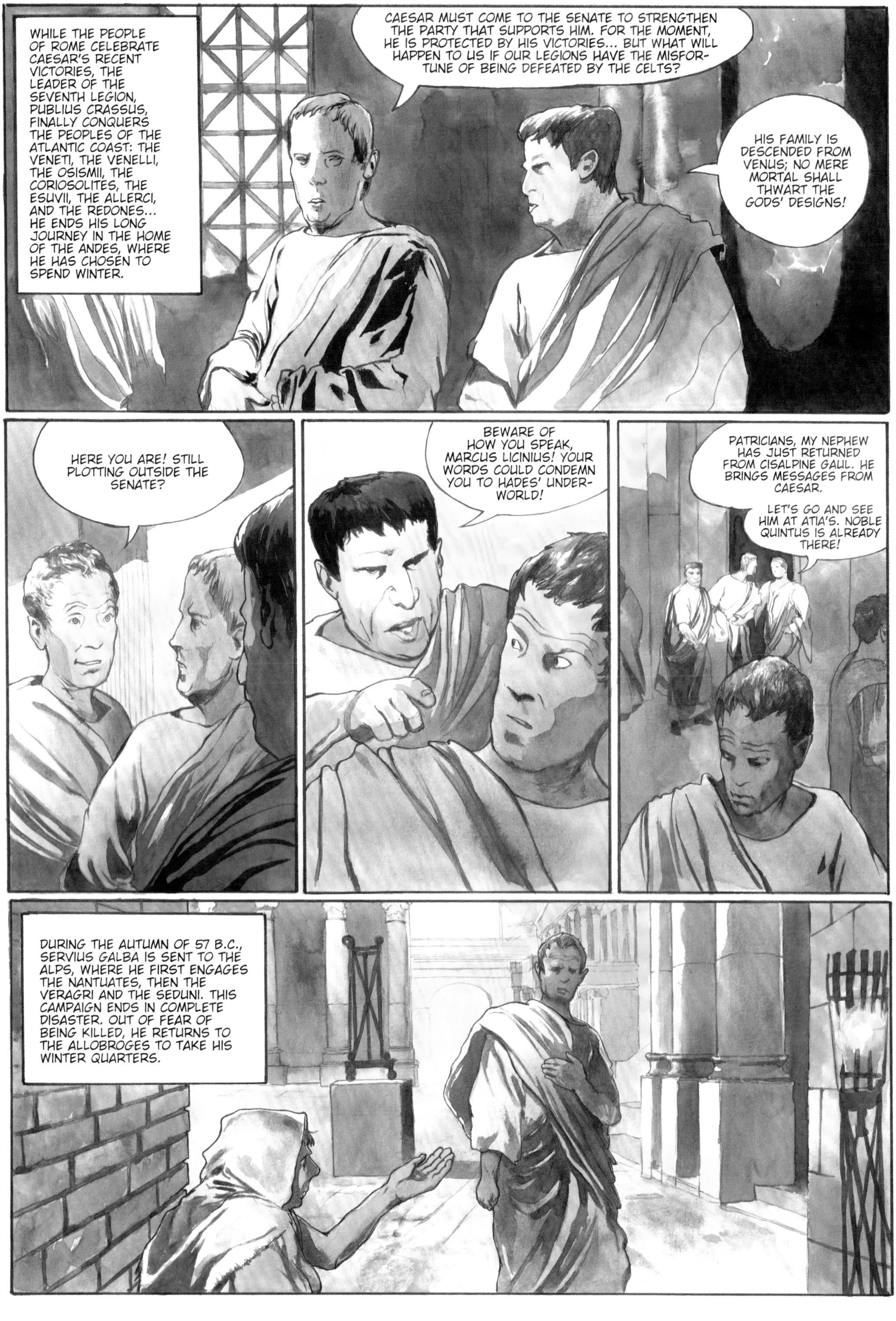
WHILE THE PEOPLE OF ROME CELEBRATE CAESAR'S RECENT VICTORIES, THE LEADER OF THE SEVENTH LEGION, PUBLIUS CRASSUS, FINALLY CONQUERS THE PEOPLES OF THE ATLANTIC COAST: THE VENETI, THE VENELLI, THE OSISMII, THE CORIOSOLITES, THE ESUVII, THE ALLERCI, AND THE REDONES... HE ENDS HIS LONG JOURNEY IN THE HOME OF THE ANDES, WHERE HE HAS CHOSEN TO SPEND WINTER.
CAESAR MUST COME TO THE SENATE TO STRENGTHEN THE PARTY THAT SUPPORTS HIM. FOR THE MOMENT, HE IS PROTECTED BY HIS VICTORIES... BUT WHAT WILL HAPPEN TO US IF OUR LEGIONS HAVE THE MISFORTUNE OF BEING DEFEATED BY THE CELTS?
HIS FAMILY IS DESCENDED FROM VENUS; NO MERE MORTAL SHALL THWART THE GODS' DESIGNS!
HERE YOU ARE! STILL PLOTTING OUTSIDE THE SENATE?
BEWARE OF HOW YOU SPEAK, MARCUS LICINIUS! YOUR WORDS COULD CONDEMN YOU TO HADES' UNDERWORLD!
PATRICIANS, MY NEPHEW HAS JUST RETURNED FROM CISALPINE GAUL. HE BRINGS MESSAGES FROM CAESAR.
LET'S GO AND SEE HIM AT ATIA'S. NOBLE QUINTUS IS ALREADY THERE!
DURING THE AUTUMN OF 57 B.C., SERVIUS GALBA IS SENT TO THE ALPS, WHERE HE FIRST ENGAGES THE NANTUATES, THEN THE VERAGRI AND THE SEDUNI. THIS CAMPAIGN ENDS IN COMPLETE DISASTER. OUT OF FEAR OF BEING KILLED, HE RETURNS TO THE ALLOBROGES TO TAKE HIS WINTER QUARTERS.

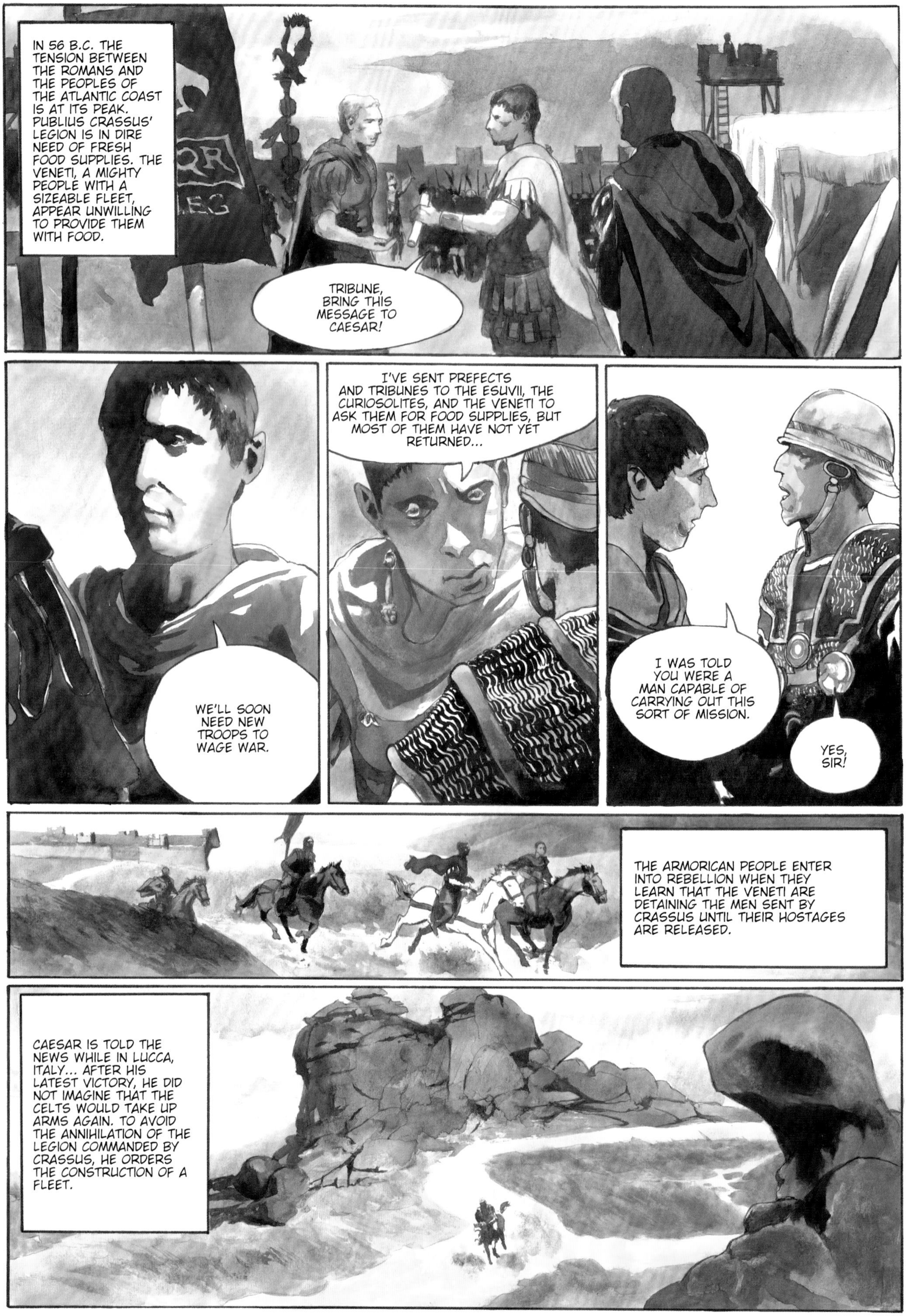
IN 56 B.C. THE TENSION BETWEEN THE ROMANS AND THE PEOPLES OF THE ATLANTIC COAST IS AT ITS PEAK. PUBLIUS CRASSUS' LEGION IS IN DIRE NEED OF FRESH FOOD SUPPLIES. THE VENETI, A MIGHTY PEOPLE WITH A SIZEABLE FLEET, APPEAR UNWILLING TO PROVIDE THEM WITH FOOD.
TRIBUNE, BRING THIS MESSAGE TO CAESAR!
WE'LL SOON NEED NEW TROOPS TO WAGE WAR.
I'VE SENT PREFECTS AND TRIBUNES TO THE ESUVII, THE CURIOSOLITES, AND THE VENETI TO ASK THEM FOR FOOD SUPPLIES, BUT MOST OF THEM HAVE NOT YET RETURNED...
I WAS TOLD YOU WERE A MAN CAPABLE OF CARRYING OUT THIS SORT OF MISSION.
YES, SIR!
THE ARMORICAN PEOPLE ENTER INTO REBELLION WHEN THEY LEARN THAT THE VENETI ARE DETAINING THE MEN SENT BY CRASSUS UNTIL THEIR HOSTAGES ARE RELEASED.
CAESAR IS TOLD THE NEWS WHILE IN LUCCA, ITALY... AFTER HIS LATEST VICTORY, HE DID NOT IMAGINE THAT THE CELTS WOULD TAKE UP ARMS AGAIN. TO AVOID THE ANNIHILATION OF THE LEGION COMMANDED BY CRASSUS, HE ORDERS THE CONSTRUCTION OF A FLEET.

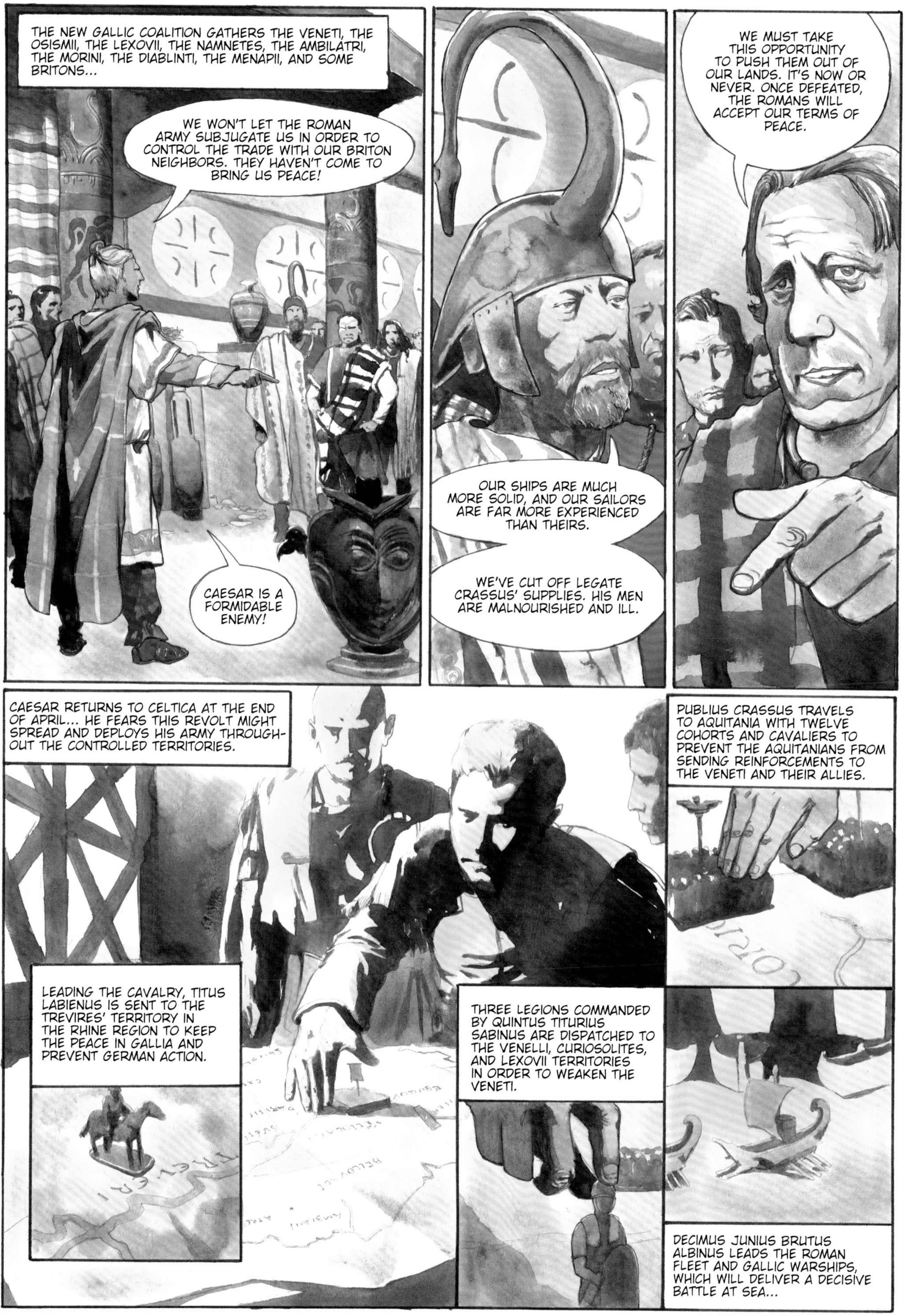
THE NEW GALLIC COALITION GATHERS THE VENETI, THE OSISMII, THE LEXOVII, THE NAMNETES, THE AMBILATRI, THE MORINI, THE DIABLINTI, THE MENAPII, AND SOME BRITONS...
WE WON'T LET THE ROMAN ARMY SUBJUGATE US IN ORDER TO CONTROL THE TRADE WITH OUR BRITON NEIGHBORS. THEY HAVEN'T COME TO BRING US PEACE!
CAESAR IS A FORMIDABLE ENEMY!
OUR SHIPS ARE MUCH MORE SOLID, AND OUR SAILORS ARE FAR MORE EXPERIENCED THAN THEIRS.
WE'VE CUT OFF LEGATE CRASSUS' SUPPLIES. HIS MEN ARE MALNOURISHED AND ILL.
WE MUST TAKE THIS OPPORTUNITY TO PUSH THEM OUT OF OUR LANDS. IT'S NOW OR NEVER. ONCE DEFEATED, THE ROMANS WILL ACCEPT OUR TERMS OF PEACE.
CAESAR RETURNS TO CELTICA AT THE END OF APRIL... HE FEARS THIS REVOLT MIGHT SPREAD AND DEPLOYS HIS ARMY THROUGHOUT THE CONTROLLED TERRITORIES.
PUBLIUS CRASSUS TRAVELS TO AQUITANIA WITH TWELVE COHORTS AND CAVALIERS TO PREVENT THE AQUITANIANS FROM SENDING REINFORCEMENTS TO THE VENETI AND THEIR ALLIES.
LEADING THE CAVALRY, TITUS LABIENUS IS SENT TO THE TREVIRES' TERRITORY IN THE RHINE REGION TO KEEP THE PEACE IN GALLIA AND PREVENT GERMAN ACTION.
THREE LEGIONS COMMANDED BY QUINTUS TITURIUS SABINUS ARE DISPATCHED TO THE VENELLI, CURIOSOLITES, AND LEXOVII TERRITORIES IN ORDER TO WEAKEN THE VENETI.
DECIMUS JUNIUS BRUTUS ALBINUS LEADS THE ROMAN FLEET AND GALLIC WARSHIPS, WHICH WILL DELIVER A DECISIVE BATTLE AT SEA...

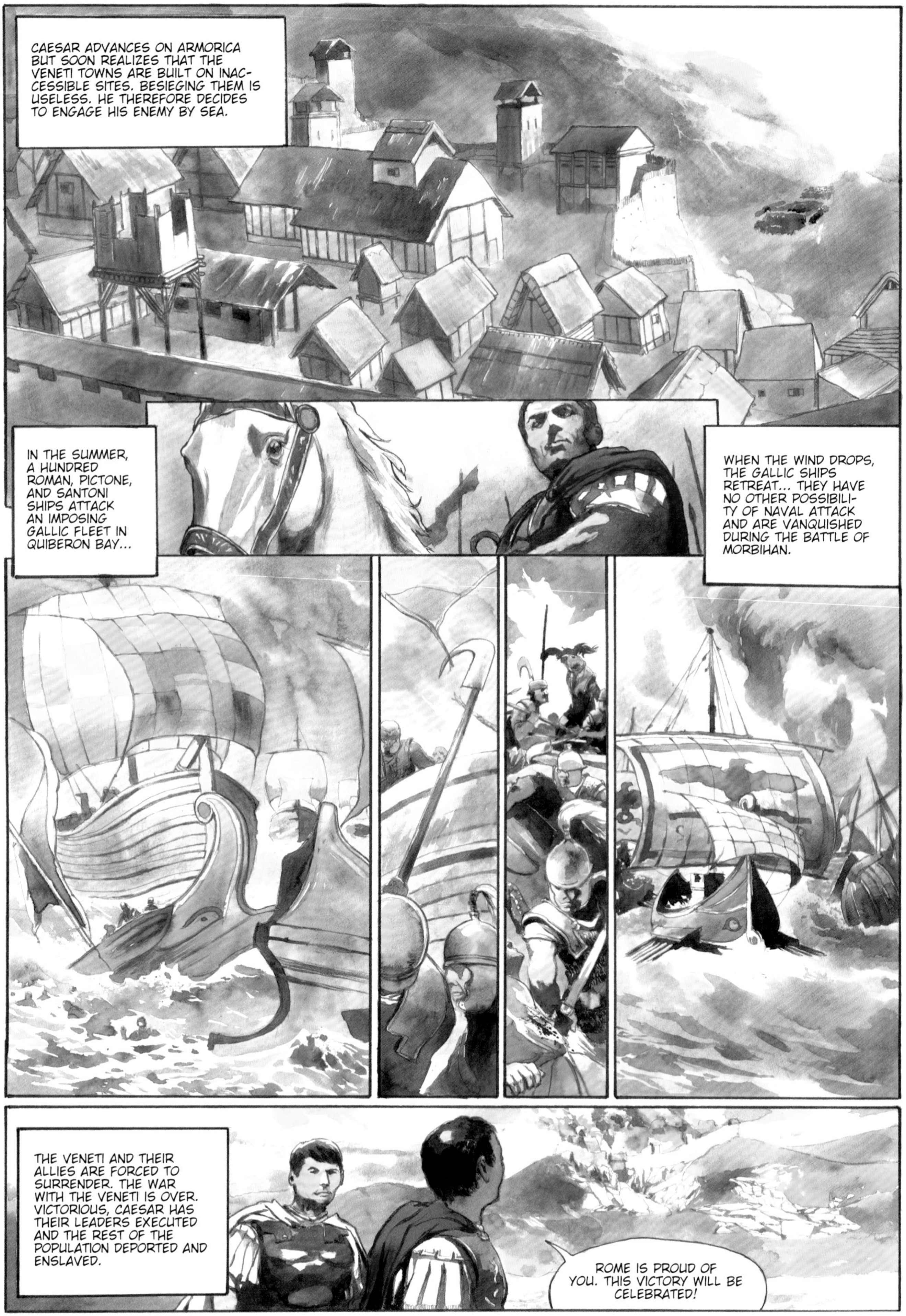
CAESAR ADVANCES ON ARMORICA BUT SOON REALIZES THAT THE VENETI TOWNS ARE BUILT ON INACCESSIBLE SITES. BESIEGING THEM IS USELESS. HE THEREFORE DECIDES TO ENGAGE HIS ENEMY BY SEA.
IN THE SUMMER, A HUNDRED ROMAN, PICTONE, AND SANTONI SHIPS ATTACK AN IMPOSING GALLIC FLEET IN QUIBERON BAY...
WHEN THE WIND DROPS, THE GALLIC SHIPS RETREAT... THEY HAVE NO OTHER POSSIBILITY OF NAVAL ATTACK AND ARE VANQUISHED DURING THE BATTLE OF MORBIHAN.
THE VENETI AND THEIR ALLIES ARE FORCED TO SURRENDER. THE WAR WITH THE VENETI IS OVER. VICTORIOUS, CAESAR HAS THEIR LEADERS EXECUTED AND THE REST OF THE POPULATION DEPORTED AND ENSLAVED.
ROME IS PROUD OF YOU. THIS VICTORY WILL BE CELEBRATED!

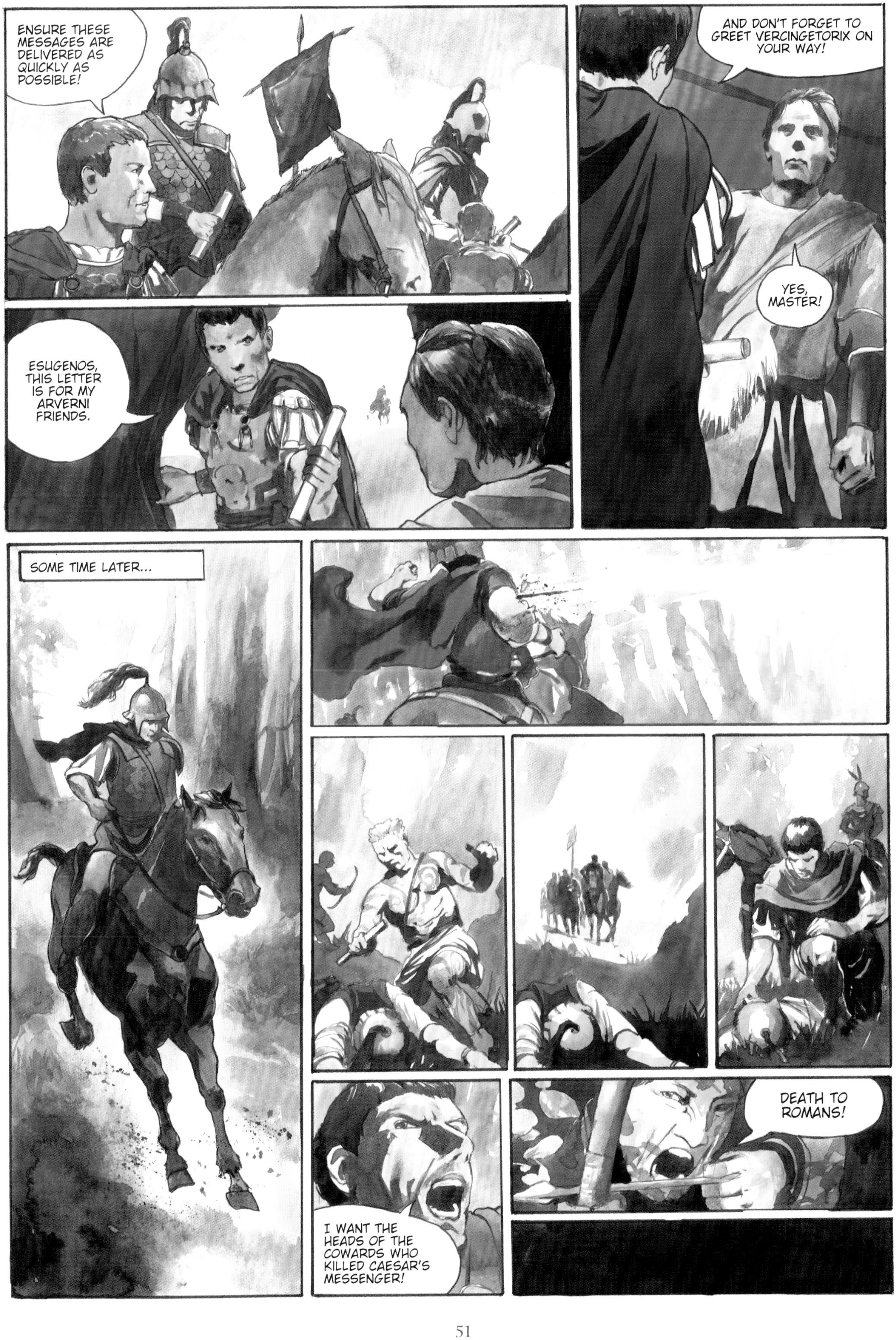
ENSURE THESE MESSAGES ARE DELIVERED AS QUICKLY AS POSSIBLE!
AND DON'T FORGET TO GREET VERCINGETORIX ON YOUR WAY!
ESUGENOS, THIS LETTER IS FOR MY ARVERNI FRIENDS.
YES, MASTER!
SOME TIME LATER...
I WANT THE HEADS OF THE COWARDS WHO KILLED CAESAR'S MESSENGER!
DEATH TO ROMANS!

LEADING THREE LEGIONS, QUINTUS TITURIUS SABINUS STARTS A CAMPAIGN AGAINST THE VENELLI. VIRIDORIX, THEIR CHIEF, HAS RECEIVED THE SUPPORT OF THE AULERCI, THE EBUROVICES, AND THE LEXOVII... THE CONFRONTATION BECOMES INEVITABLE...

CENTURION, THEY'RE COMING FROM THE NORTH!

SPREAD THE RUMOR THAT CAESAR IS DEFEATED... OUR ENEMIES MUST THINK WE'RE HOPELESS AND AFRAID TO FIGHT IN THE PLAINS.

LET THE GAULS ATTACK FIRST, AND THEN WE'LL REACT ACCORDINGLY.

OUR MEN ARE READY TO FIGHT STRAIGHT AWAY.

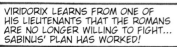

VIRIDORIX LEARNS FROM ONE OF HIS LIEUTENANTS THAT THE ROMANS ARE NO LONGER WILLING TO FIGHT... SABINUS' PLAN HAS WORKED!

THE NEXT MORNING...

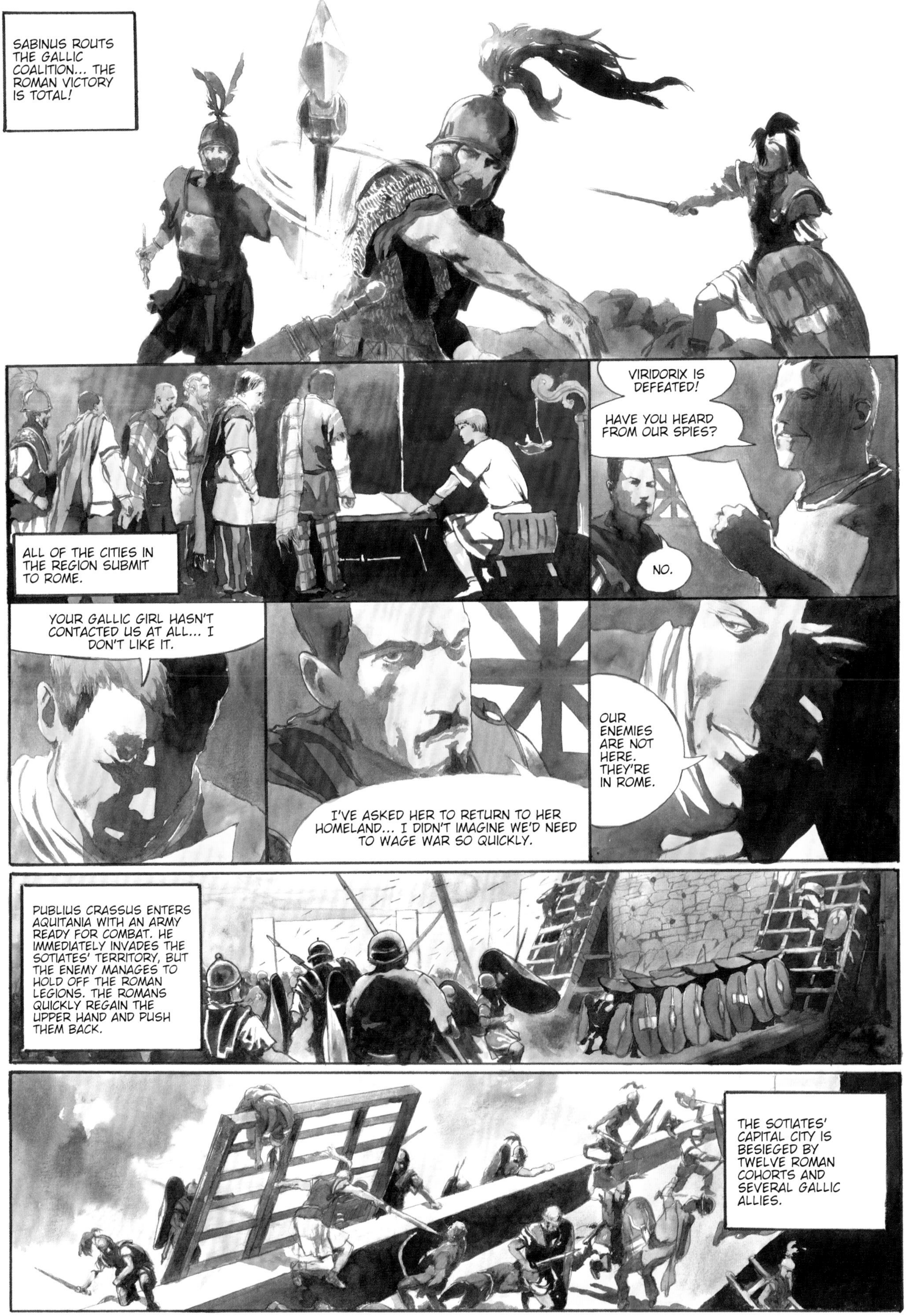
SABINUS ROUTS THE GALLIC COALITION... THE ROMAN VICTORY IS TOTAL!
ALL OF THE CITIES IN THE REGION SUBMIT TO ROME.
VIRIDORIX IS DEFEATED!
HAVE YOU HEARD FROM OUR SPIES?
NO.
YOUR GALLIC GIRL HASN'T CONTACTED US AT ALL... I DON'T LIKE IT.
I'VE ASKED HER TO RETURN TO HER HOMELAND... I DIDN'T IMAGINE WE'D NEED TO WAGE WAR SO QUICKLY.
OUR ENEMIES ARE NOT HERE. THEY'RE IN ROME.
PUBLIUS CRASSUS ENTERS AQUITANIA WITH AN ARMY READY FOR COMBAT. HE IMMEDIATELY INVADES THE SOTIATES' TERRITORY, BUT THE ENEMY MANAGES TO HOLD OFF THE ROMAN LEGIONS. THE ROMANS QUICKLY REGAIN THE UPPER HAND AND PUSH THEM BACK.
THE SOTIATES' CAPITAL CITY IS BESIEGED BY TWELVE ROMAN COHORTS AND SEVERAL GALLIC ALLIES.

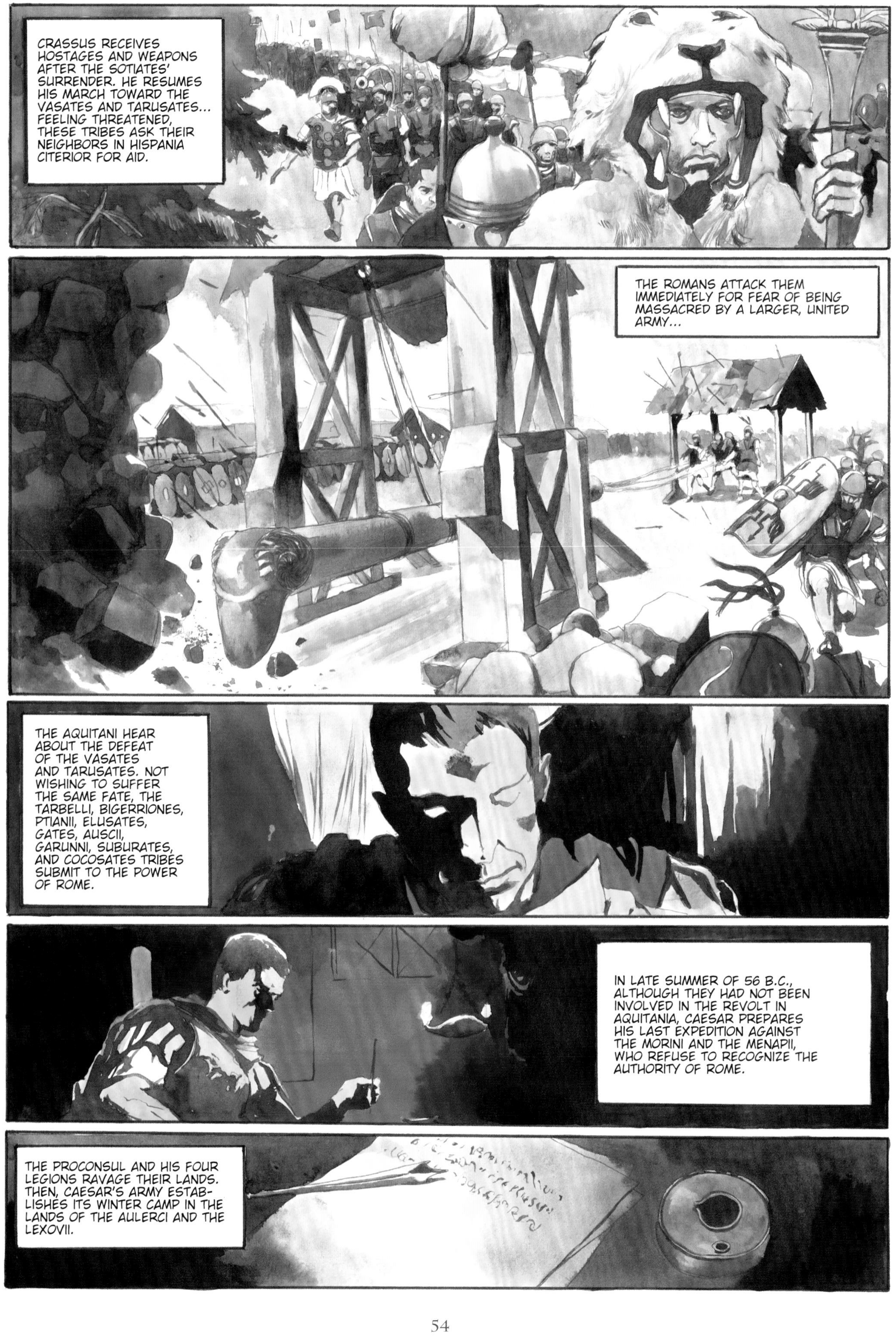
CRASSUS RECEIVES HOSTAGES AND WEAPONS AFTER THE SOTIATES' SURRENDER. HE RESUMES HIS MARCH TOWARD THE VASATES AND TARUSATES... FEELING THREATENED, THESE TRIBES ASK THEIR NEIGHBORS IN HISPANIA CITERIOR FOR AID.
THE ROMANS ATTACK THEM IMMEDIATELY FOR FEAR OF BEING MASSACRED BY A LARGER, UNITED ARMY...
THE AQUITANI HEAR ABOUT THE DEFEAT OF THE VASATES AND TARUSATES. NOT WISHING TO SUFFER THE SAME FATE, THE TARBELLI, BIGERRIONES, PTIANII, ELUSATES, GATES, AUSCII, GARUNNI, SUBURATES, AND COCOSATES TRIBES SUBMIT TO THE POWER OF ROME.
IN LATE SUMMER OF 56 B.C., ALTHOUGH THEY HAD NOT BEEN INVOLVED IN THE REVOLT IN AQUITANIA, CAESAR PREPARES HIS LAST EXPEDITION AGAINST THE MORINI AND THE MENAPII, WHO REFUSE TO RECOGNIZE THE AUTHORITY OF ROME.
THE PROCONSUL AND HIS FOUR LEGIONS RAVAGE THEIR LANDS. THEN, CAESAR'S ARMY ESTABLISHES ITS WINTER CAMP IN THE LANDS OF THE AULERCI AND THE LEXOVII.

I DON'T UNDERSTAND...

WHO ARE YOU, OLD MAN?

I KNEW CELTILLUS, YOUR FATHER... A GREAT MAN WHO UNITED ALL THE GAULS DURING THE ARVERNI REIGN.

VERCINGETORIX, ARE YOU SURE THAT YOUR STEPS LEAD YOU IN THE RIGHT DIRECTION?

HASN'T YOUR MOTHER TOLD YOU? I DOUBT IT... SHE WAS RIGHT TO PROTECT YOU, BUT TIMES HAVE CHANGED, AND YOU MUST NOW KNOW THE TRUTH!

HE WAS MURDERED IN THE MOST COWARDLY MANNER...

YES... BY MEN WHO CHOSE TO DIVIDE US! TRAITORS WHO UNDER-STAND NOTHING ABOUT OUR GODS AND HAVE CHOSEN TO SIDE WITH THE ROMANS.

DO YOU REALLY BELIEVE THAT CAESAR HAS COME TO CELTICA WITH THE SOLE INTENTION OF HELPING ITS TRIBES? DO YOU THINK HE WILL GO BACK TO ROME WITHOUT CONQUER-ING OUR LANDS?

HE HAS COME HERE TO ENSLAVE US ALL!

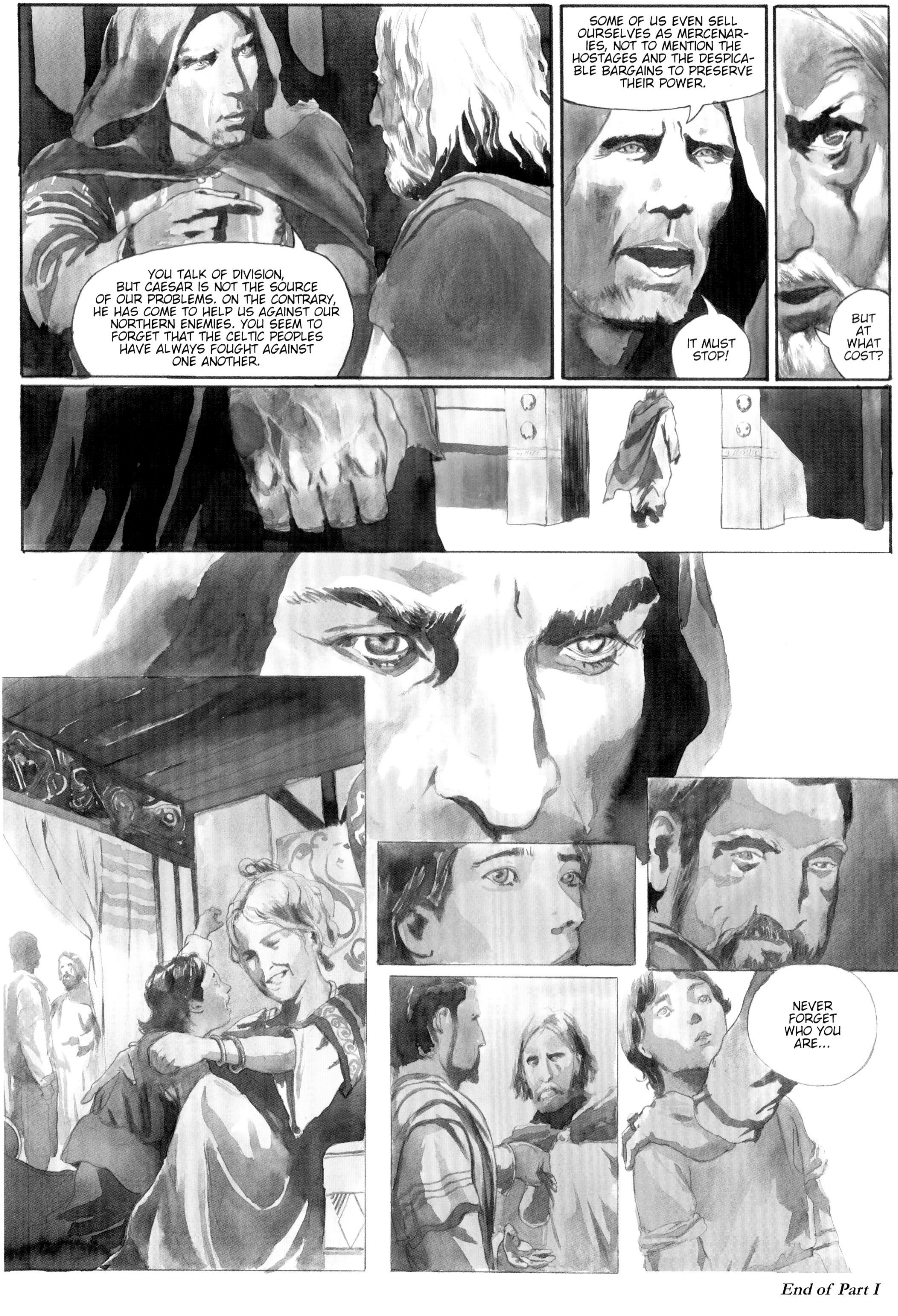
YOU TALK OF DIVISION, BUT CAESAR IS NOT THE SOURCE OF OUR PROBLEMS. ON THE CONTRARY, HE HAS COME TO HELP US AGAINST OUR NORTHERN ENEMIES. YOU SEEM TO FORGET THAT THE CELTIC PEOPLES HAVE ALWAYS FOUGHT AGAINST ONE ANOTHER.
SOME OF US EVEN SELL OURSELVES AS MERCENARIES, NOT TO MENTION THE HOSTAGES AND THE DESPICABLE BARGAINS TO PRESERVE THEIR POWER.
IT MUST STOP!
BUT AT WHAT COST?
NEVER FORGET WHO YOU ARE...

*End of Part I*

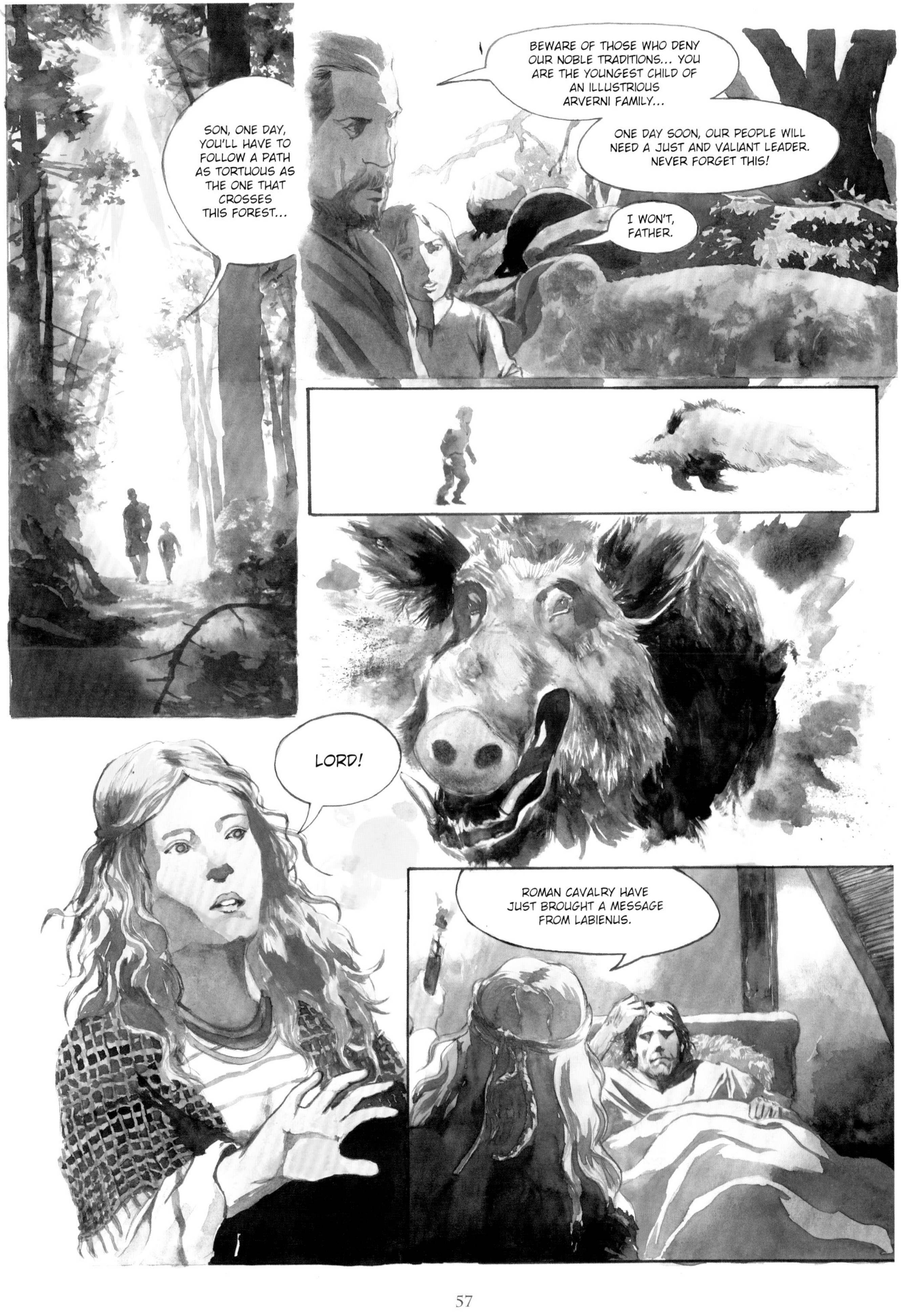
SON, ONE DAY, YOU'LL HAVE TO FOLLOW A PATH AS TORTUOUS AS THE ONE THAT CROSSES THIS FOREST...
BEWARE OF THOSE WHO DENY OUR NOBLE TRADITIONS... YOU ARE THE YOUNGEST CHILD OF AN ILLUSTRIOUS ARVERNI FAMILY...
ONE DAY SOON, OUR PEOPLE WILL NEED A JUST AND VALIANT LEADER. NEVER FORGET THIS!
I WON'T, FATHER.
LORD!
ROMAN CAVALRY HAVE JUST BROUGHT A MESSAGE FROM LABIENUS.

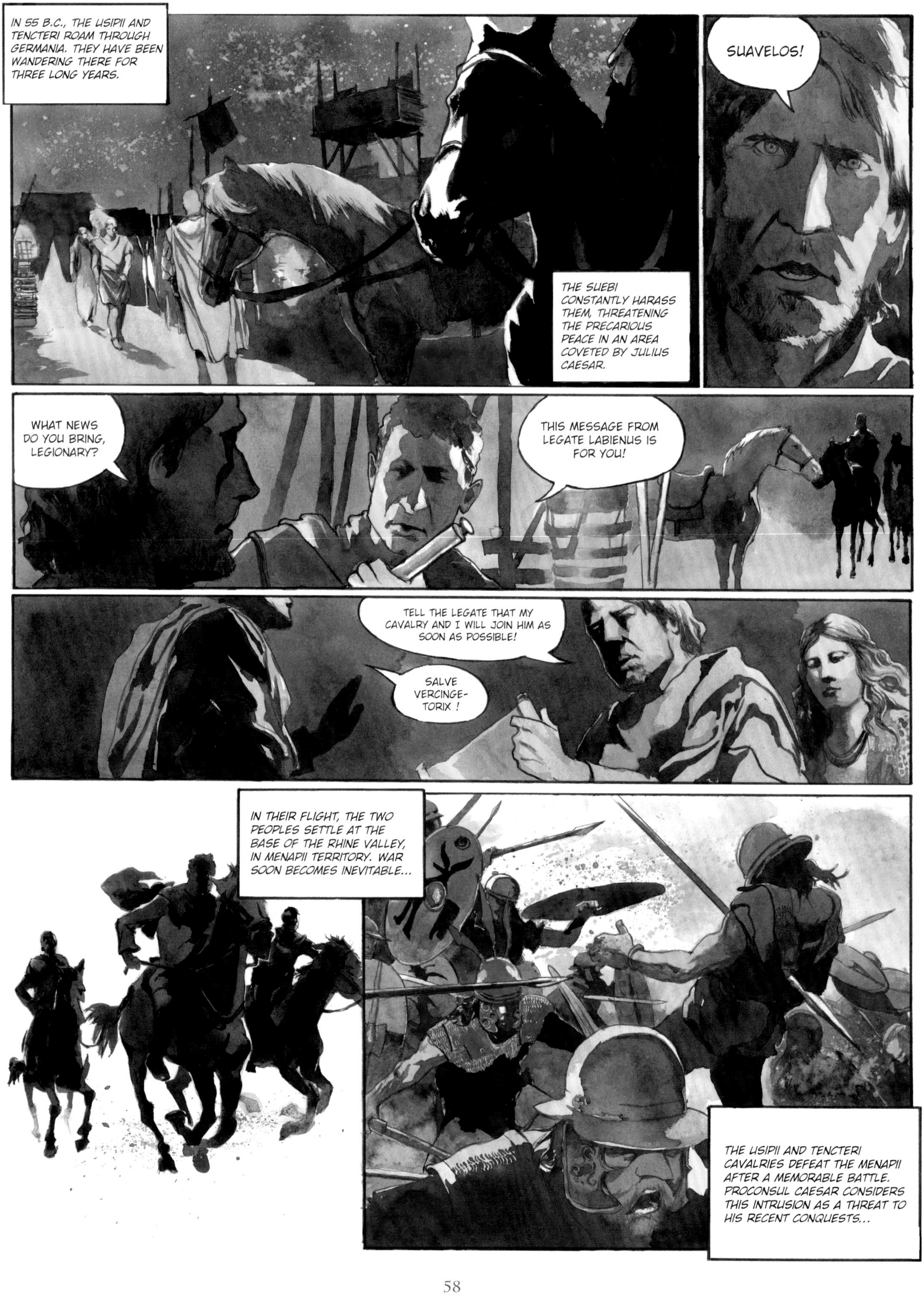
IN 55 B.C., THE USIPII AND TENCTERI ROAM THROUGH GERMANIA. THEY HAVE BEEN WANDERING THERE FOR THREE LONG YEARS.
THE SUEBI CONSTANTLY HARASS THEM, THREATENING THE PRECARIOUS PEACE IN AN AREA COVETED BY JULIUS CAESAR.
SUAVELOS!
WHAT NEWS DO YOU BRING, LEGIONARY?
THIS MESSAGE FROM LEGATE LABIENUS IS FOR YOU!
TELL THE LEGATE THAT MY CAVALRY AND I WILL JOIN HIM AS SOON AS POSSIBLE!
SALVE VERCINGE-TORIX !
IN THEIR FLIGHT, THE TWO PEOPLES SETTLE AT THE BASE OF THE RHINE VALLEY, IN MENAPII TERRITORY. WAR SOON BECOMES INEVITABLE...
THE USIPII AND TENCTERI CAVALRIES DEFEAT THE MENAPII AFTER A MEMORABLE BATTLE. PROCONSUL CAESAR CONSIDERS THIS INTRUSION AS A THREAT TO HIS RECENT CONQUESTS...

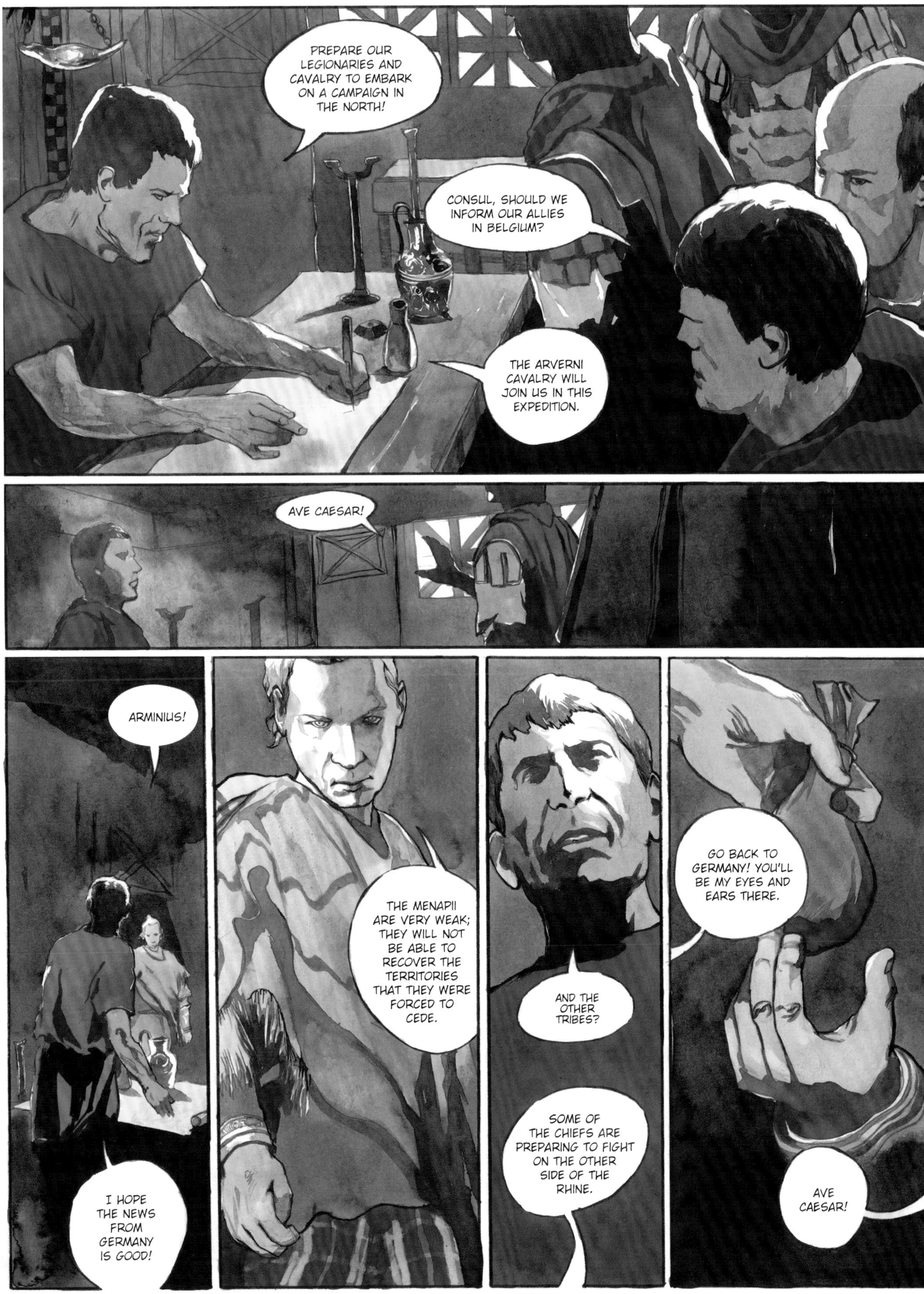
PREPARE OUR LEGIONARIES AND CAVALRY TO EMBARK ON A CAMPAIGN IN THE NORTH!
CONSUL, SHOULD WE INFORM OUR ALLIES IN BELGIUM?
THE ARVERNI CAVALRY WILL JOIN US IN THIS EXPEDITION.
AVE CAESAR!
ARMINIUS!
I HOPE THE NEWS FROM GERMANY IS GOOD!
THE MENAPII ARE VERY WEAK; THEY WILL NOT BE ABLE TO RECOVER THE TERRITORIES THAT THEY WERE FORCED TO CEDE.
AND THE OTHER TRIBES?
SOME OF THE CHIEFS ARE PREPARING TO FIGHT ON THE OTHER SIDE OF THE RHINE.
GO BACK TO GERMANY! YOU'LL BE MY EYES AND EARS THERE.
AVE CAESAR!

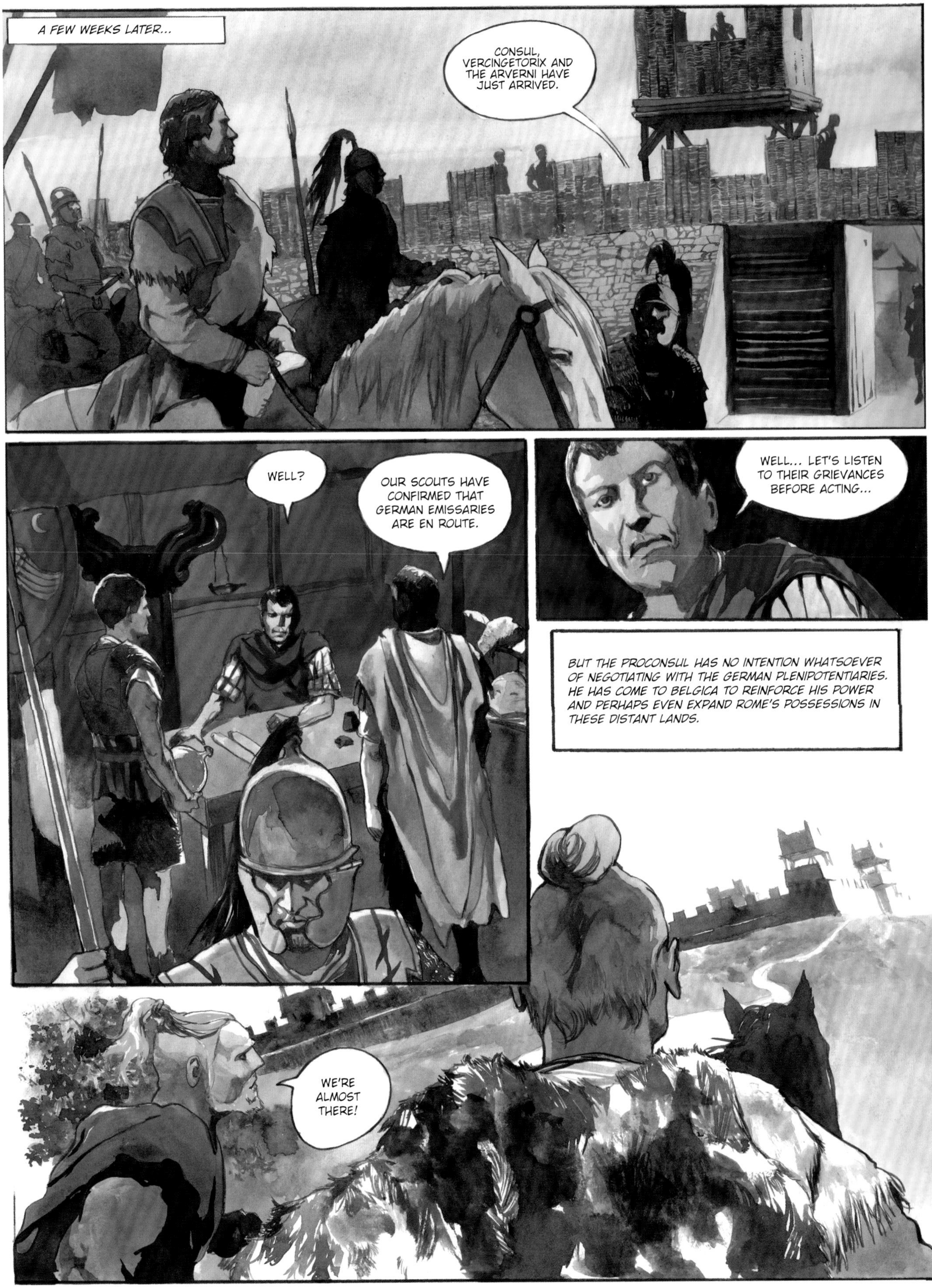
A FEW WEEKS LATER...
CONSUL, VERCINGETORIX AND THE ARVERNI HAVE JUST ARRIVED.
WELL?
OUR SCOUTS HAVE CONFIRMED THAT GERMAN EMISSARIES ARE EN ROUTE.
WELL... LET'S LISTEN TO THEIR GRIEVANCES BEFORE ACTING...
BUT THE PROCONSUL HAS NO INTENTION WHATSOEVER OF NEGOTIATING WITH THE GERMAN PLENIPOTENTIARIES. HE HAS COME TO BELGICA TO REINFORCE HIS POWER AND PERHAPS EVEN EXPAND ROME'S POSSESSIONS IN THESE DISTANT LANDS.
WE'RE ALMOST THERE!

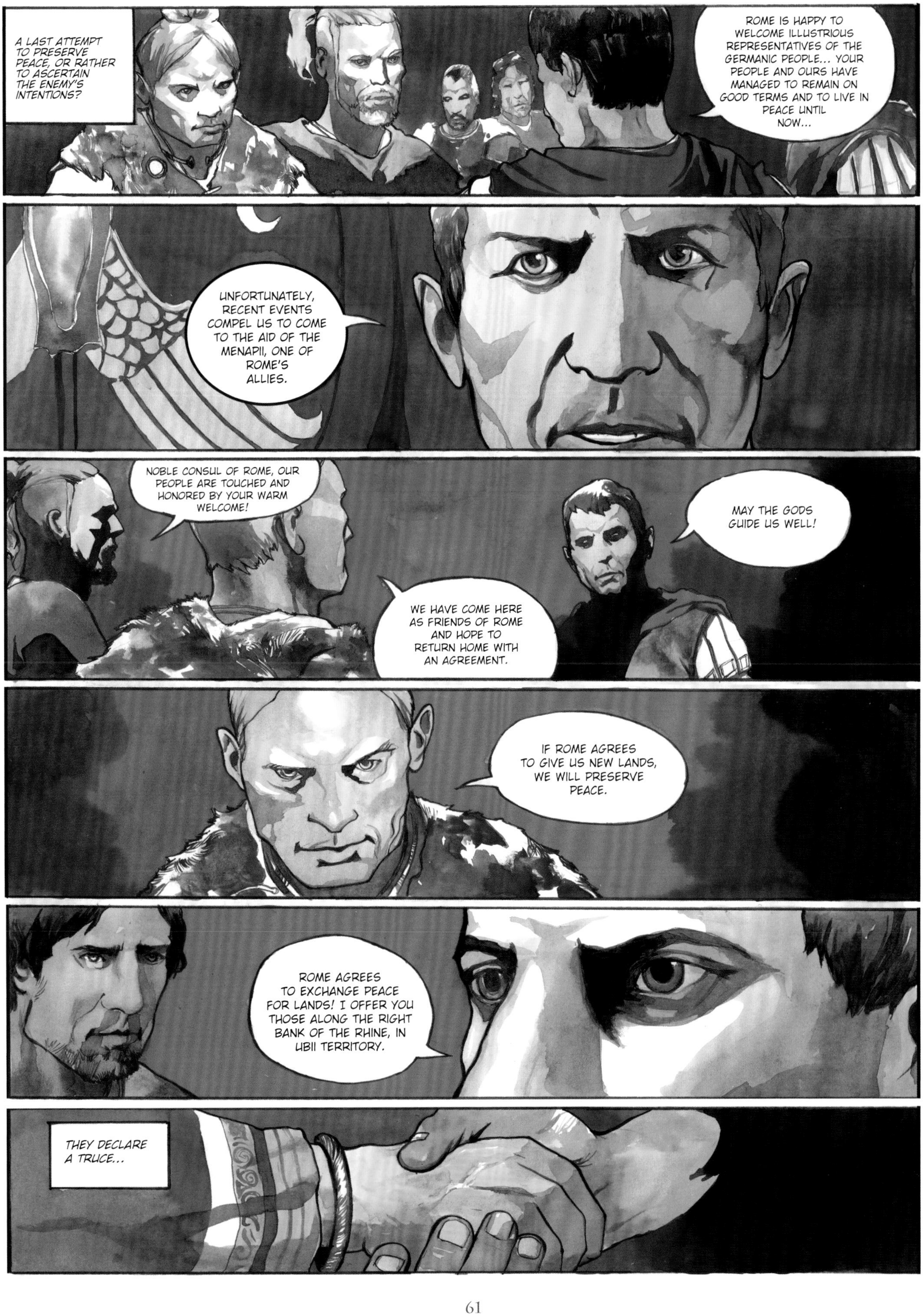
A LAST ATTEMPT TO PRESERVE PEACE, OR RATHER TO ASCERTAIN THE ENEMY'S INTENTIONS?
ROME IS HAPPY TO WELCOME ILLUSTRIOUS REPRESENTATIVES OF THE GERMANIC PEOPLE... YOUR PEOPLE AND OURS HAVE MANAGED TO REMAIN ON GOOD TERMS AND TO LIVE IN PEACE UNTIL NOW...
UNFORTUNATELY, RECENT EVENTS COMPEL US TO COME TO THE AID OF THE MENAPII, ONE OF ROME'S ALLIES.
NOBLE CONSUL OF ROME, OUR PEOPLE ARE TOUCHED AND HONORED BY YOUR WARM WELCOME!
WE HAVE COME HERE AS FRIENDS OF ROME AND HOPE TO RETURN HOME WITH AN AGREEMENT.
MAY THE GODS GUIDE US WELL!
IF ROME AGREES TO GIVE US NEW LANDS, WE WILL PRESERVE PEACE.
ROME AGREES TO EXCHANGE PEACE FOR LANDS! I OFFER YOU THOSE ALONG THE RIGHT BANK OF THE RHINE, IN UBII TERRITORY.
THEY DECLARE A TRUCE...

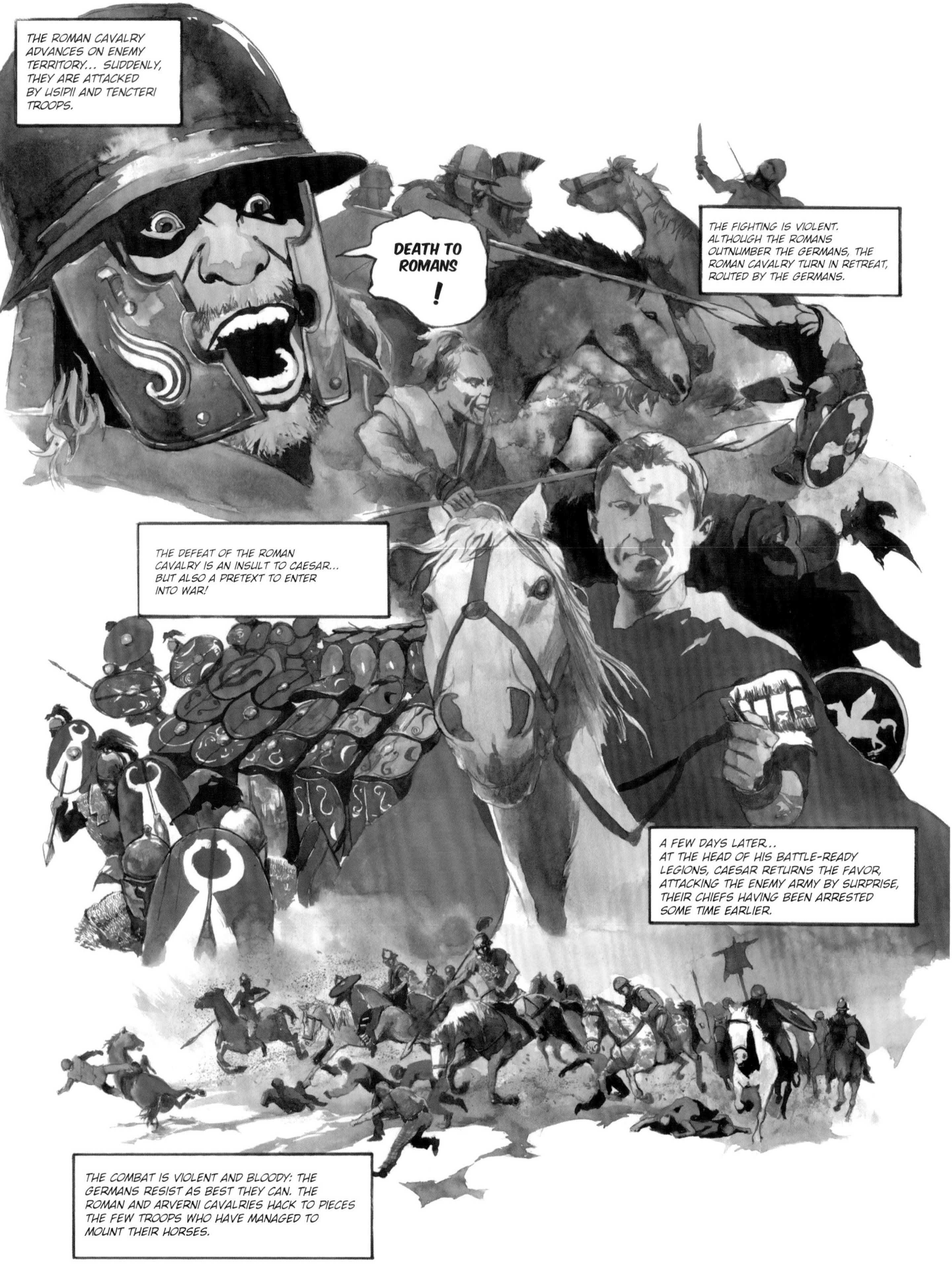
THE ROMAN CAVALRY ADVANCES ON ENEMY TERRITORY... SUDDENLY, THEY ARE ATTACKED BY USIPII AND TENCTERI TROOPS.
DEATH TO ROMANS !
THE FIGHTING IS VIOLENT. ALTHOUGH THE ROMANS OUTNUMBER THE GERMANS, THE ROMAN CAVALRY TURN IN RETREAT, ROUTED BY THE GERMANS.
THE DEFEAT OF THE ROMAN CAVALRY IS AN INSULT TO CAESAR... BUT ALSO A PRETEXT TO ENTER INTO WAR!
A FEW DAYS LATER... AT THE HEAD OF HIS BATTLE-READY LEGIONS, CAESAR RETURNS THE FAVOR, ATTACKING THE ENEMY ARMY BY SURPRISE, THEIR CHIEFS HAVING BEEN ARRESTED SOME TIME EARLIER.
THE COMBAT IS VIOLENT AND BLOODY: THE GERMANS RESIST AS BEST THEY CAN. THE ROMAN AND ARVERNI CAVALRIES HACK TO PIECES THE FEW TROOPS WHO HAVE MANAGED TO MOUNT THEIR HORSES.

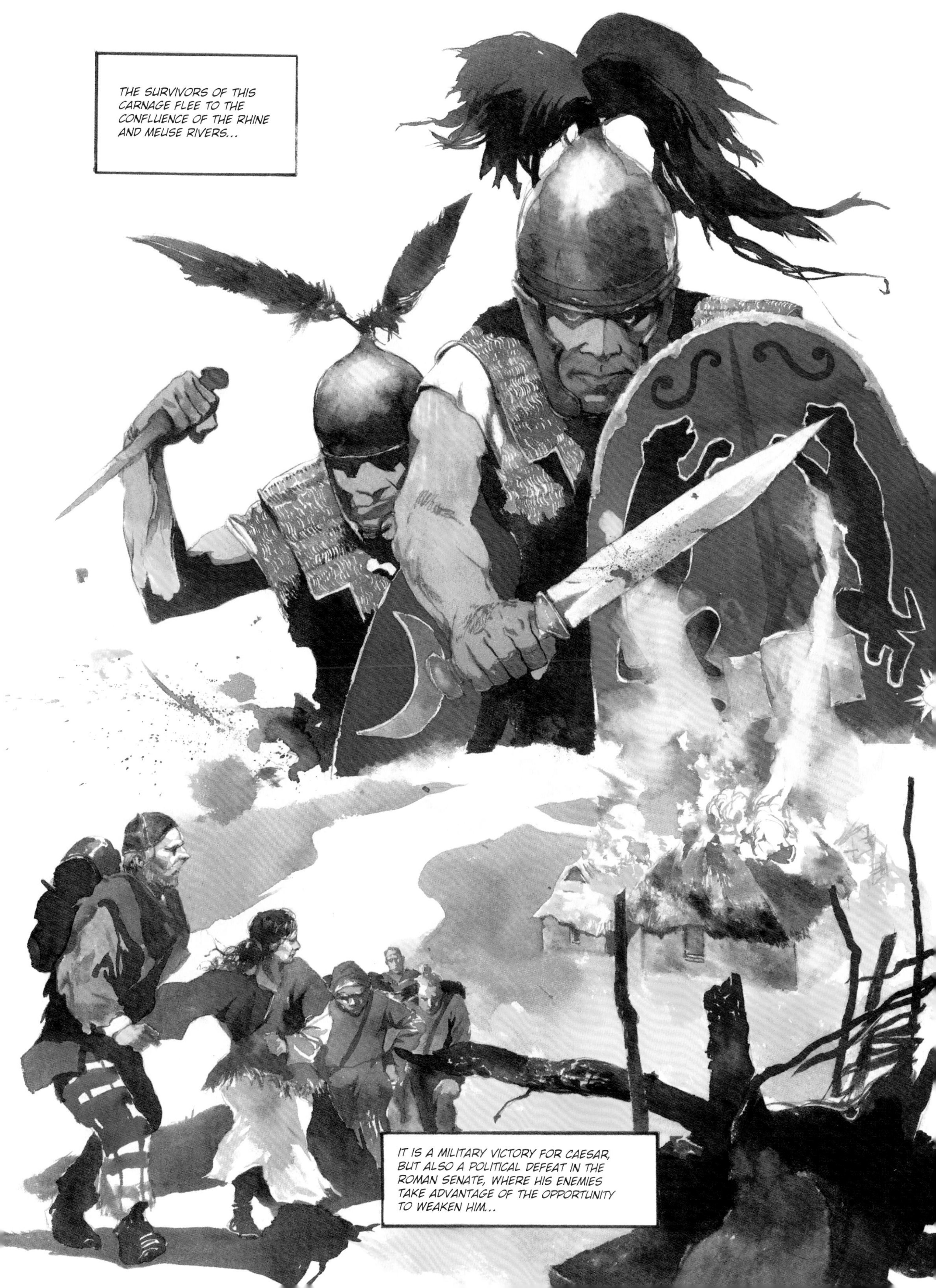
THE SURVIVORS OF THIS CARNAGE FLEE TO THE CONFLUENCE OF THE RHINE AND MEUSE RIVERS...
IT IS A MILITARY VICTORY FOR CAESAR, BUT ALSO A POLITICAL DEFEAT IN THE ROMAN SENATE, WHERE HIS ENEMIES TAKE ADVANTAGE OF THE OPPORTUNITY TO WEAKEN HIM...

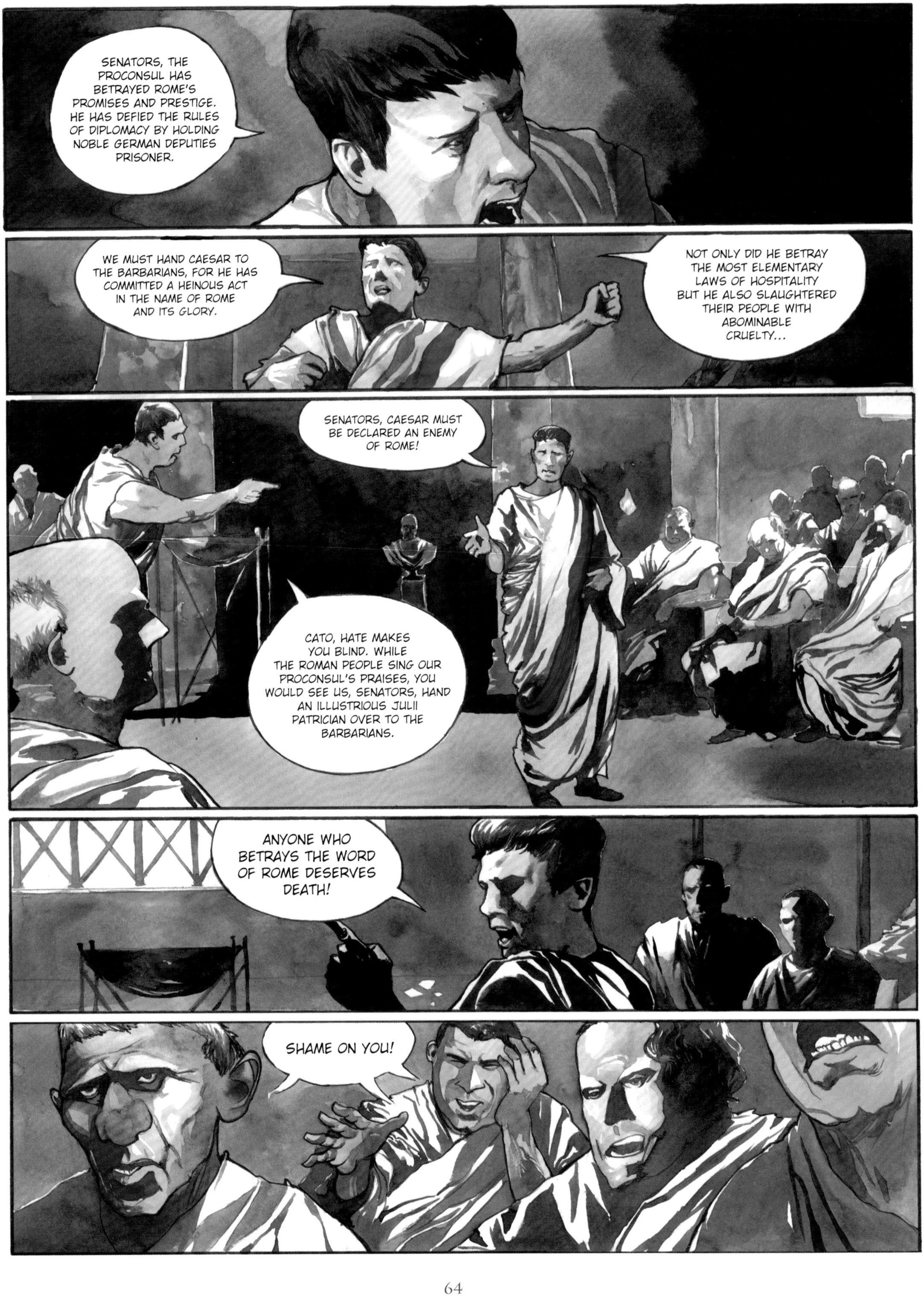
SENATORS, THE PROCONSUL HAS BETRAYED ROME'S PROMISES AND PRESTIGE. HE HAS DEFIED THE RULES OF DIPLOMACY BY HOLDING NOBLE GERMAN DEPUTIES PRISONER.
WE MUST HAND CAESAR TO THE BARBARIANS, FOR HE HAS COMMITTED A HEINOUS ACT IN THE NAME OF ROME AND ITS GLORY.
NOT ONLY DID HE BETRAY THE MOST ELEMENTARY LAWS OF HOSPITALITY BUT HE ALSO SLAUGHTERED THEIR PEOPLE WITH ABOMINABLE CRUELTY...
SENATORS, CAESAR MUST BE DECLARED AN ENEMY OF ROME!
CATO, HATE MAKES YOU BLIND. WHILE THE ROMAN PEOPLE SING OUR PROCONSUL'S PRAISES, YOU WOULD SEE US, SENATORS, HAND AN ILLUSTRIOUS JULII PATRICIAN OVER TO THE BARBARIANS.
ANYONE WHO BETRAYS THE WORD OF ROME DESERVES DEATH!
SHAME ON YOU!

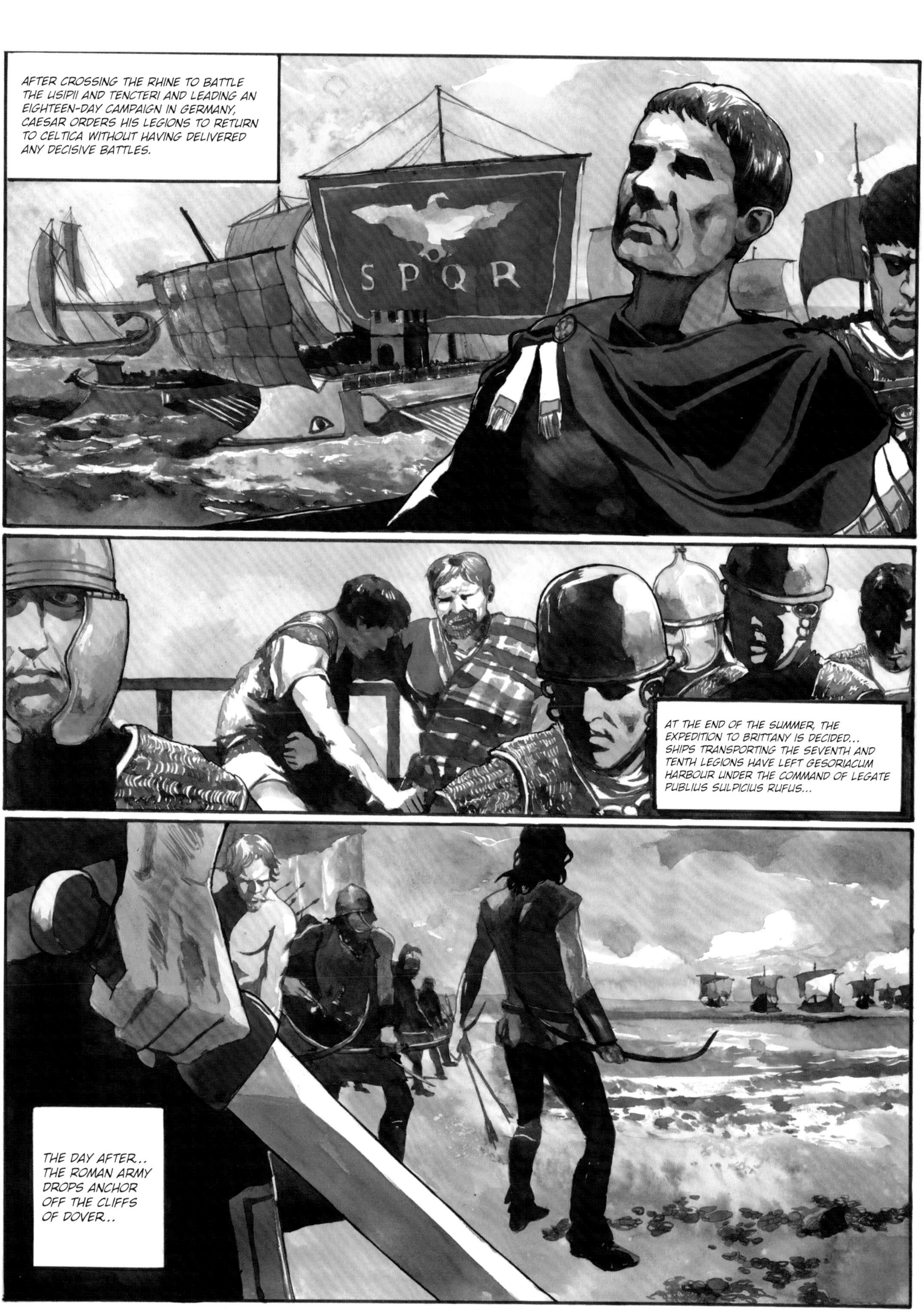
AFTER CROSSING THE RHINE TO BATTLE THE USIPII AND TENCTERI AND LEADING AN EIGHTEEN-DAY CAMPAIGN IN GERMANY, CAESAR ORDERS HIS LEGIONS TO RETURN TO CELTICA WITHOUT HAVING DELIVERED ANY DECISIVE BATTLES.
SPQR
AT THE END OF THE SUMMER, THE EXPEDITION TO BRITTANY IS DECIDED... SHIPS TRANSPORTING THE SEVENTH AND TENTH LEGIONS HAVE LEFT GESORIACUM HARBOUR UNDER THE COMMAND OF LEGATE PUBLIUS SULPICIUS RUFUS...
THE DAY AFTER... THE ROMAN ARMY DROPS ANCHOR OFF THE CLIFFS OF DOVER...

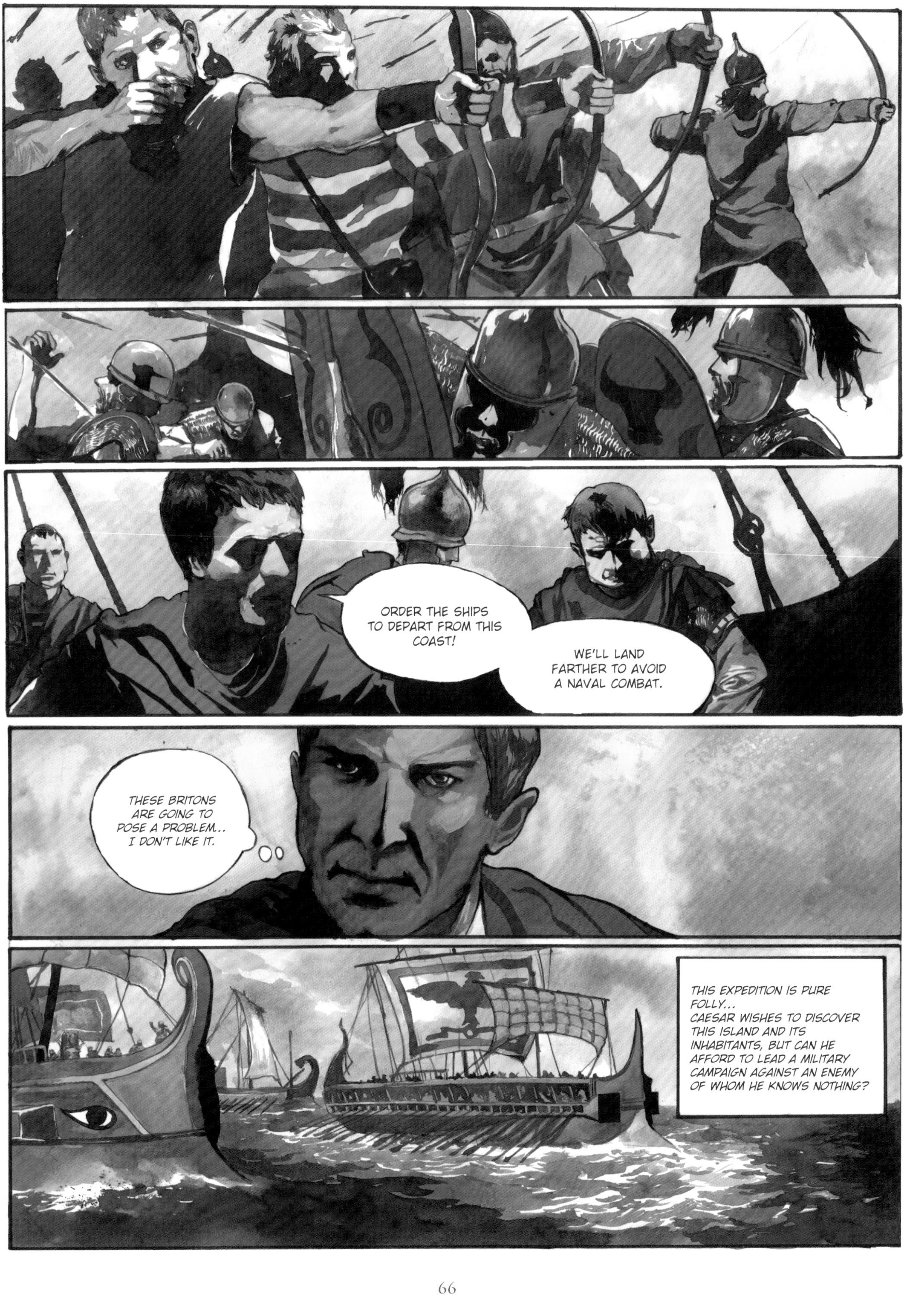
ORDER THE SHIPS TO DEPART FROM THIS COAST!
WE'LL LAND FARTHER TO AVOID A NAVAL COMBAT.
THESE BRITONS ARE GOING TO POSE A PROBLEM... I DON'T LIKE IT.
THIS EXPEDITION IS PURE FOLLY... CAESAR WISHES TO DISCOVER THIS ISLAND AND ITS INHABITANTS, BUT CAN HE AFFORD TO LEAD A MILITARY CAMPAIGN AGAINST AN ENEMY OF WHOM HE KNOWS NOTHING?

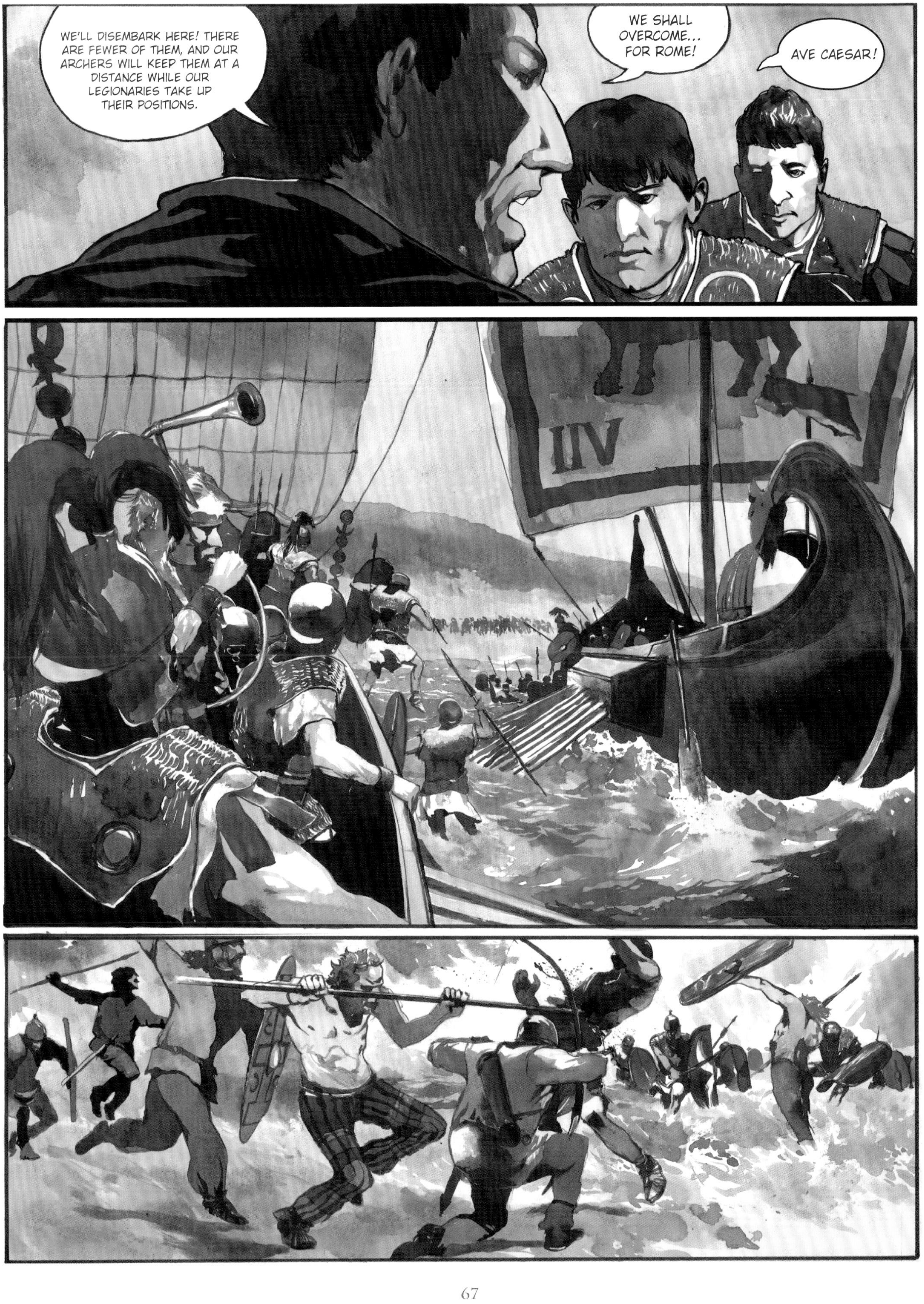
WE'LL DISEMBARK HERE! THERE ARE FEWER OF THEM, AND OUR ARCHERS WILL KEEP THEM AT A DISTANCE WHILE OUR LEGIONARIES TAKE UP THEIR POSITIONS.
WE SHALL OVERCOME... FOR ROME!
AVE CAESAR!
IIV

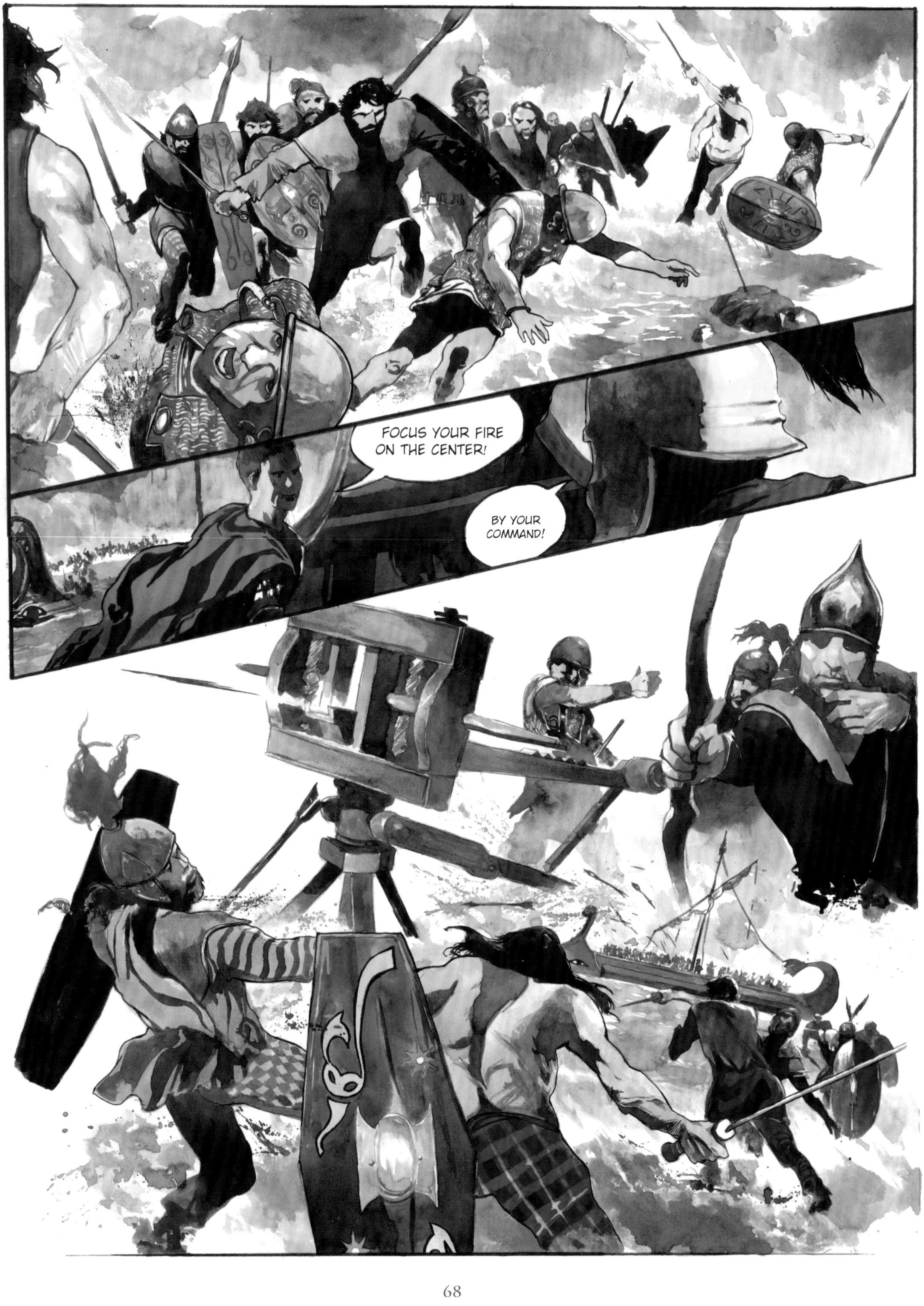
FOCUS YOUR FIRE ON THE CENTER!
BY YOUR COMMAND!

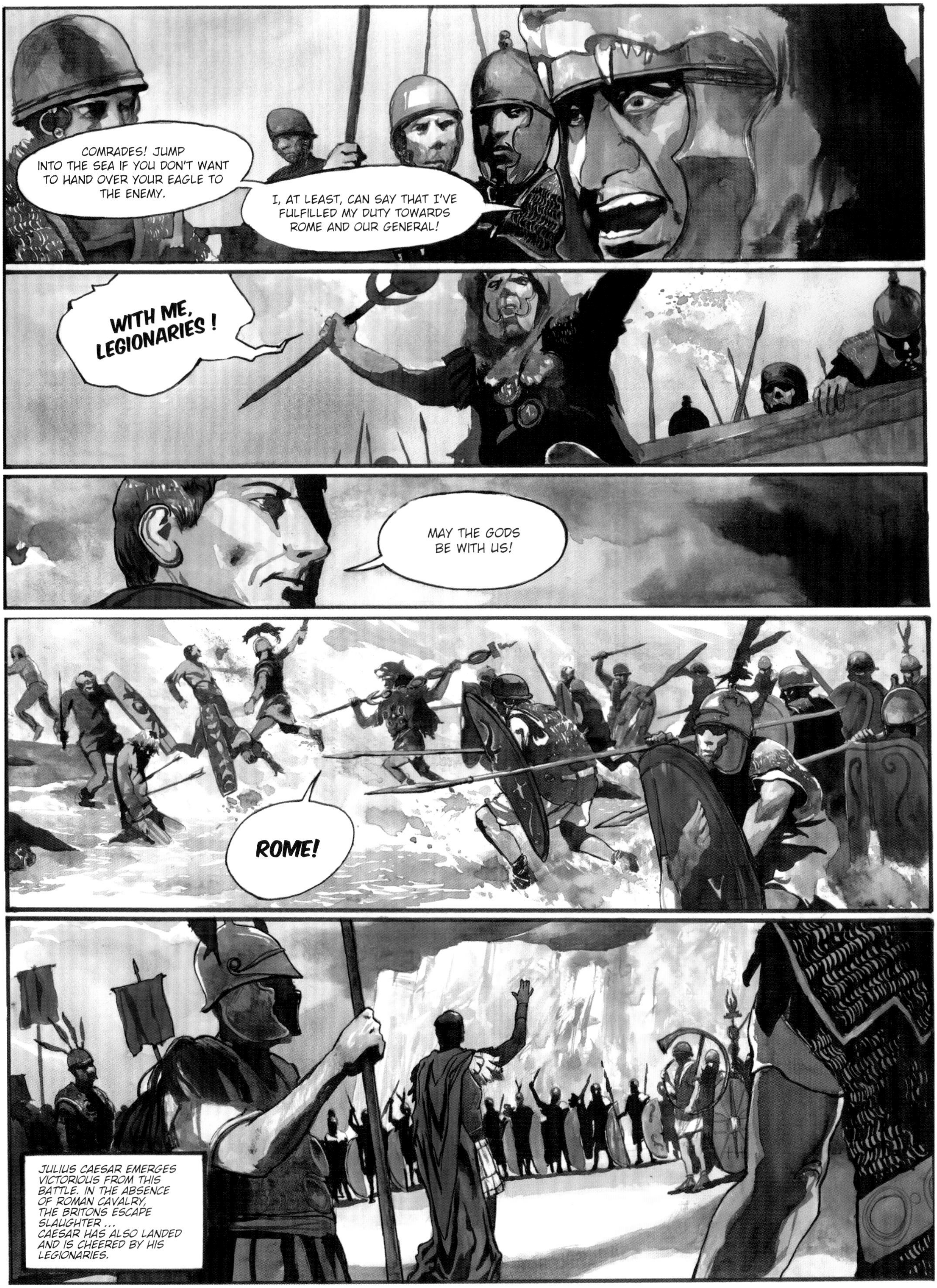
COMRADES! JUMP INTO THE SEA IF YOU DON'T WANT TO HAND OVER YOUR EAGLE TO THE ENEMY.
I, AT LEAST, CAN SAY THAT I'VE FULFILLED MY DUTY TOWARDS ROME AND OUR GENERAL!
WITH ME, LEGIONARIES !
MAY THE GODS BE WITH US!
ROME!
JULIUS CAESAR EMERGES VICTORIOUS FROM THIS BATTLE. IN THE ABSENCE OF ROMAN CAVALRY, THE BRITONS ESCAPE SLAUGHTER ... CAESAR HAS ALSO LANDED AND IS CHEERED BY HIS LEGIONARIES.

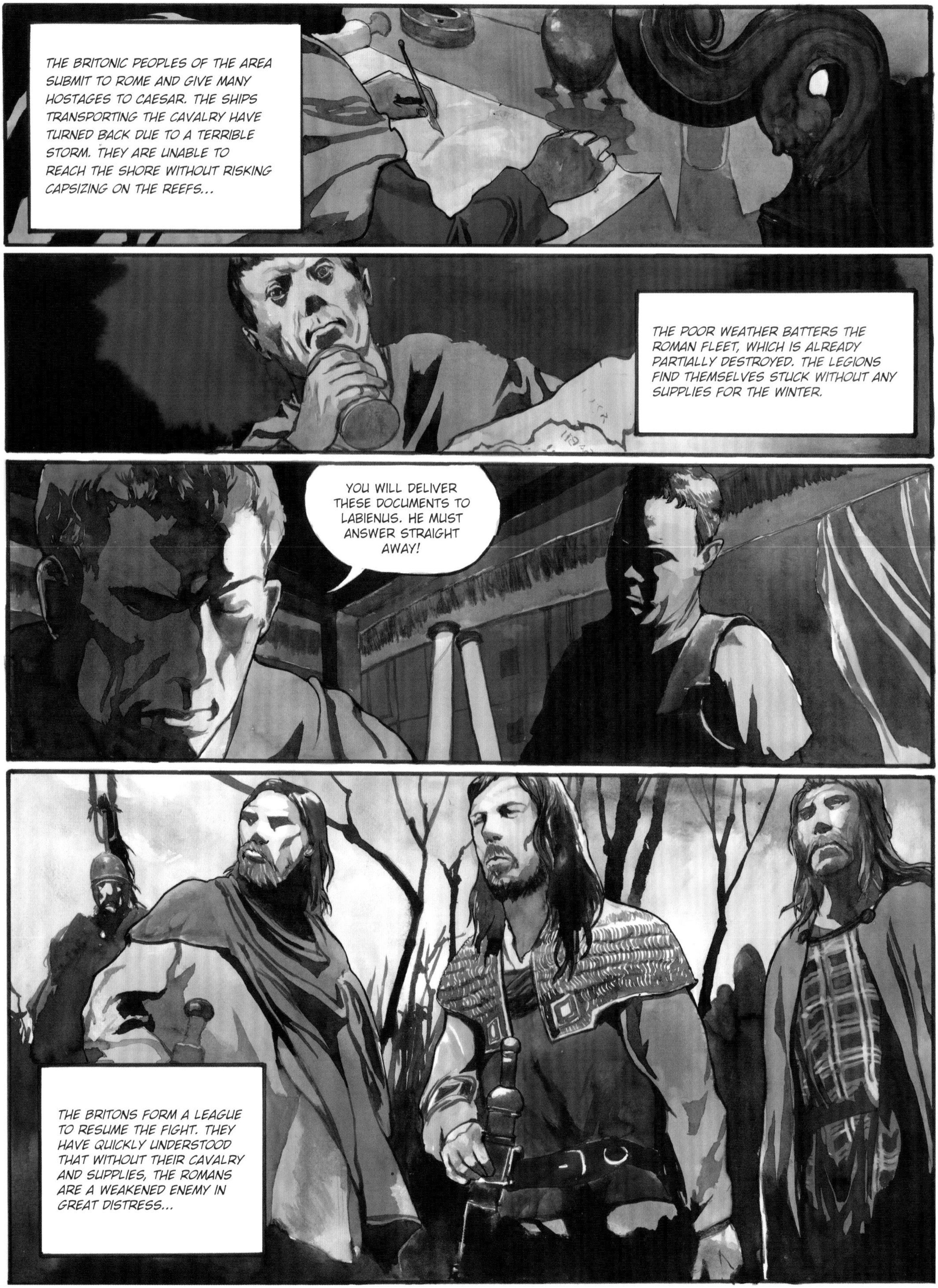
THE BRITONIC PEOPLES OF THE AREA SUBMIT TO ROME AND GIVE MANY HOSTAGES TO CAESAR. THE SHIPS TRANSPORTING THE CAVALRY HAVE TURNED BACK DUE TO A TERRIBLE STORM. THEY ARE UNABLE TO REACH THE SHORE WITHOUT RISKING CAPSIZING ON THE REEFS...
THE POOR WEATHER BATTERS THE ROMAN FLEET, WHICH IS ALREADY PARTIALLY DESTROYED. THE LEGIONS FIND THEMSELVES STUCK WITHOUT ANY SUPPLIES FOR THE WINTER.
YOU WILL DELIVER THESE DOCUMENTS TO LABIENUS. HE MUST ANSWER STRAIGHT AWAY!
THE BRITONS FORM A LEAGUE TO RESUME THE FIGHT. THEY HAVE QUICKLY UNDERSTOOD THAT WITHOUT THEIR CAVALRY AND SUPPLIES, THE ROMANS ARE A WEAKENED ENEMY IN GREAT DISTRESS...

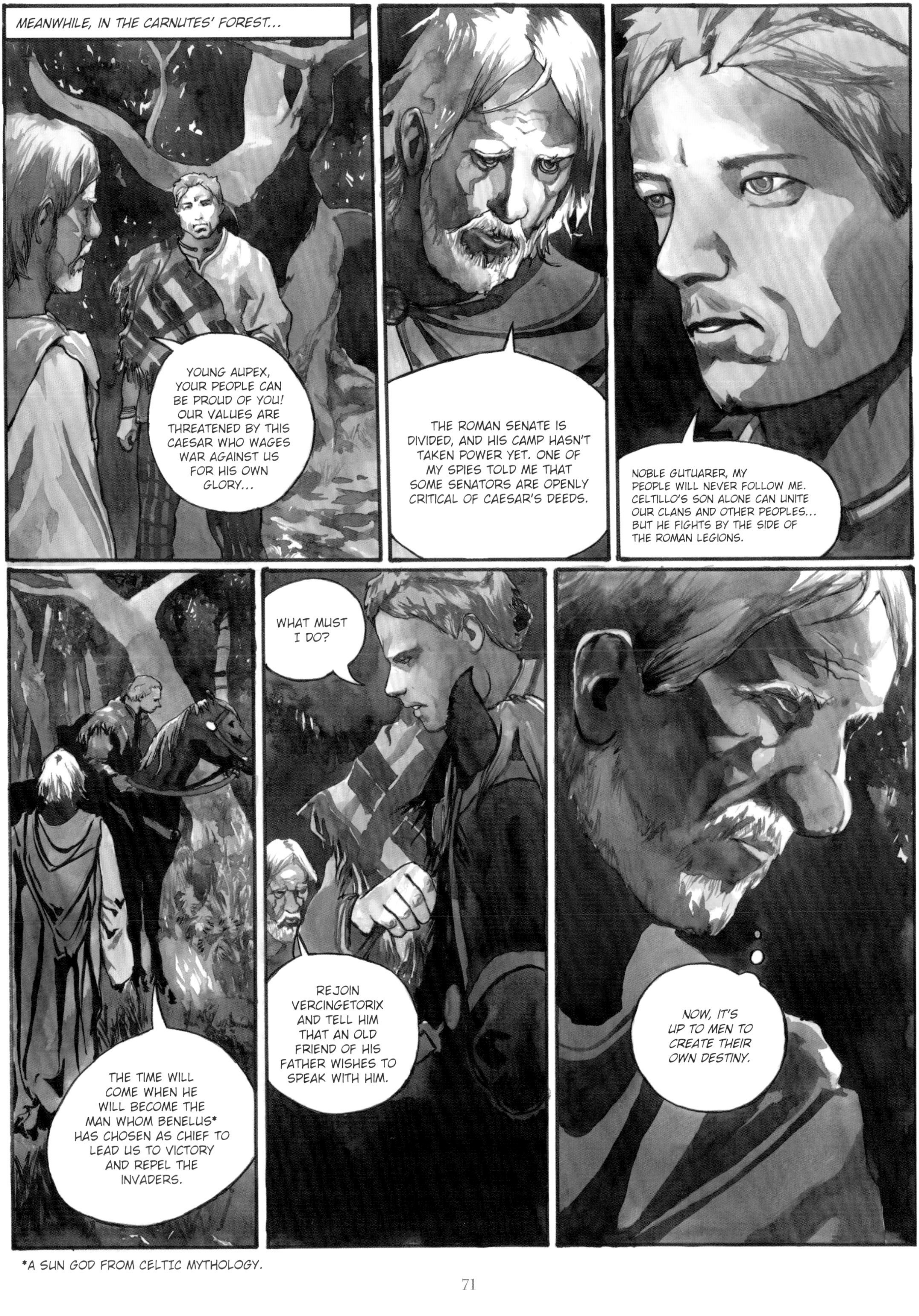
MEANWHILE, IN THE CARNUTES' FOREST...
YOUNG AUPEX, YOUR PEOPLE CAN BE PROUD OF YOU! OUR VALUES ARE THREATENED BY THIS CAESAR WHO WAGES WAR AGAINST US FOR HIS OWN GLORY...
THE ROMAN SENATE IS DIVIDED, AND HIS CAMP HASN'T TAKEN POWER YET. ONE OF MY SPIES TOLD ME THAT SOME SENATORS ARE OPENLY CRITICAL OF CAESAR'S DEEDS.
NOBLE GUTUARER, MY PEOPLE WILL NEVER FOLLOW ME. CELTILLO'S SON ALONE CAN UNITE OUR CLANS AND OTHER PEOPLES... BUT HE FIGHTS BY THE SIDE OF THE ROMAN LEGIONS.
THE TIME WILL COME WHEN HE WILL BECOME THE MAN WHOM BENELUS* HAS CHOSEN AS CHIEF TO LEAD US TO VICTORY AND REPEL THE INVADERS.
WHAT MUST I DO?
REJOIN VERCINGETORIX AND TELL HIM THAT AN OLD FRIEND OF HIS FATHER WISHES TO SPEAK WITH HIM.
NOW, IT'S UP TO MEN TO CREATE THEIR OWN DESTINY.

*A SUN GOD FROM CELTIC MYTHOLOGY.

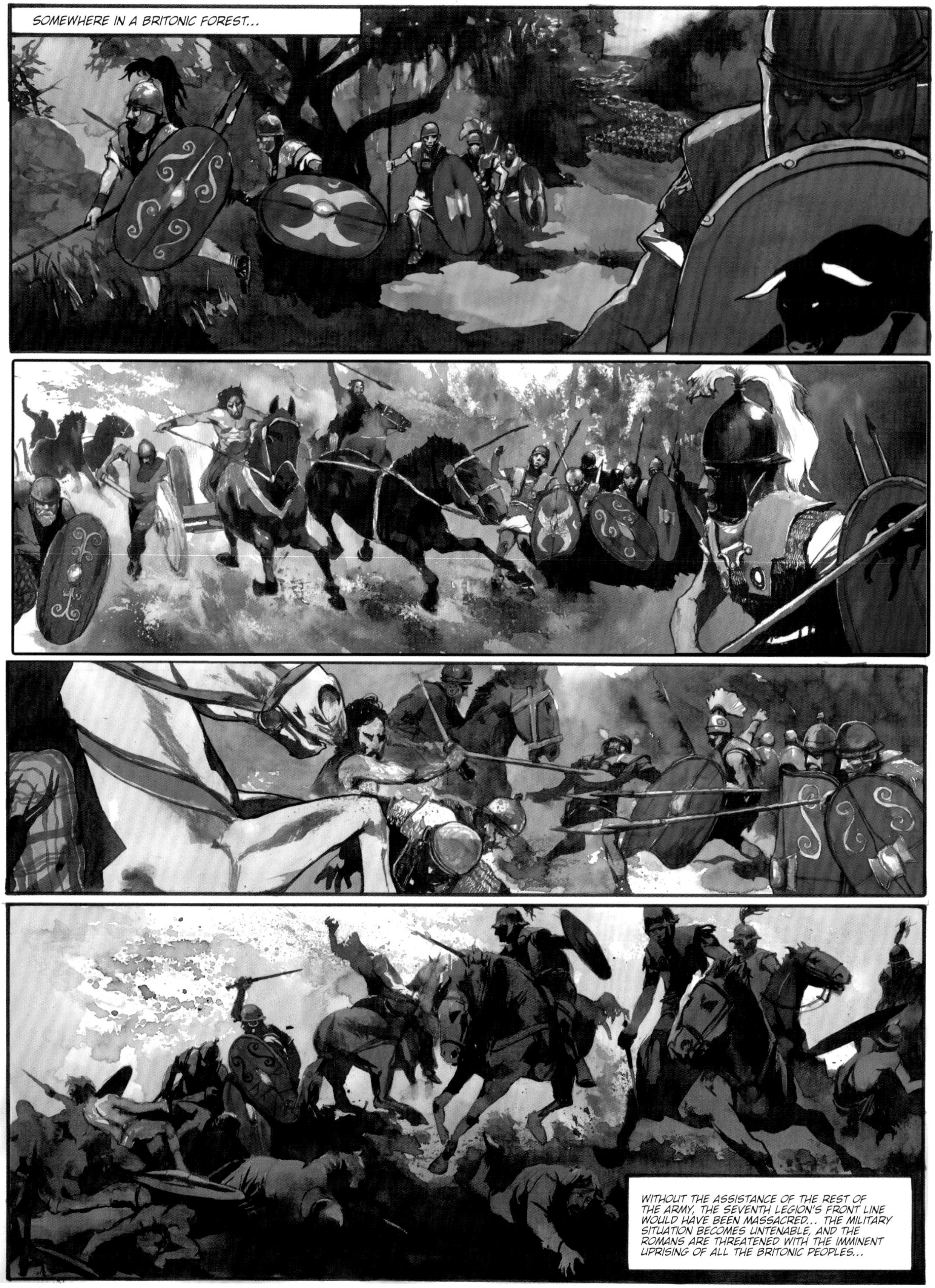
SOMEWHERE IN A BRITONIC FOREST...
WITHOUT THE ASSISTANCE OF THE REST OF THE ARMY, THE SEVENTH LEGION'S FRONT LINE WOULD HAVE BEEN MASSACRED... THE MILITARY SITUATION BECOMES UNTENABLE, AND THE ROMANS ARE THREATENED WITH THE IMMINENT UPRISING OF ALL THE BRITONIC PEOPLES...

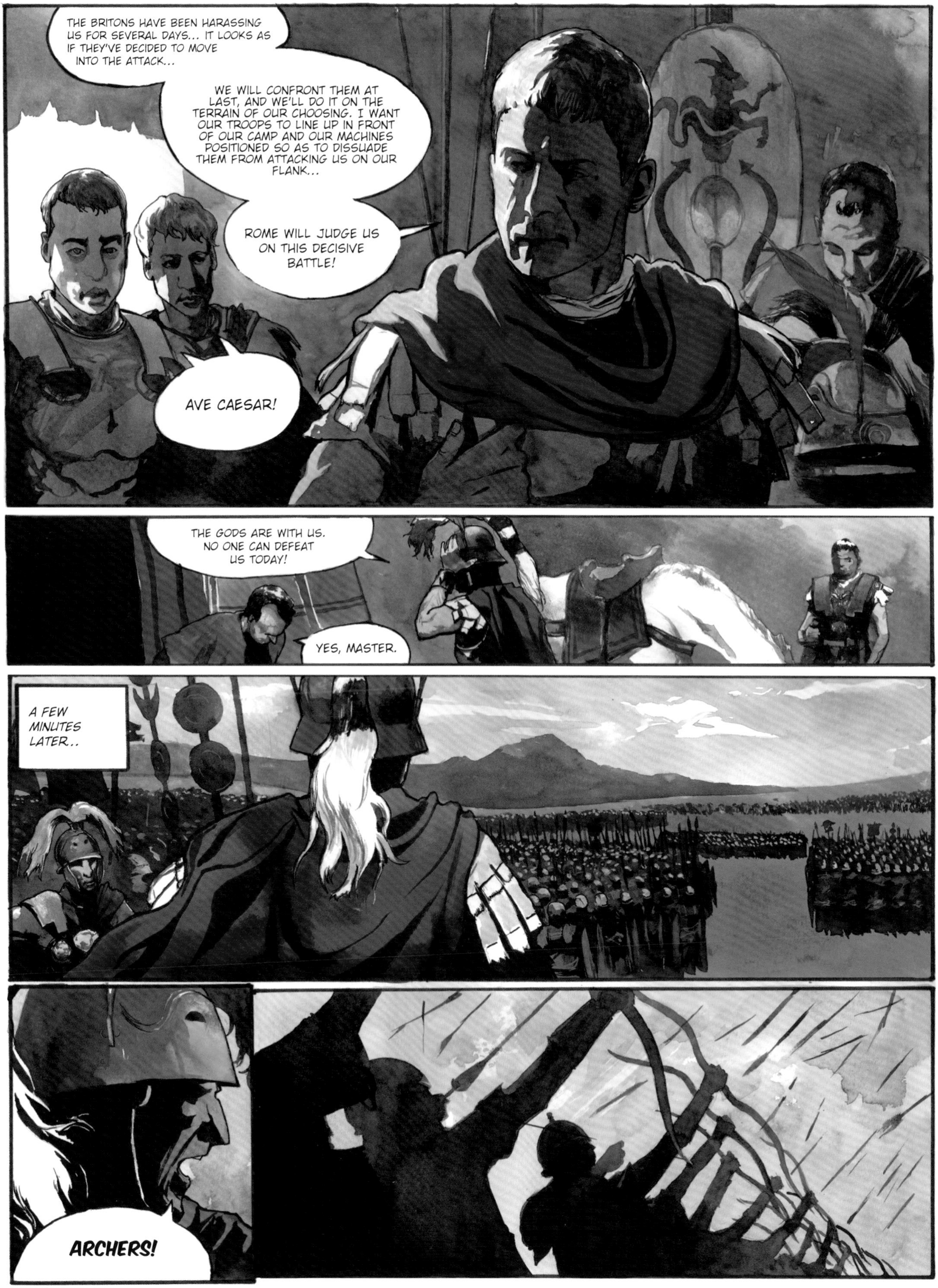
THE BRITONS HAVE BEEN HARASSING US FOR SEVERAL DAYS... IT LOOKS AS IF THEY'VE DECIDED TO MOVE INTO THE ATTACK...
WE WILL CONFRONT THEM AT LAST, AND WE'LL DO IT ON THE TERRAIN OF OUR CHOOSING. I WANT OUR TROOPS TO LINE UP IN FRONT OF OUR CAMP AND OUR MACHINES POSITIONED SO AS TO DISSUADE THEM FROM ATTACKING US ON OUR FLANK...
ROME WILL JUDGE US ON THIS DECISIVE BATTLE!
AVE CAESAR!
THE GODS ARE WITH US. NO ONE CAN DEFEAT US TODAY!
YES, MASTER.
A FEW MINUTES LATER...
ARCHERS!

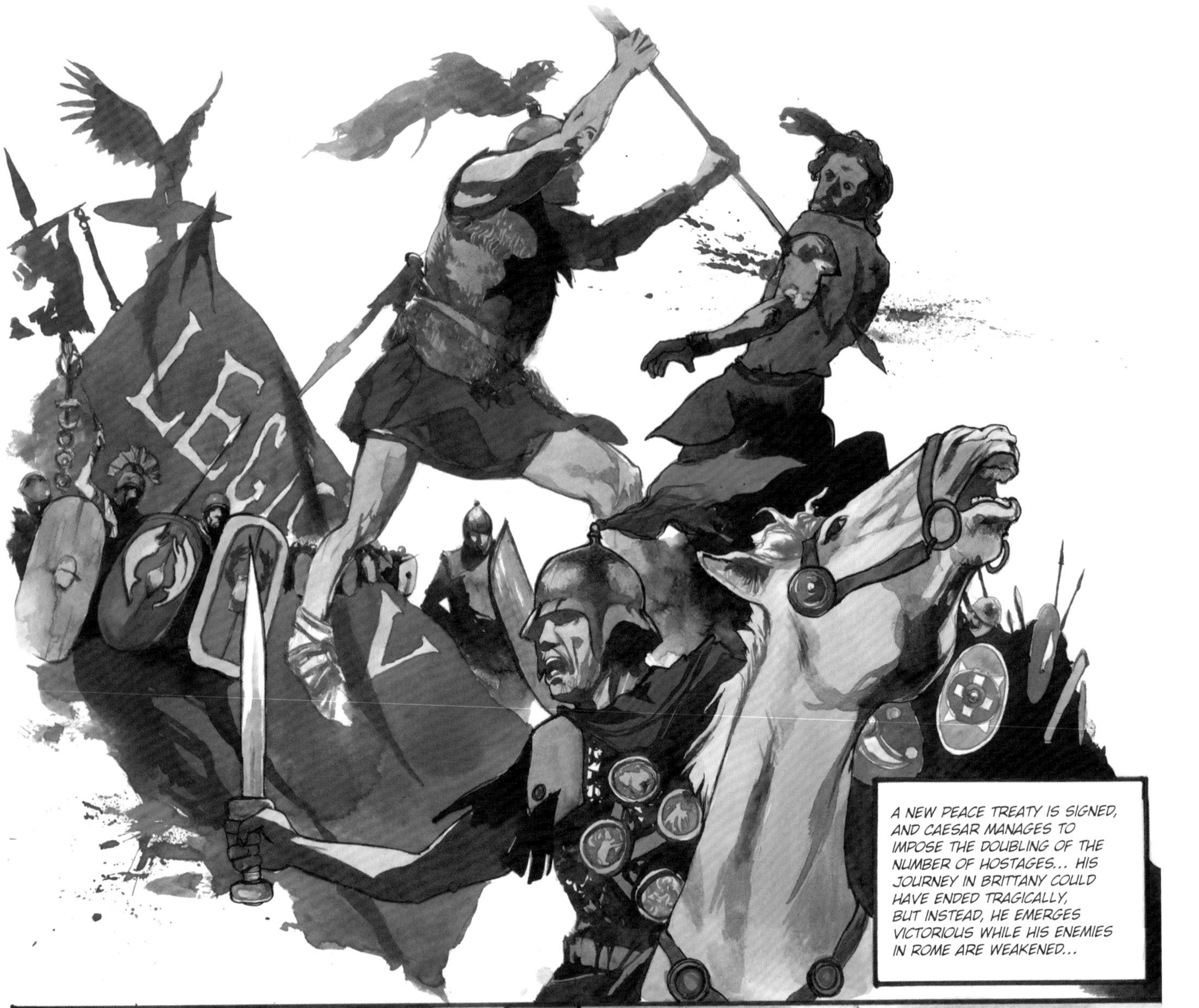
LEGIO
V
A NEW PEACE TREATY IS SIGNED, AND CAESAR MANAGES TO IMPOSE THE DOUBLING OF THE NUMBER OF HOSTAGES... HIS JOURNEY IN BRITTANY COULD HAVE ENDED TRAGICALLY, BUT INSTEAD, HE EMERGES VICTORIOUS WHILE HIS ENEMIES IN ROME ARE WEAKENED...

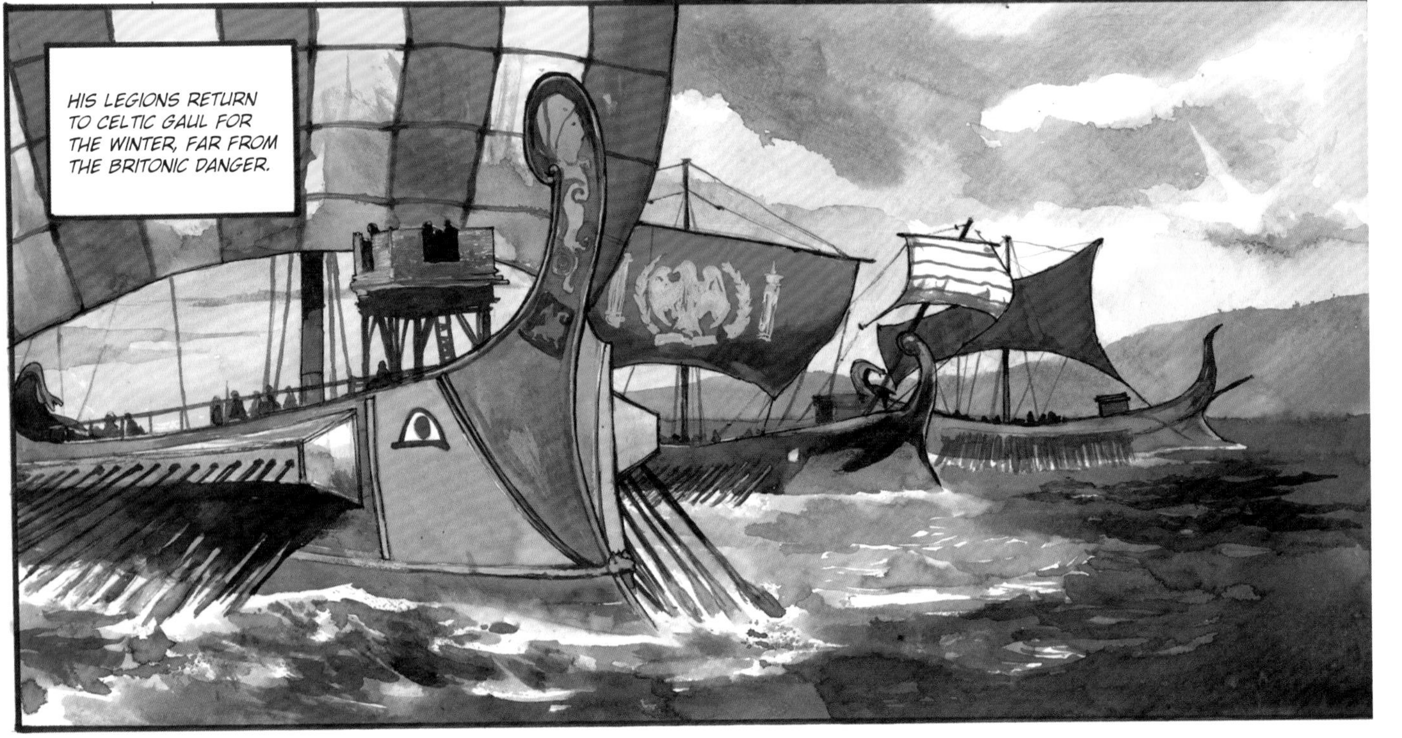
HIS LEGIONS RETURN TO CELTIC GAUL FOR THE WINTER, FAR FROM THE BRITONIC DANGER.

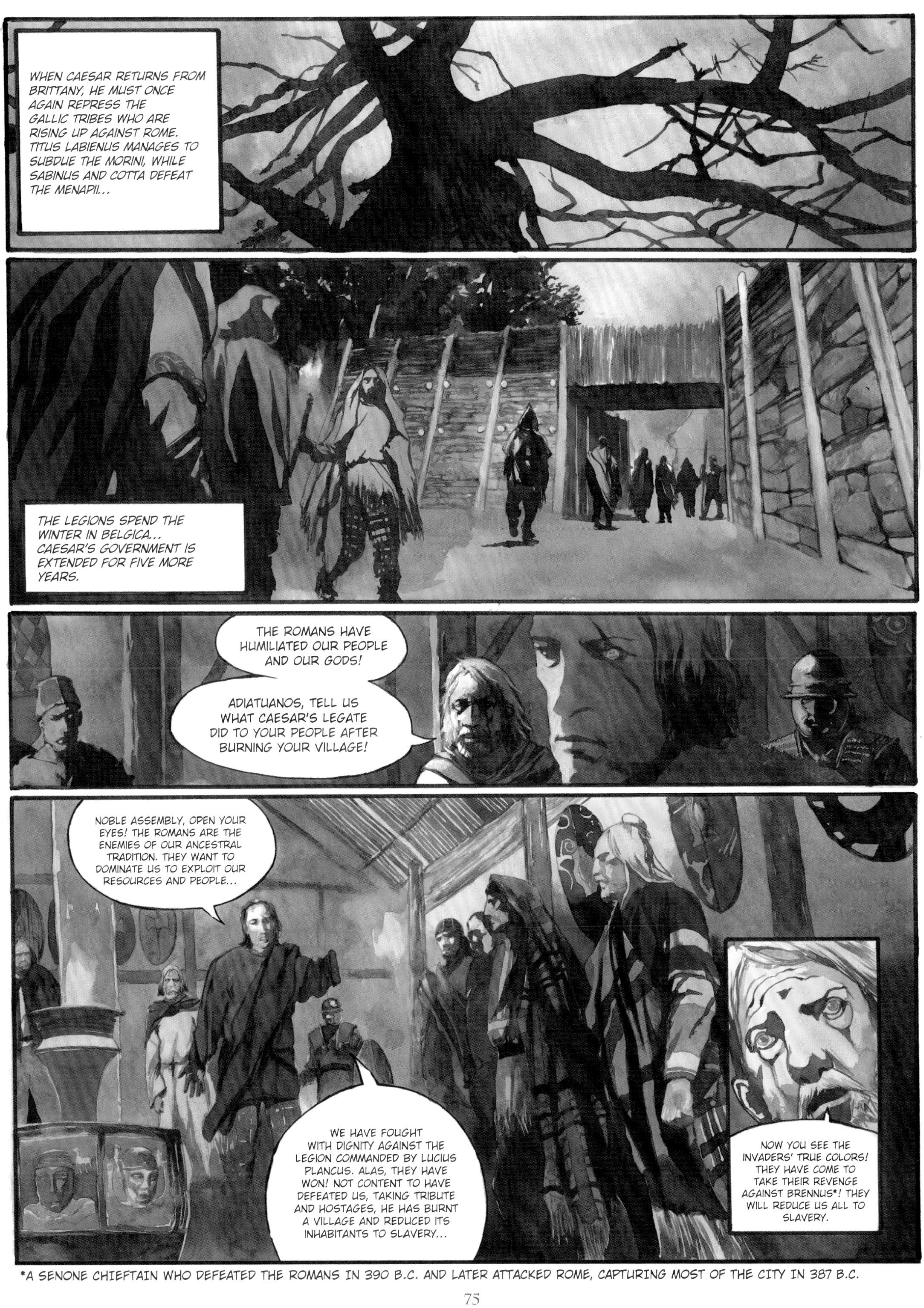
WHEN CAESAR RETURNS FROM BRITTANY, HE MUST ONCE AGAIN REPRESS THE GALLIC TRIBES WHO ARE RISING UP AGAINST ROME. TITUS LABIENUS MANAGES TO SUBDUE THE MORINI, WHILE SABINUS AND COTTA DEFEAT THE MENAPII...
THE LEGIONS SPEND THE WINTER IN BELGICA... CAESAR'S GOVERNMENT IS EXTENDED FOR FIVE MORE YEARS.
THE ROMANS HAVE HUMILIATED OUR PEOPLE AND OUR GODS!
ADIATUANOS, TELL US WHAT CAESAR'S LEGATE DID TO YOUR PEOPLE AFTER BURNING YOUR VILLAGE!
NOBLE ASSEMBLY, OPEN YOUR EYES! THE ROMANS ARE THE ENEMIES OF OUR ANCESTRAL TRADITION. THEY WANT TO DOMINATE US TO EXPLOIT OUR RESOURCES AND PEOPLE...
WE HAVE FOUGHT WITH DIGNITY AGAINST THE LEGION COMMANDED BY LUCIUS PLANCUS. ALAS, THEY HAVE WON! NOT CONTENT TO HAVE DEFEATED US, TAKING TRIBUTE AND HOSTAGES, HE HAS BURNT A VILLAGE AND REDUCED ITS INHABITANTS TO SLAVERY...
NOW YOU SEE THE INVADERS' TRUE COLORS! THEY HAVE COME TO TAKE THEIR REVENGE AGAINST BRENNUS*! THEY WILL REDUCE US ALL TO SLAVERY.

*A SENONE CHIEFTAIN WHO DEFEATED THE ROMANS IN 390 B.C. AND LATER ATTACKED ROME, CAPTURING MOST OF THE CITY IN 387 B.C.

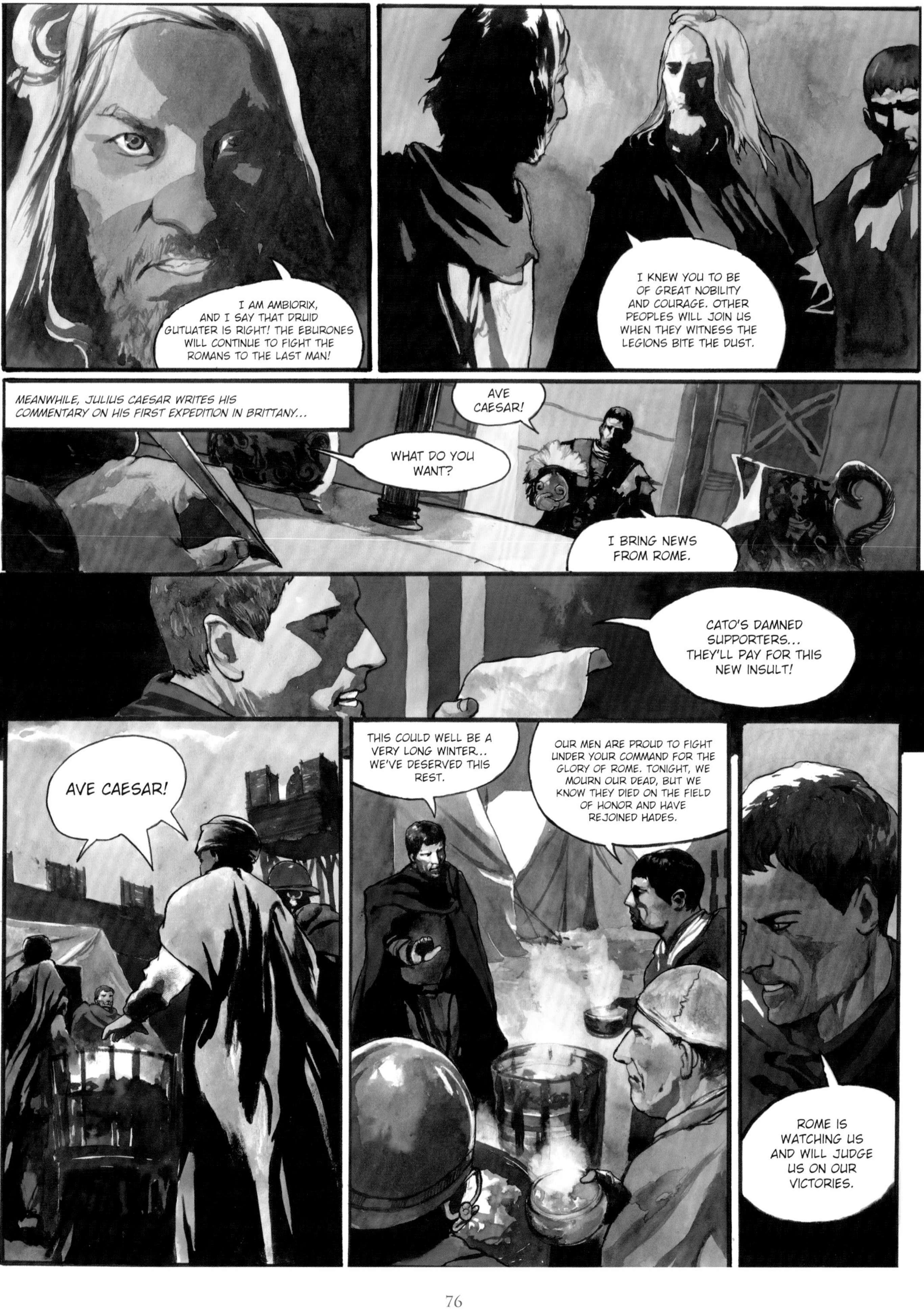
I AM AMBIORIX, AND I SAY THAT DRUID GUTUATER IS RIGHT! THE EBURONES WILL CONTINUE TO FIGHT THE ROMANS TO THE LAST MAN!
I KNEW YOU TO BE OF GREAT NOBILITY AND COURAGE. OTHER PEOPLES WILL JOIN US WHEN THEY WITNESS THE LEGIONS BITE THE DUST.
MEANWHILE, JULIUS CAESAR WRITES HIS COMMENTARY ON HIS FIRST EXPEDITION IN BRITTANY...
AVE CAESAR!
WHAT DO YOU WANT?
I BRING NEWS FROM ROME.
CATO'S DAMNED SUPPORTERS... THEY'LL PAY FOR THIS NEW INSULT!
AVE CAESAR!
THIS COULD WELL BE A VERY LONG WINTER... WE'VE DESERVED THIS REST.
OUR MEN ARE PROUD TO FIGHT UNDER YOUR COMMAND FOR THE GLORY OF ROME. TONIGHT, WE MOURN OUR DEAD, BUT WE KNOW THEY DIED ON THE FIELD OF HONOR AND HAVE REJOINED HADES.
ROME IS WATCHING US AND WILL JUDGE US ON OUR VICTORIES.

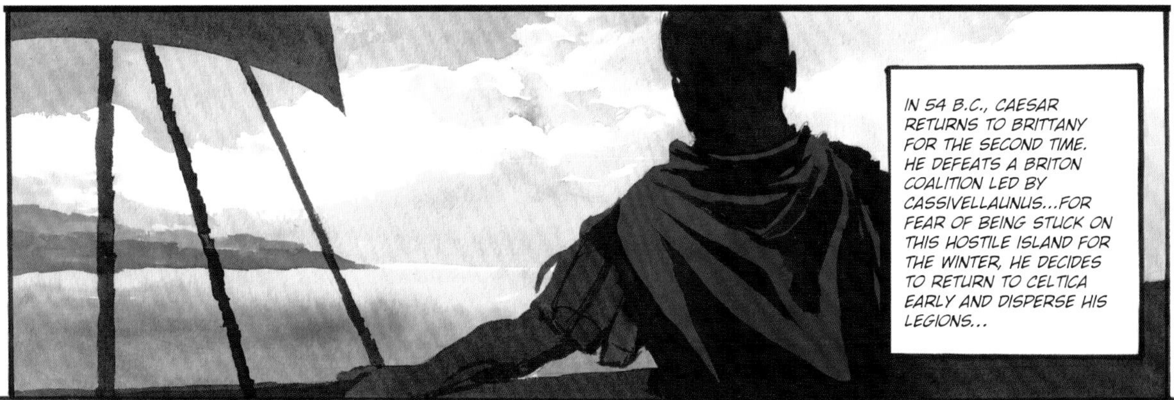
IN 54 B.C., CAESAR RETURNS TO BRITTANY FOR THE SECOND TIME. HE DEFEATS A BRITON COALITION LED BY CASSIVELLAUNUS...FOR FEAR OF BEING STUCK ON THIS HOSTILE ISLAND FOR THE WINTER, HE DECIDES TO RETURN TO CELTICA EARLY AND DISPERSE HIS LEGIONS...
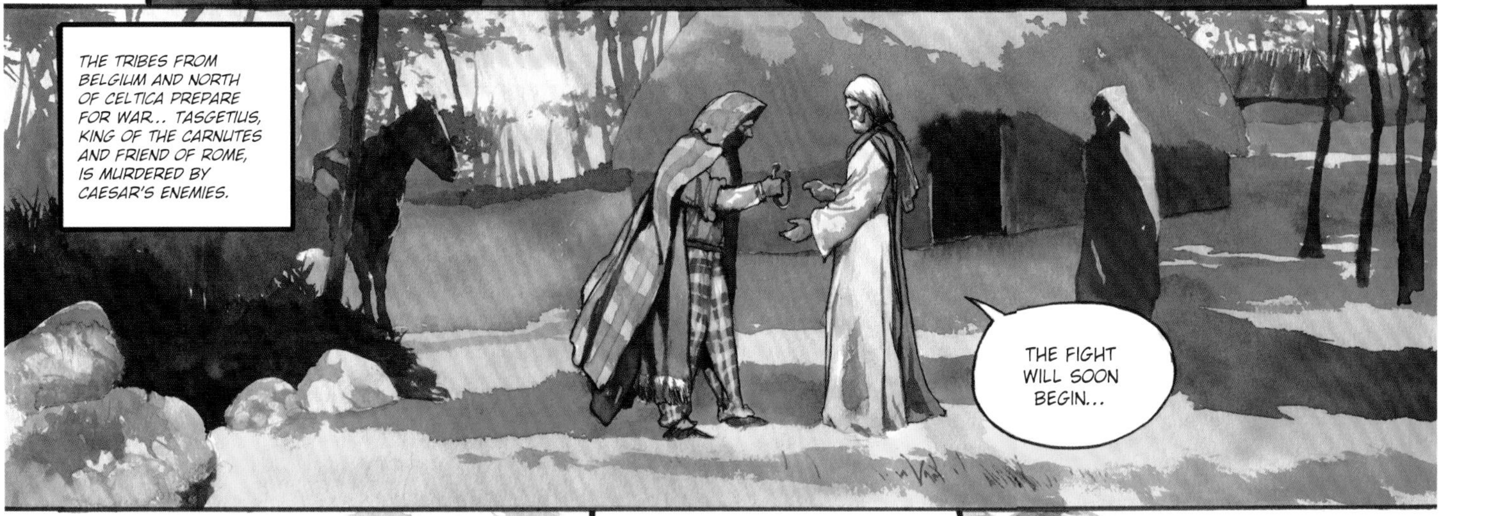
THE TRIBES FROM BELGIUM AND NORTH OF CELTICA PREPARE FOR WAR... TASGETIUS, KING OF THE CARNUTES AND FRIEND OF ROME, IS MURDERED BY CAESAR'S ENEMIES.
THE FIGHT WILL SOON BEGIN...
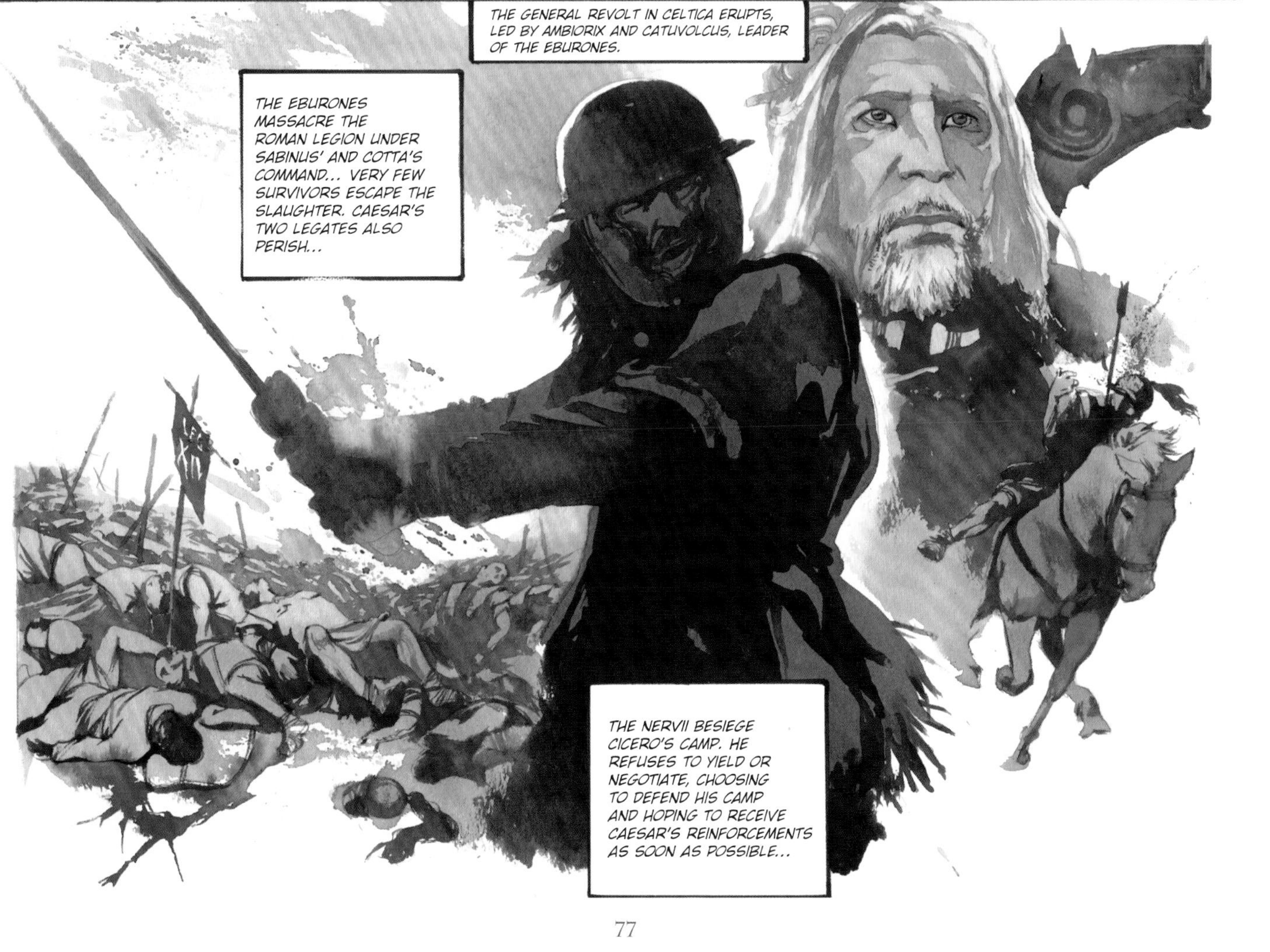
THE GENERAL REVOLT IN CELTICA ERUPTS, LED BY AMBIORIX AND CATUVOLCUS, LEADER OF THE EBURONES.
THE EBURONES MASSACRE THE ROMAN LEGION UNDER SABINUS' AND COTTA'S COMMAND... VERY FEW SURVIVORS ESCAPE THE SLAUGHTER. CAESAR'S TWO LEGATES ALSO PERISH...
THE NERVII BESIEGE CICERO'S CAMP. HE REFUSES TO YIELD OR NEGOTIATE, CHOOSING TO DEFEND HIS CAMP AND HOPING TO RECEIVE CAESAR'S REINFORCEMENTS AS SOON AS POSSIBLE...

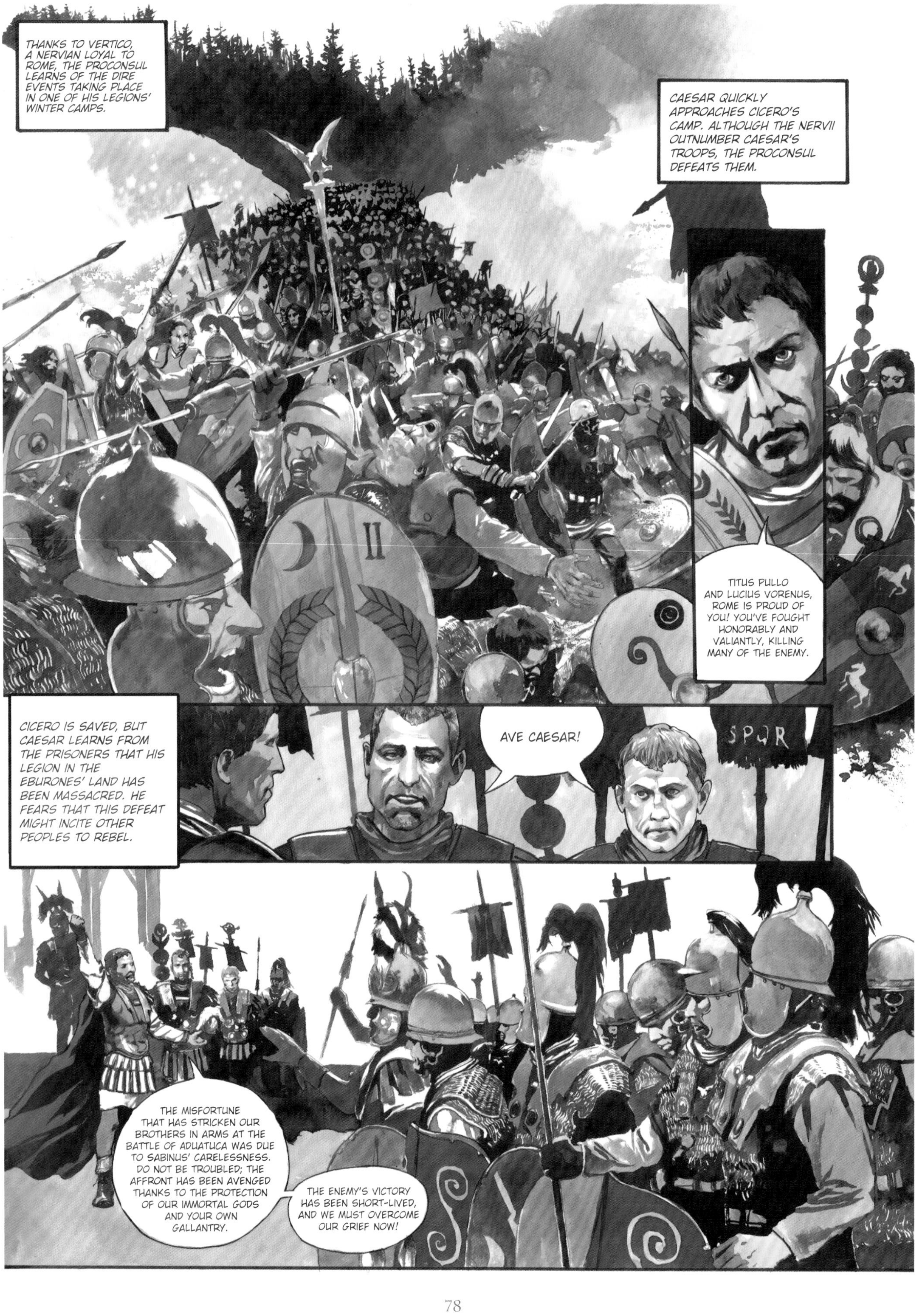
THANKS TO VERTICO, A NERVIAN LOYAL TO ROME, THE PROCONSUL LEARNS OF THE DIRE EVENTS TAKING PLACE IN ONE OF HIS LEGIONS' WINTER CAMPS.
CAESAR QUICKLY APPROACHES CICERO'S CAMP. ALTHOUGH THE NERVII OUTNUMBER CAESAR'S TROOPS, THE PROCONSUL DEFEATS THEM.
TITUS PULLO AND LUCIUS VORENUS, ROME IS PROUD OF YOU! YOU'VE FOUGHT HONORABLY AND VALIANTLY, KILLING MANY OF THE ENEMY.
CICERO IS SAVED, BUT CAESAR LEARNS FROM THE PRISONERS THAT HIS LEGION IN THE EBURONES' LAND HAS BEEN MASSACRED. HE FEARS THAT THIS DEFEAT MIGHT INCITE OTHER PEOPLES TO REBEL.
AVE CAESAR!
SPQR
THE MISFORTUNE THAT HAS STRICKEN OUR BROTHERS IN ARMS AT THE BATTLE OF ADUATUCA WAS DUE TO SABINUS' CARELESSNESS. DO NOT BE TROUBLED; THE AFFRONT HAS BEEN AVENGED THANKS TO THE PROTECTION OF OUR IMMORTAL GODS AND YOUR OWN GALLANTRY.
THE ENEMY'S VICTORY HAS BEEN SHORT-LIVED, AND WE MUST OVERCOME OUR GRIEF NOW!

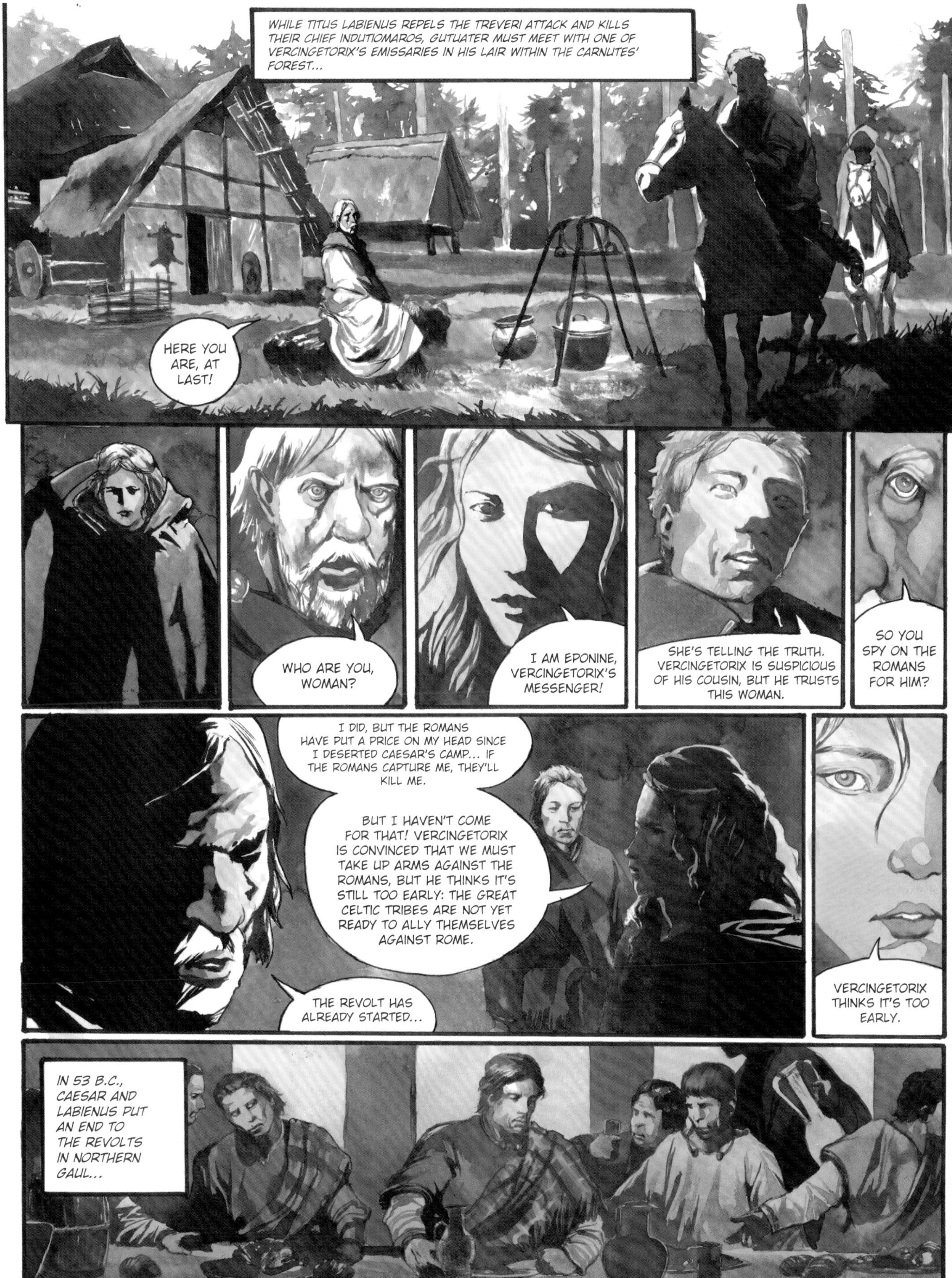
WHILE TITUS LABIENUS REPELS THE TREVERI ATTACK AND KILLS THEIR CHIEF INDUTIOMAROS, GUTUATER MUST MEET WITH ONE OF VERCINGETORIX'S EMISSARIES IN HIS LAIR WITHIN THE CARNUTES' FOREST...
HERE YOU ARE, AT LAST!
WHO ARE YOU, WOMAN?
I AM EPONINE, VERCINGETORIX'S MESSENGER!
SHE'S TELLING THE TRUTH. VERCINGETORIX IS SUSPICIOUS OF HIS COUSIN, BUT HE TRUSTS THIS WOMAN.
SO YOU SPY ON THE ROMANS FOR HIM?
I DID, BUT THE ROMANS HAVE PUT A PRICE ON MY HEAD SINCE I DESERTED CAESAR'S CAMP... IF THE ROMANS CAPTURE ME, THEY'LL KILL ME.
BUT I HAVEN'T COME FOR THAT! VERCINGETORIX IS CONVINCED THAT WE MUST TAKE UP ARMS AGAINST THE ROMANS, BUT HE THINKS IT'S STILL TOO EARLY: THE GREAT CELTIC TRIBES ARE NOT YET READY TO ALLY THEMSELVES AGAINST ROME.
THE REVOLT HAS ALREADY STARTED...
VERCINGETORIX THINKS IT'S TOO EARLY.
IN 53 B.C., CAESAR AND LABIENUS PUT AN END TO THE REVOLTS IN NORTHERN GAUL...

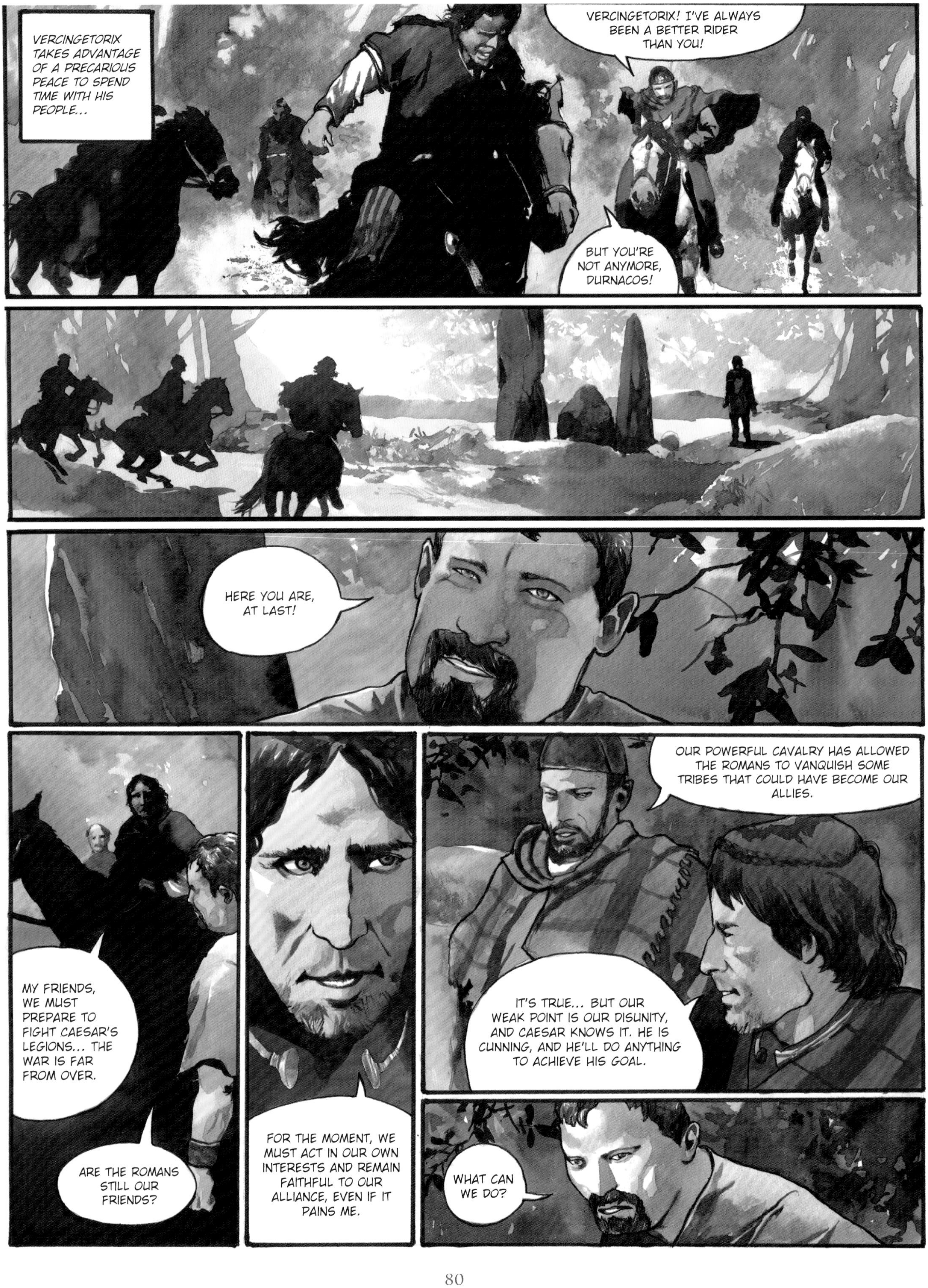
VERCINGETORIX TAKES ADVANTAGE OF A PRECARIOUS PEACE TO SPEND TIME WITH HIS PEOPLE...
VERCINGETORIX! I'VE ALWAYS BEEN A BETTER RIDER THAN YOU!
BUT YOU'RE NOT ANYMORE, DURNACOS!
HERE YOU ARE, AT LAST!
MY FRIENDS, WE MUST PREPARE TO FIGHT CAESAR'S LEGIONS... THE WAR IS FAR FROM OVER.
ARE THE ROMANS STILL OUR FRIENDS?
FOR THE MOMENT, WE MUST ACT IN OUR OWN INTERESTS AND REMAIN FAITHFUL TO OUR ALLIANCE, EVEN IF IT PAINS ME.
OUR POWERFUL CAVALRY HAS ALLOWED THE ROMANS TO VANQUISH SOME TRIBES THAT COULD HAVE BECOME OUR ALLIES.
IT'S TRUE... BUT OUR WEAK POINT IS OUR DISUNITY, AND CAESAR KNOWS IT. HE IS CUNNING, AND HE'LL DO ANYTHING TO ACHIEVE HIS GOAL.
WHAT CAN WE DO?

THIS IS EPONINE, MY MOST PRECIOUS ASSET.

A WOMAN!

YES, BELLORIX! SHE TOOK RISKS FOR OUR PEOPLE, AND WITHOUT HER HELP, I WOULD NEVER HAVE KNOWN CAESAR'S INTENTIONS.

WHO ARE YOU?

I'M ONE OF CAESAR'S ENEMIES!

HE'S MY ENEMY TOO!

AH! AH! AHA! AH! AH!

AH! AH!

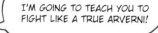

I'M GOING TO TEACH YOU TO FIGHT LIKE A TRUE ARVERNI!

WE'LL SEE ABOUT THAT!

81

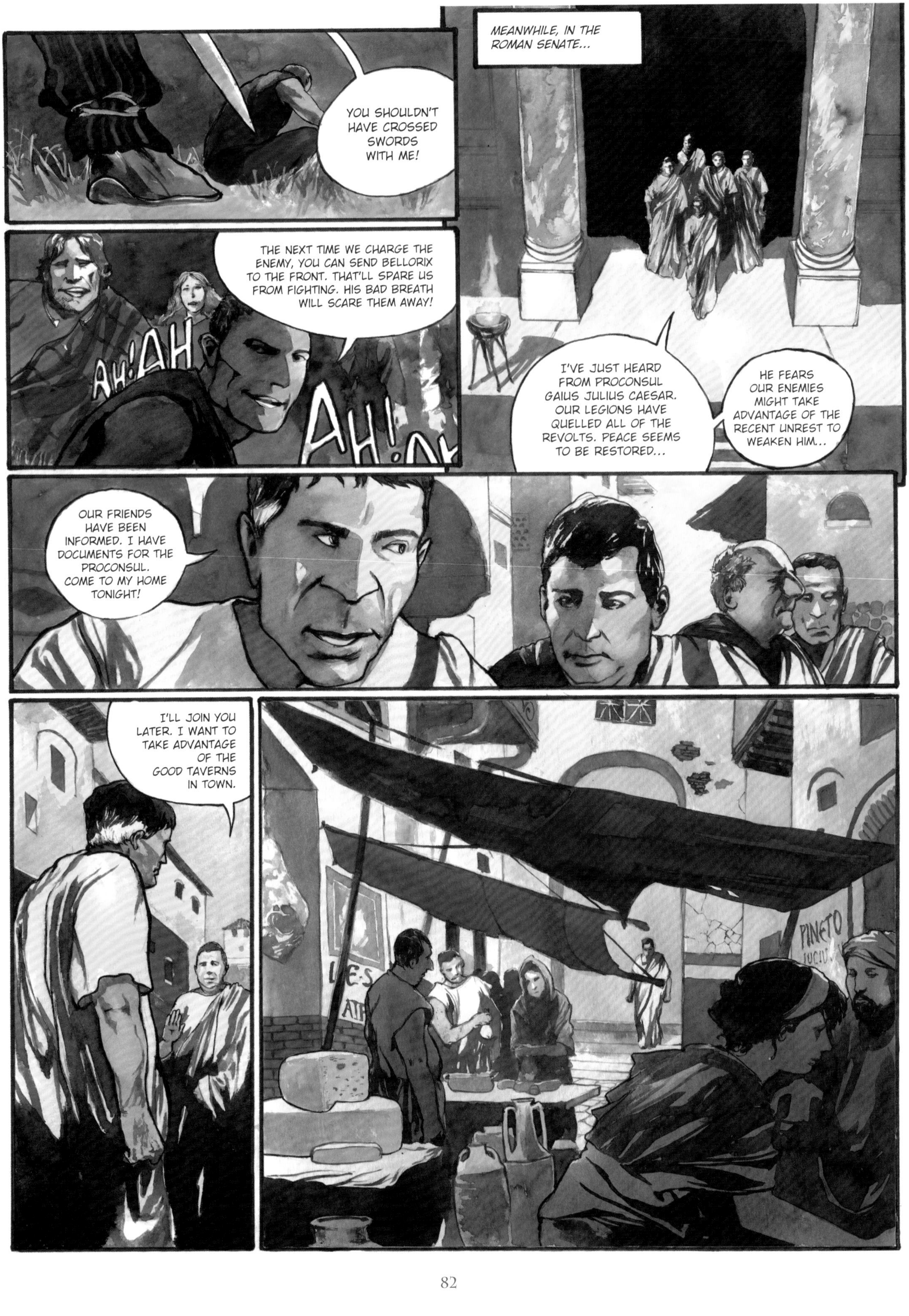
YOU SHOULDN'T HAVE CROSSED SWORDS WITH ME!
THE NEXT TIME WE CHARGE THE ENEMY, YOU CAN SEND BELLORIX TO THE FRONT. THAT'LL SPARE US FROM FIGHTING. HIS BAD BREATH WILL SCARE THEM AWAY!
AH!AH
AH!
MEANWHILE, IN THE ROMAN SENATE...
I'VE JUST HEARD FROM PROCONSUL GAIUS JULIUS CAESAR. OUR LEGIONS HAVE QUELLED ALL OF THE REVOLTS. PEACE SEEMS TO BE RESTORED...
HE FEARS OUR ENEMIES MIGHT TAKE ADVANTAGE OF THE RECENT UNREST TO WEAKEN HIM...
OUR FRIENDS HAVE BEEN INFORMED. I HAVE DOCUMENTS FOR THE PROCONSUL. COME TO MY HOME TONIGHT!
I'LL JOIN YOU LATER. I WANT TO TAKE ADVANTAGE OF THE GOOD TAVERNS IN TOWN.
PINETO

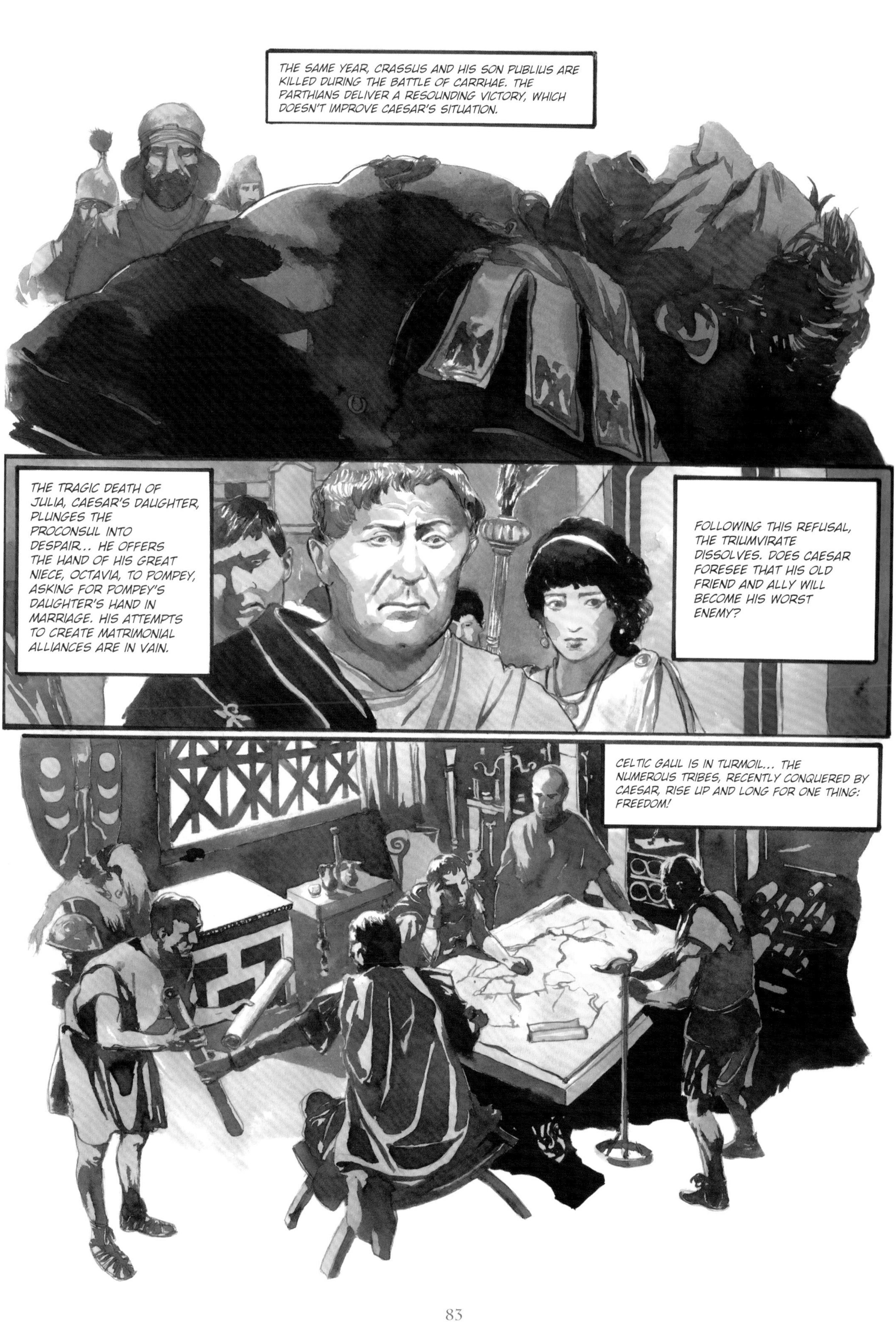
THE SAME YEAR, CRASSUS AND HIS SON PUBLIUS ARE KILLED DURING THE BATTLE OF CARRHAE. THE PARTHIANS DELIVER A RESOUNDING VICTORY, WHICH DOESN'T IMPROVE CAESAR'S SITUATION.
THE TRAGIC DEATH OF JULIA, CAESAR'S DAUGHTER, PLUNGES THE PROCONSUL INTO DESPAIR... HE OFFERS THE HAND OF HIS GREAT NIECE, OCTAVIA, TO POMPEY, ASKING FOR POMPEY'S DAUGHTER'S HAND IN MARRIAGE. HIS ATTEMPTS TO CREATE MATRIMONIAL ALLIANCES ARE IN VAIN.
FOLLOWING THIS REFUSAL, THE TRIUMVIRATE DISSOLVES. DOES CAESAR FORESEE THAT HIS OLD FRIEND AND ALLY WILL BECOME HIS WORST ENEMY?
CELTIC GAUL IS IN TURMOIL... THE NUMEROUS TRIBES, RECENTLY CONQUERED BY CAESAR, RISE UP AND LONG FOR ONE THING: FREEDOM!

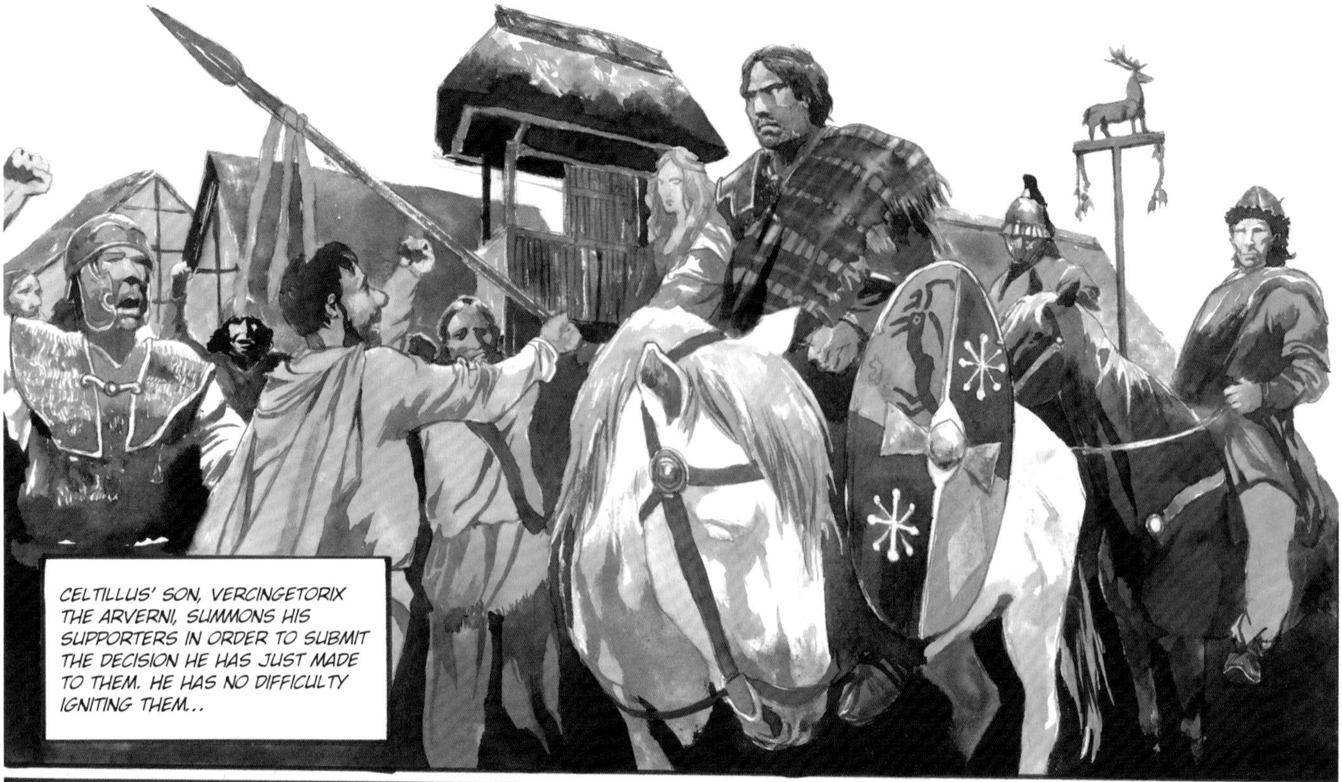
CELTILLUS' SON, VERCINGETORIX THE ARVERNI, SUMMONS HIS SUPPORTERS IN ORDER TO SUBMIT THE DECISION HE HAS JUST MADE TO THEM. HE HAS NO DIFFICULTY IGNITING THEM...

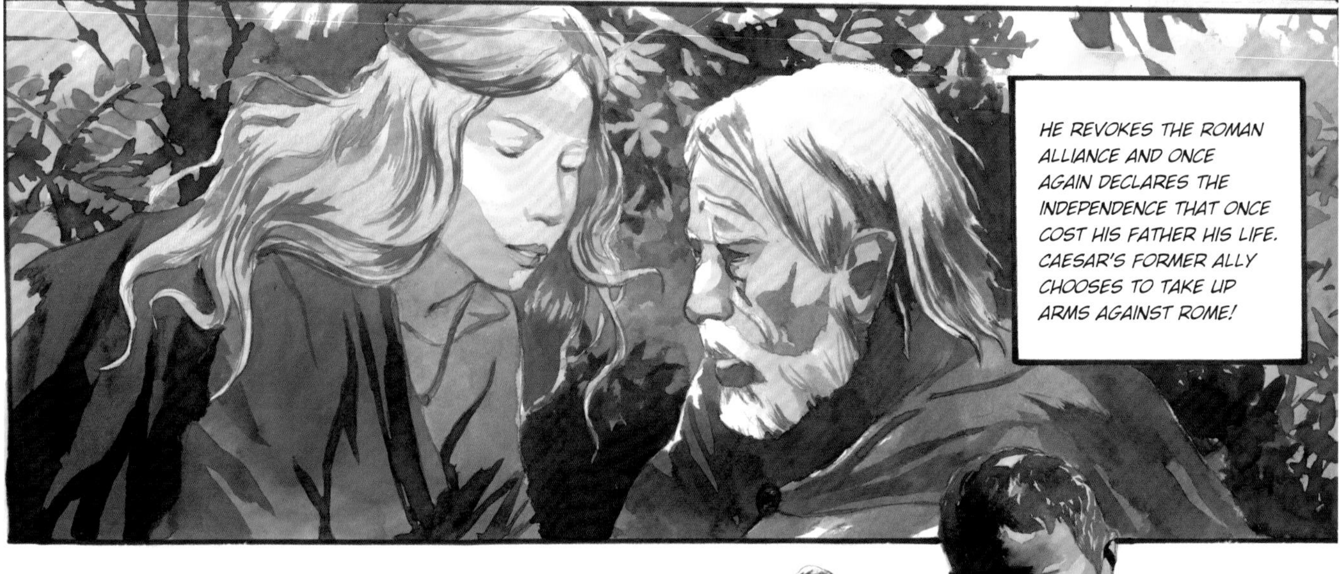
HE REVOKES THE ROMAN ALLIANCE AND ONCE AGAIN DECLARES THE INDEPENDENCE THAT ONCE COST HIS FATHER HIS LIFE. CAESAR'S FORMER ALLY CHOOSES TO TAKE UP ARMS AGAINST ROME!

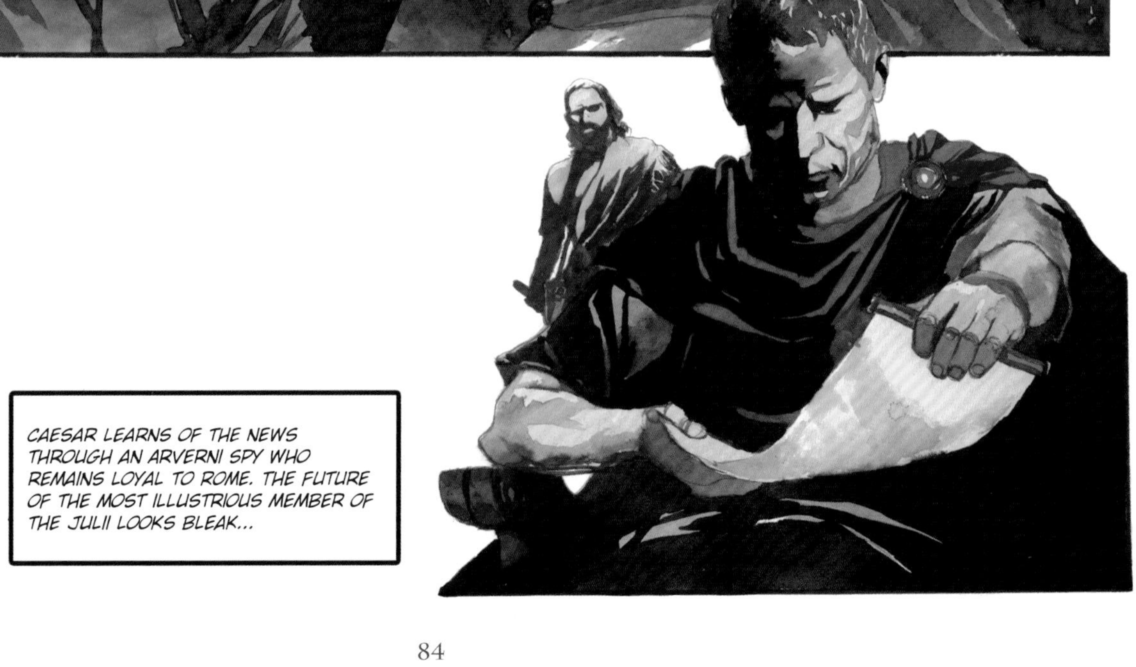
CAESAR LEARNS OF THE NEWS THROUGH AN ARVERNI SPY WHO REMAINS LOYAL TO ROME. THE FUTURE OF THE MOST ILLUSTRIOUS MEMBER OF THE JULII LOOKS BLEAK...

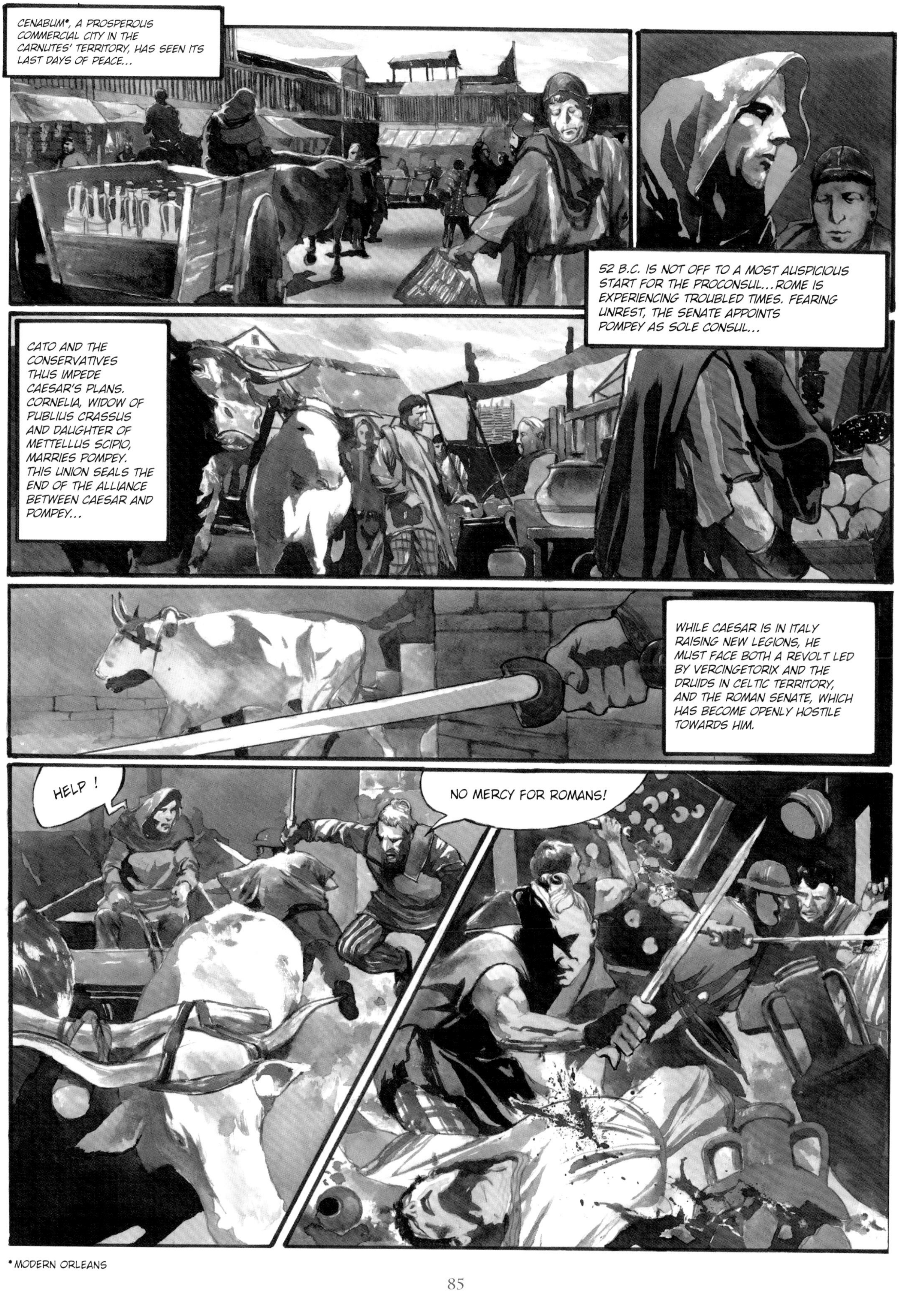
CENABUM*, A PROSPEROUS COMMERCIAL CITY IN THE CARNUTES' TERRITORY, HAS SEEN ITS LAST DAYS OF PEACE...
52 B.C. IS NOT OFF TO A MOST AUSPICIOUS START FOR THE PROCONSUL... ROME IS EXPERIENCING TROUBLED TIMES. FEARING UNREST, THE SENATE APPOINTS POMPEY AS SOLE CONSUL...
CATO AND THE CONSERVATIVES THUS IMPEDE CAESAR'S PLANS. CORNELIA, WIDOW OF PUBLIUS CRASSUS AND DAUGHTER OF METTELLUS SCIPIO, MARRIES POMPEY. THIS UNION SEALS THE END OF THE ALLIANCE BETWEEN CAESAR AND POMPEY...
WHILE CAESAR IS IN ITALY RAISING NEW LEGIONS, HE MUST FACE BOTH A REVOLT LED BY VERCINGETORIX AND THE DRUIDS IN CELTIC TERRITORY, AND THE ROMAN SENATE, WHICH HAS BECOME OPENLY HOSTILE TOWARDS HIM.
HELP !
NO MERCY FOR ROMANS!

* MODERN ORLEANS

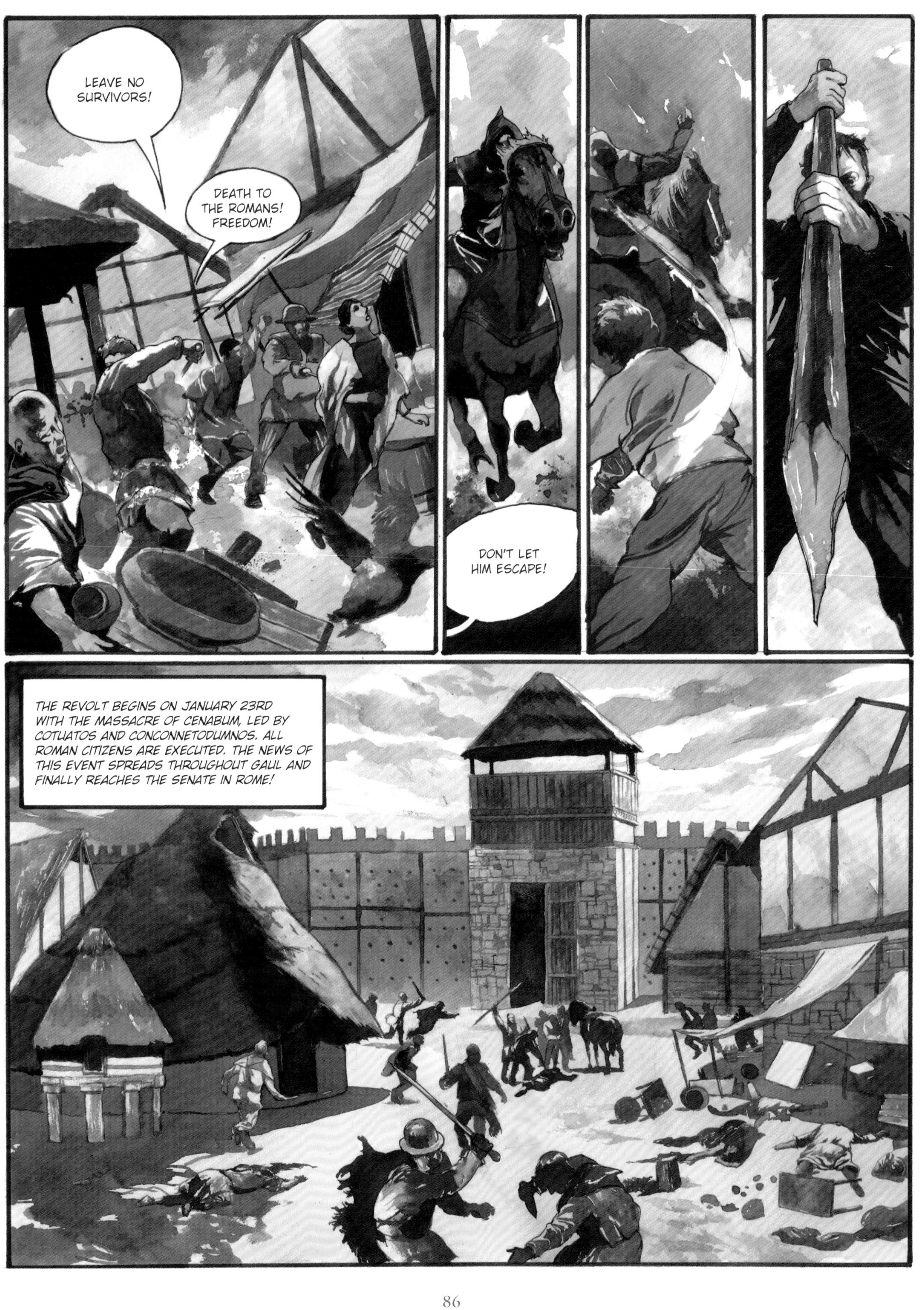
LEAVE NO SURVIVORS!
DEATH TO THE ROMANS! FREEDOM!
DON'T LET HIM ESCAPE!
THE REVOLT BEGINS ON JANUARY 23RD WITH THE MASSACRE OF CENABUM, LED BY COTUATOS AND CONCONNETODUMNOS. ALL ROMAN CITIZENS ARE EXECUTED. THE NEWS OF THIS EVENT SPREADS THROUGHOUT GAUL AND FINALLY REACHES THE SENATE IN ROME!

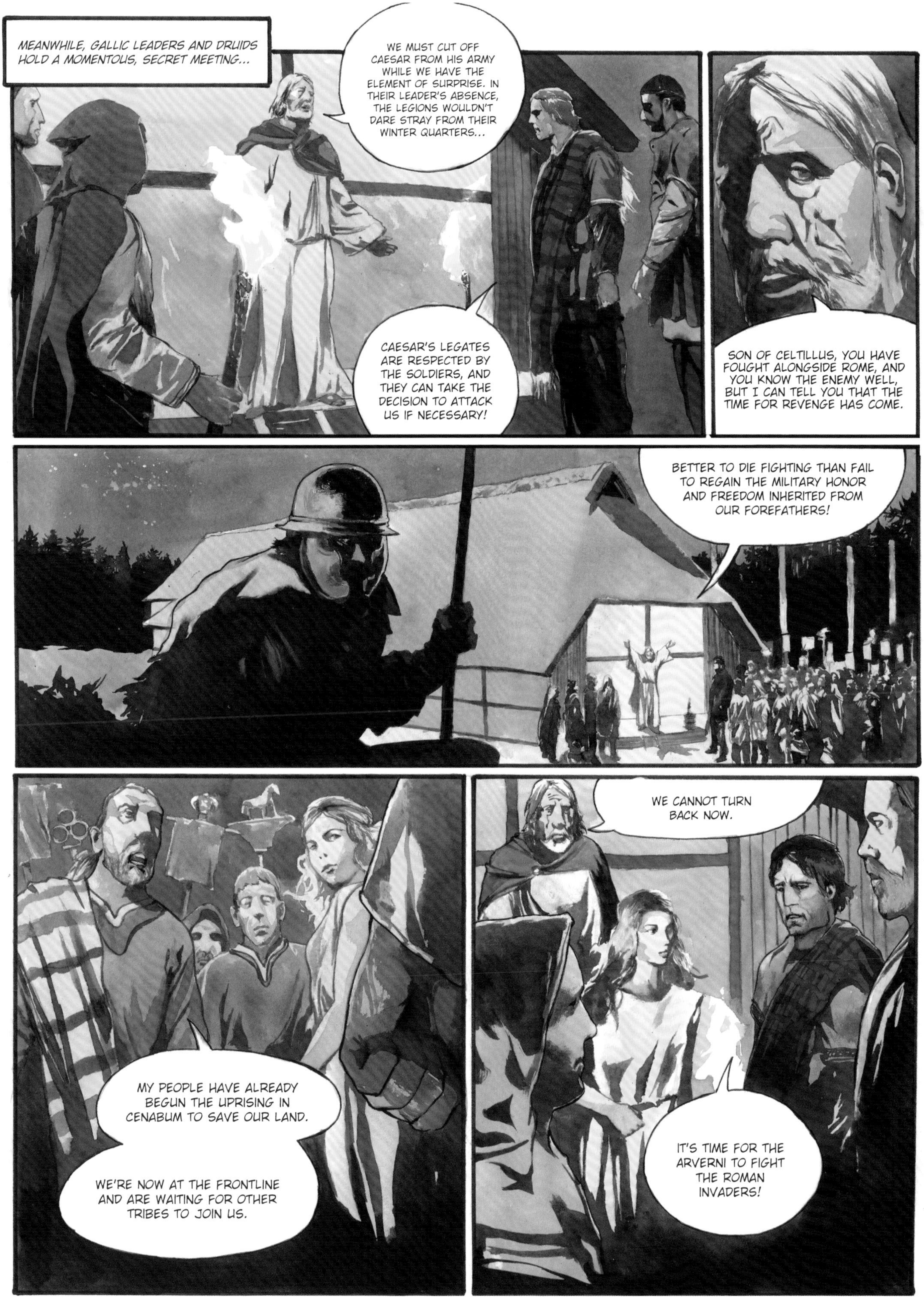
MEANWHILE, GALLIC LEADERS AND DRUIDS HOLD A MOMENTOUS, SECRET MEETING...
WE MUST CUT OFF CAESAR FROM HIS ARMY WHILE WE HAVE THE ELEMENT OF SURPRISE. IN THEIR LEADER'S ABSENCE, THE LEGIONS WOULDN'T DARE STRAY FROM THEIR WINTER QUARTERS...
CAESAR'S LEGATES ARE RESPECTED BY THE SOLDIERS, AND THEY CAN TAKE THE DECISION TO ATTACK US IF NECESSARY!
SON OF CELTILLUS, YOU HAVE FOUGHT ALONGSIDE ROME, AND YOU KNOW THE ENEMY WELL, BUT I CAN TELL YOU THAT THE TIME FOR REVENGE HAS COME.
BETTER TO DIE FIGHTING THAN FAIL TO REGAIN THE MILITARY HONOR AND FREEDOM INHERITED FROM OUR FOREFATHERS!
MY PEOPLE HAVE ALREADY BEGUN THE UPRISING IN CENABUM TO SAVE OUR LAND.
WE'RE NOW AT THE FRONTLINE AND ARE WAITING FOR OTHER TRIBES TO JOIN US.
WE CANNOT TURN BACK NOW.
IT'S TIME FOR THE ARVERNI TO FIGHT THE ROMAN INVADERS!

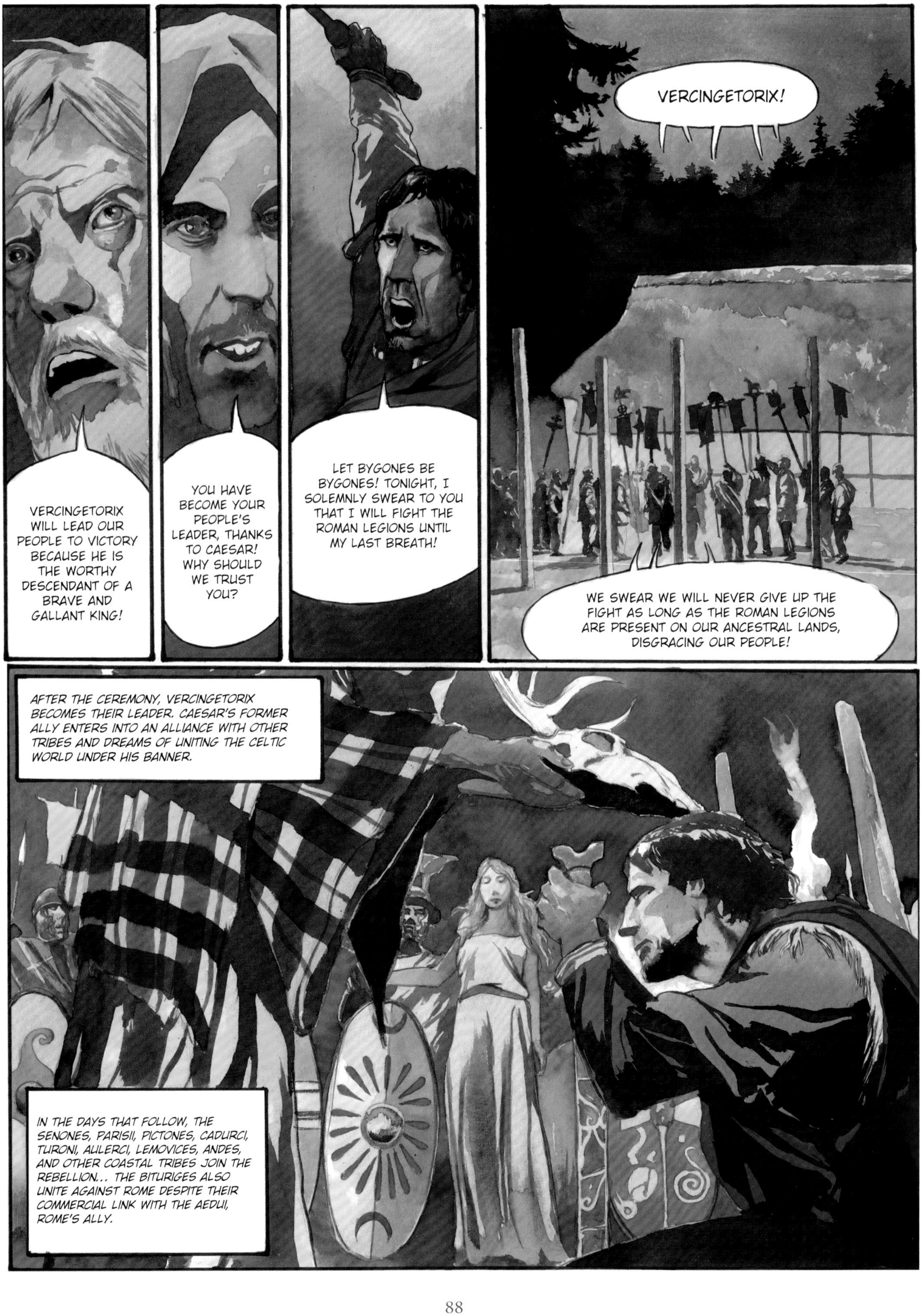
VERCINGETORIX WILL LEAD OUR PEOPLE TO VICTORY BECAUSE HE IS THE WORTHY DESCENDANT OF A BRAVE AND GALLANT KING!
YOU HAVE BECOME YOUR PEOPLE'S LEADER, THANKS TO CAESAR! WHY SHOULD WE TRUST YOU?
LET BYGONES BE BYGONES! TONIGHT, I SOLEMNLY SWEAR TO YOU THAT I WILL FIGHT THE ROMAN LEGIONS UNTIL MY LAST BREATH!
VERCINGETORIX!
WE SWEAR WE WILL NEVER GIVE UP THE FIGHT AS LONG AS THE ROMAN LEGIONS ARE PRESENT ON OUR ANCESTRAL LANDS, DISGRACING OUR PEOPLE!
AFTER THE CEREMONY, VERCINGETORIX BECOMES THEIR LEADER. CAESAR'S FORMER ALLY ENTERS INTO AN ALLIANCE WITH OTHER TRIBES AND DREAMS OF UNITING THE CELTIC WORLD UNDER HIS BANNER.
IN THE DAYS THAT FOLLOW, THE SENONES, PARISII, PICTONES, CADURCI, TURONI, AULERCI, LEMOVICES, ANDES, AND OTHER COASTAL TRIBES JOIN THE REBELLION... THE BITURIGES ALSO UNITE AGAINST ROME DESPITE THEIR COMMERCIAL LINK WITH THE AEDUI, ROME'S ALLY.

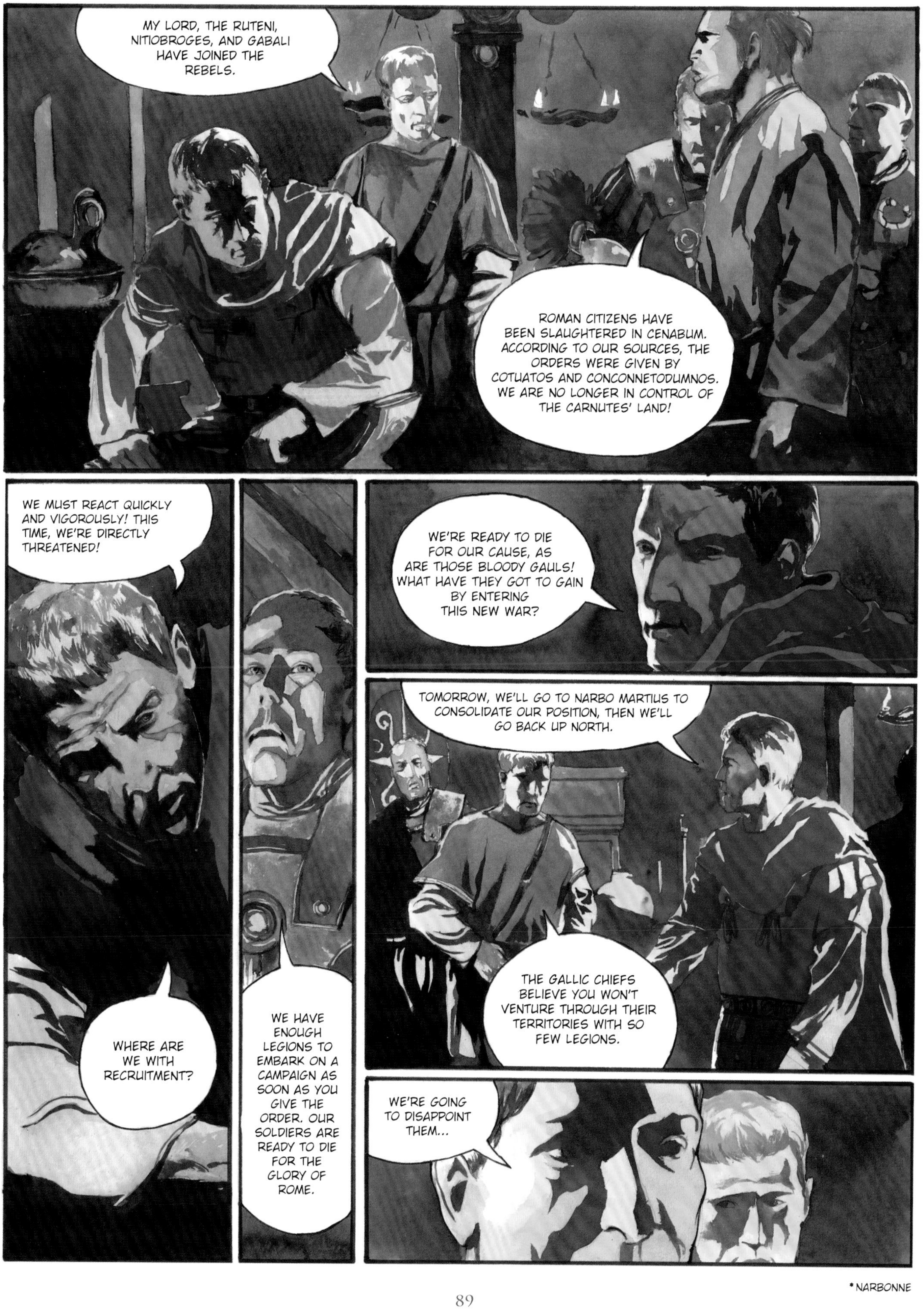
MY LORD, THE RUTENI, NITIOBROGES, AND GABALI HAVE JOINED THE REBELS.
ROMAN CITIZENS HAVE BEEN SLAUGHTERED IN CENABUM. ACCORDING TO OUR SOURCES, THE ORDERS WERE GIVEN BY COTUATOS AND CONCONNETODUMNOS. WE ARE NO LONGER IN CONTROL OF THE CARNUTES' LAND!
WE MUST REACT QUICKLY AND VIGOROUSLY! THIS TIME, WE'RE DIRECTLY THREATENED!
WHERE ARE WE WITH RECRUITMENT?
WE HAVE ENOUGH LEGIONS TO EMBARK ON A CAMPAIGN AS SOON AS YOU GIVE THE ORDER. OUR SOLDIERS ARE READY TO DIE FOR THE GLORY OF ROME.
WE'RE READY TO DIE FOR OUR CAUSE, AS ARE THOSE BLOODY GAULS! WHAT HAVE THEY GOT TO GAIN BY ENTERING THIS NEW WAR?
TOMORROW, WE'LL GO TO NARBO MARTIUS TO CONSOLIDATE OUR POSITION, THEN WE'LL GO BACK UP NORTH.
THE GALLIC CHIEFS BELIEVE YOU WON'T VENTURE THROUGH THEIR TERRITORIES WITH SO FEW LEGIONS.
WE'RE GOING TO DISAPPOINT THEM...

*NARBONNE

CAESAR LEADS HIS NEW RECRUITS TO TRANSALPINE GAUL TO ORGANIZE THE DEFENSE OF NARBO MARTIUS, HOME OF THE VOLCAE ARECOMICI, TOLOSATES, RUTENI, AND HELVII, WHERE HE UNITES HIS TROOPS.

VERCINGETORIX HOPES TO HOLD CAESAR AND HIS LEGIONS BACK IN THE ROMAN PROVINCE. HIS PLAN FAILS; CAESAR CROSSES THE CEVENNES*, SAID TO BE IMPASSABLE BEFORE SUMMER, AND REACHES THE ARVERNI BORDER, MUCH TO THE ENEMY'S SURPRISE!

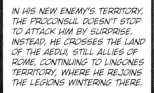

IN HIS NEW ENEMY'S TERRITORY, THE PROCONSUL DOESN'T STOP TO ATTACK HIM BY SURPRISE. INSTEAD, HE CROSSES THE LAND OF THE AEDUI, STILL ALLIES OF ROME, CONTINUING TO LINGONES TERRITORY, WHERE HE REJOINS THE LEGIONS WINTERING THERE.

THE GAULS HAVE FAILED IN THEIR ATTEMPT TO CUT CAESAR OFF FROM HIS LEGIONS...

*A RANGE OF MOUNTAINS IN MODERN SOUTH-CENTRAL FRANCE.

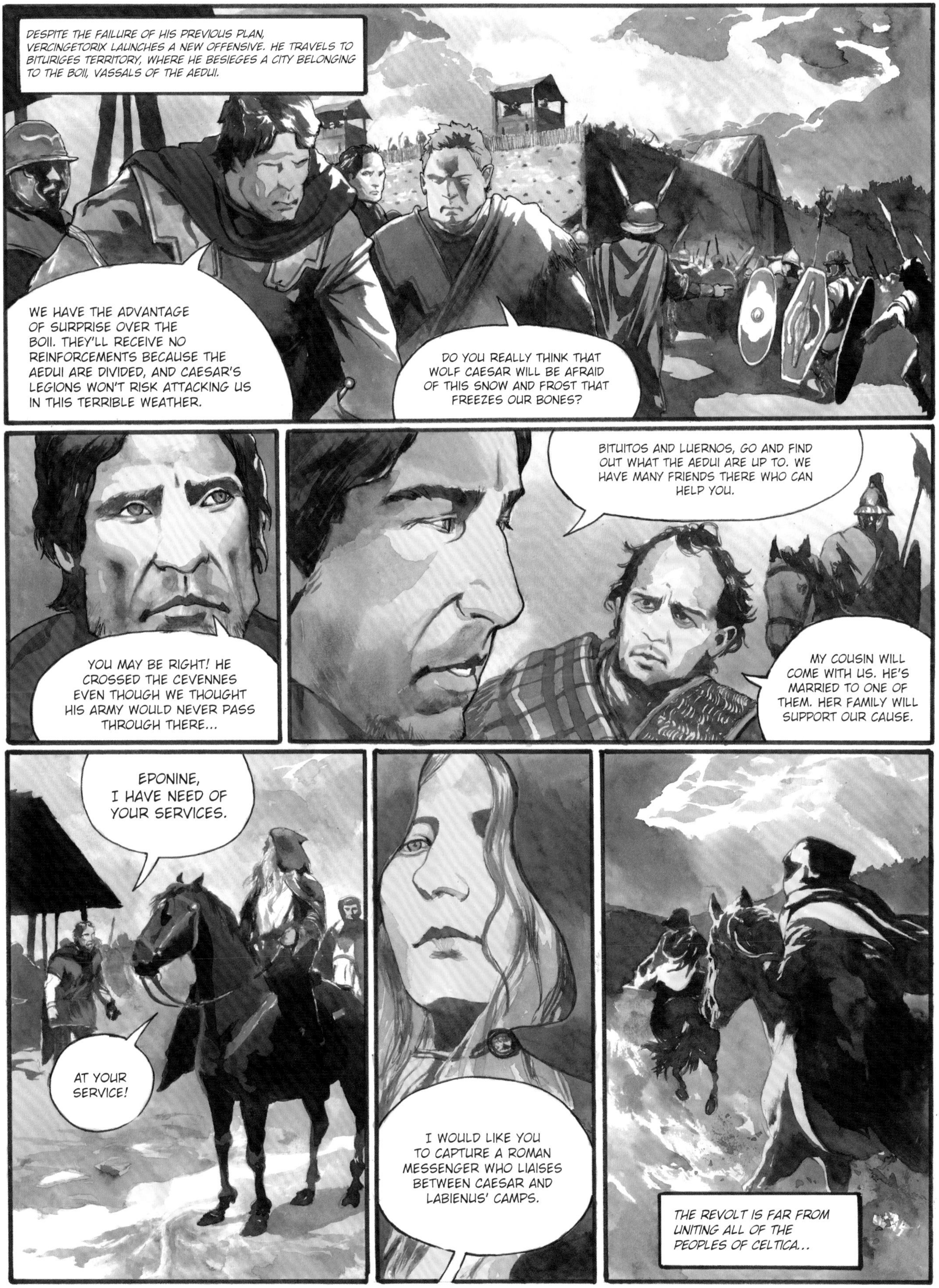
DESPITE THE FAILURE OF HIS PREVIOUS PLAN, VERCINGETORIX LAUNCHES A NEW OFFENSIVE. HE TRAVELS TO BITURIGES TERRITORY, WHERE HE BESIEGES A CITY BELONGING TO THE BOII, VASSALS OF THE AEDUI.
WE HAVE THE ADVANTAGE OF SURPRISE OVER THE BOII. THEY'LL RECEIVE NO REINFORCEMENTS BECAUSE THE AEDUI ARE DIVIDED, AND CAESAR'S LEGIONS WON'T RISK ATTACKING US IN THIS TERRIBLE WEATHER.
DO YOU REALLY THINK THAT WOLF CAESAR WILL BE AFRAID OF THIS SNOW AND FROST THAT FREEZES OUR BONES?
YOU MAY BE RIGHT! HE CROSSED THE CEVENNES EVEN THOUGH WE THOUGHT HIS ARMY WOULD NEVER PASS THROUGH THERE...
BITUITOS AND LUERNOS, GO AND FIND OUT WHAT THE AEDUI ARE UP TO. WE HAVE MANY FRIENDS THERE WHO CAN HELP YOU.
MY COUSIN WILL COME WITH US. HE'S MARRIED TO ONE OF THEM. HER FAMILY WILL SUPPORT OUR CAUSE.
EPONINE, I HAVE NEED OF YOUR SERVICES.
AT YOUR SERVICE!
I WOULD LIKE YOU TO CAPTURE A ROMAN MESSENGER WHO LIAISES BETWEEN CAESAR AND LABIENUS' CAMPS.
THE REVOLT IS FAR FROM UNITING ALL OF THE PEOPLES OF CELTICA...

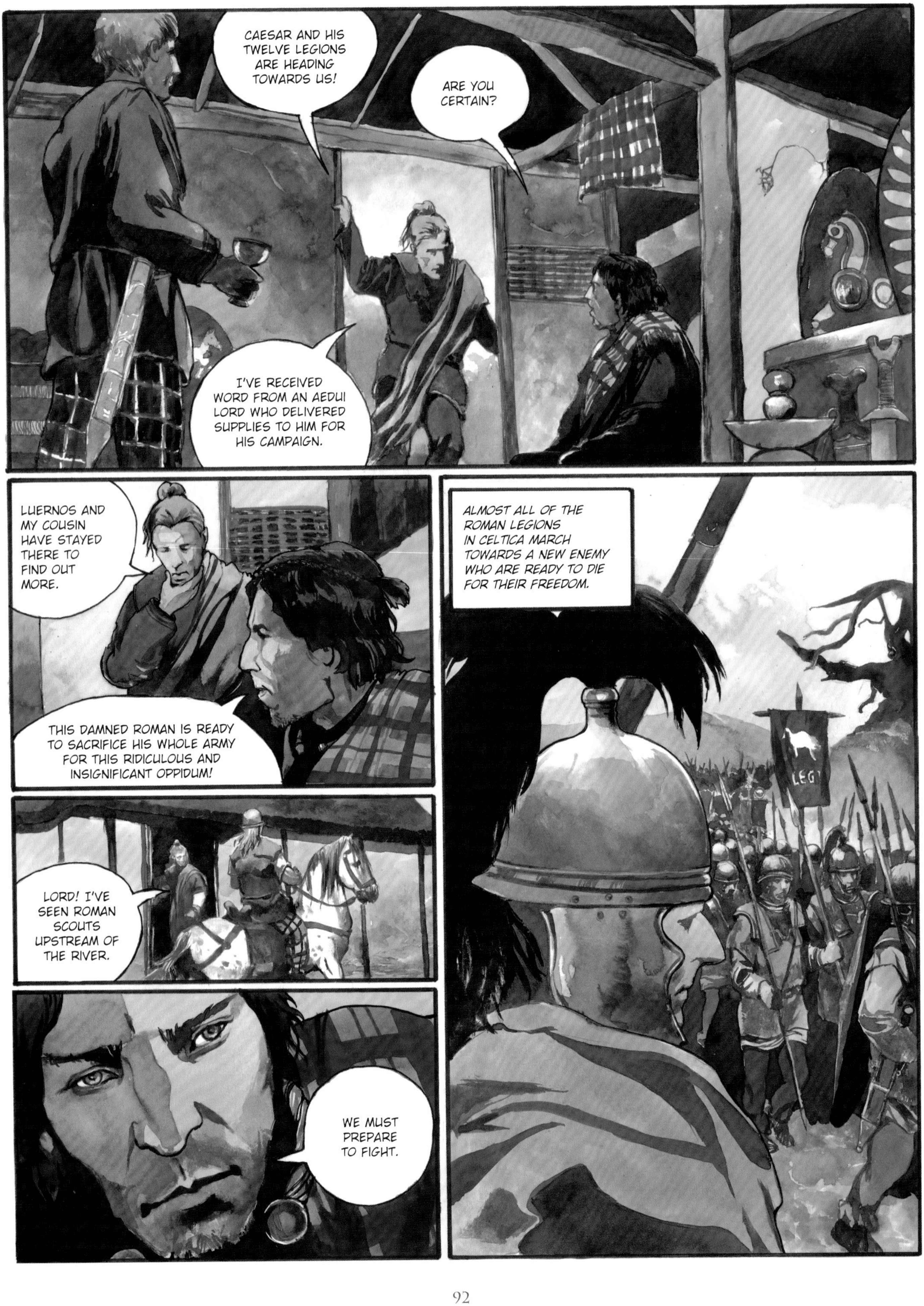
CAESAR AND HIS TWELVE LEGIONS ARE HEADING TOWARDS US!
ARE YOU CERTAIN?
I'VE RECEIVED WORD FROM AN AEDUI LORD WHO DELIVERED SUPPLIES TO HIM FOR HIS CAMPAIGN.
LUERNOS AND MY COUSIN HAVE STAYED THERE TO FIND OUT MORE.
THIS DAMNED ROMAN IS READY TO SACRIFICE HIS WHOLE ARMY FOR THIS RIDICULOUS AND INSIGNIFICANT OPPIDUM!
LORD! I'VE SEEN ROMAN SCOUTS UPSTREAM OF THE RIVER.
WE MUST PREPARE TO FIGHT.
ALMOST ALL OF THE ROMAN LEGIONS IN CELTICA MARCH TOWARDS A NEW ENEMY WHO ARE READY TO DIE FOR THEIR FREEDOM.
LEG

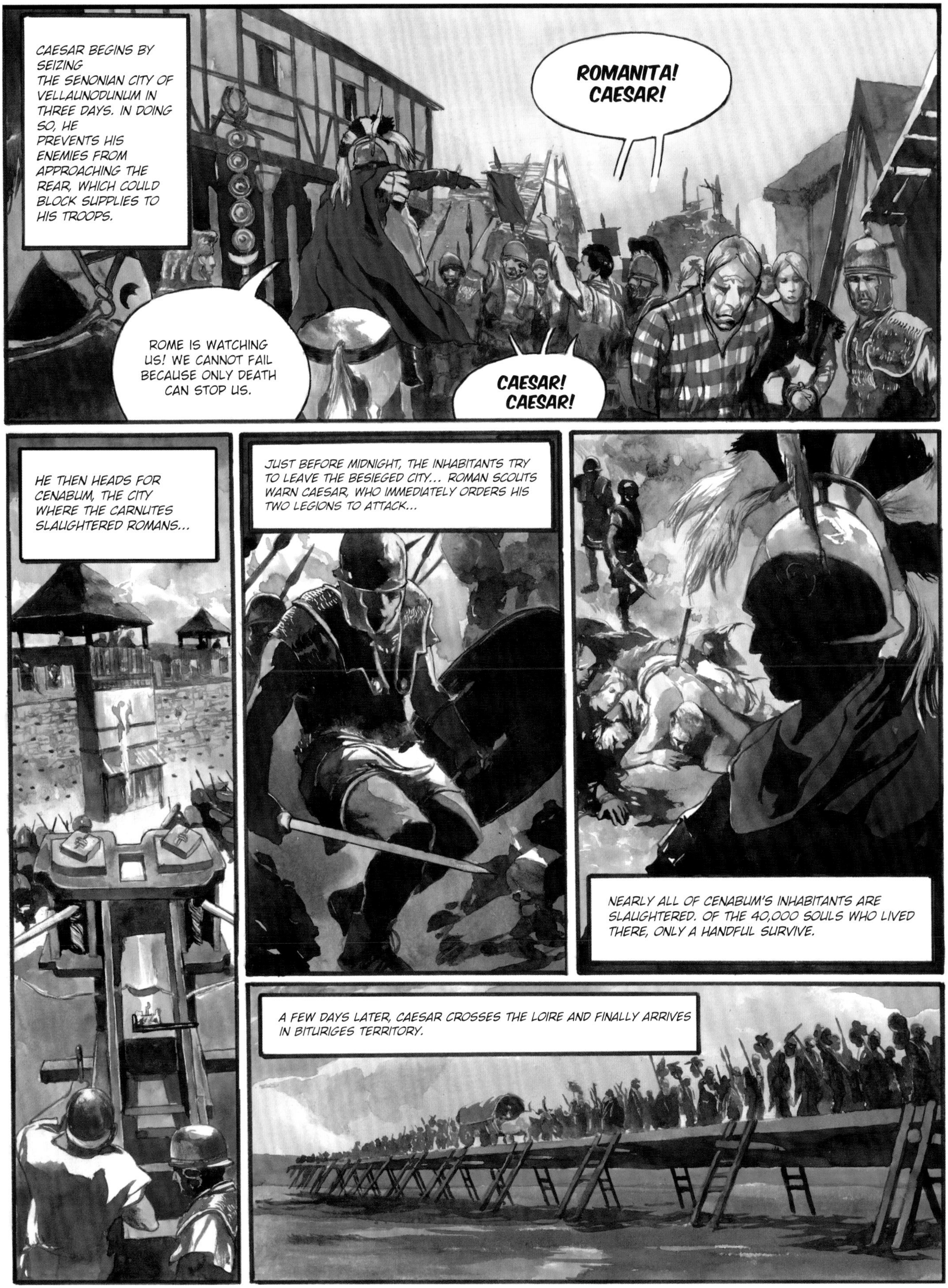

CAESAR BEGINS BY SEIZING THE SENONIAN CITY OF VELLAUNODUNUM IN THREE DAYS. IN DOING SO, HE PREVENTS HIS ENEMIES FROM APPROACHING THE REAR, WHICH COULD BLOCK SUPPLIES TO HIS TROOPS.
ROMANITA! CAESAR!
ROME IS WATCHING US! WE CANNOT FAIL BECAUSE ONLY DEATH CAN STOP US.
CAESAR! CAESAR!
HE THEN HEADS FOR CENABUM, THE CITY WHERE THE CARNUTES SLAUGHTERED ROMANS...
JUST BEFORE MIDNIGHT, THE INHABITANTS TRY TO LEAVE THE BESIEGED CITY... ROMAN SCOUTS WARN CAESAR, WHO IMMEDIATELY ORDERS HIS TWO LEGIONS TO ATTACK...
NEARLY ALL OF CENABUM'S INHABITANTS ARE SLAUGHTERED. OF THE 40,000 SOULS WHO LIVED THERE, ONLY A HANDFUL SURVIVE.
A FEW DAYS LATER, CAESAR CROSSES THE LOIRE AND FINALLY ARRIVES IN BITURIGES TERRITORY.

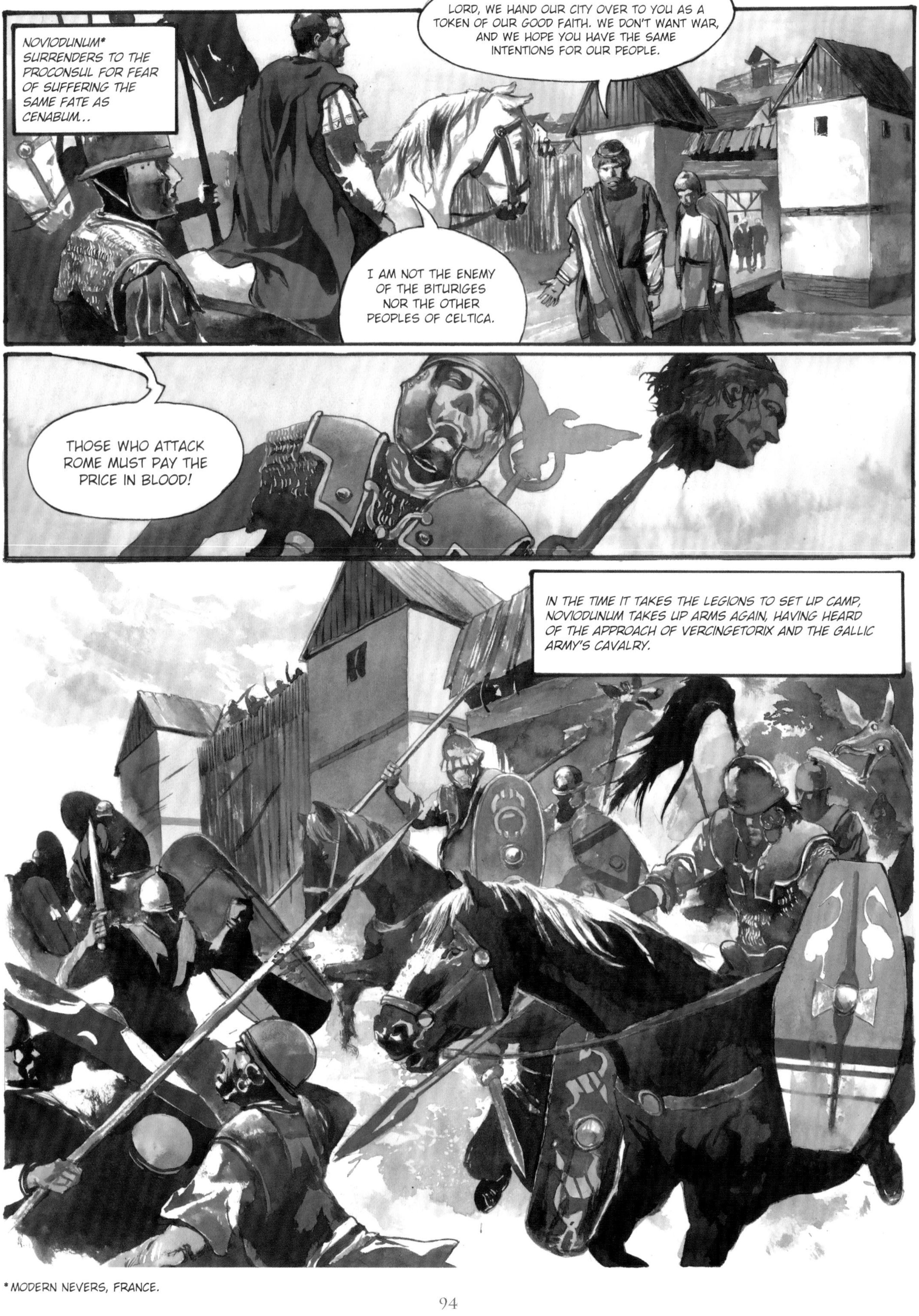
NOVIODUNUM* SURRENDERS TO THE PROCONSUL FOR FEAR OF SUFFERING THE SAME FATE AS CENABUM...
LORD, WE HAND OUR CITY OVER TO YOU AS A TOKEN OF OUR GOOD FAITH. WE DON'T WANT WAR, AND WE HOPE YOU HAVE THE SAME INTENTIONS FOR OUR PEOPLE.
I AM NOT THE ENEMY OF THE BITURIGES NOR THE OTHER PEOPLES OF CELTICA.
THOSE WHO ATTACK ROME MUST PAY THE PRICE IN BLOOD!
IN THE TIME IT TAKES THE LEGIONS TO SET UP CAMP, NOVIODUNUM TAKES UP ARMS AGAIN, HAVING HEARD OF THE APPROACH OF VERCINGETORIX AND THE GALLIC ARMY'S CAVALRY.

*MODERN NEVERS, FRANCE.

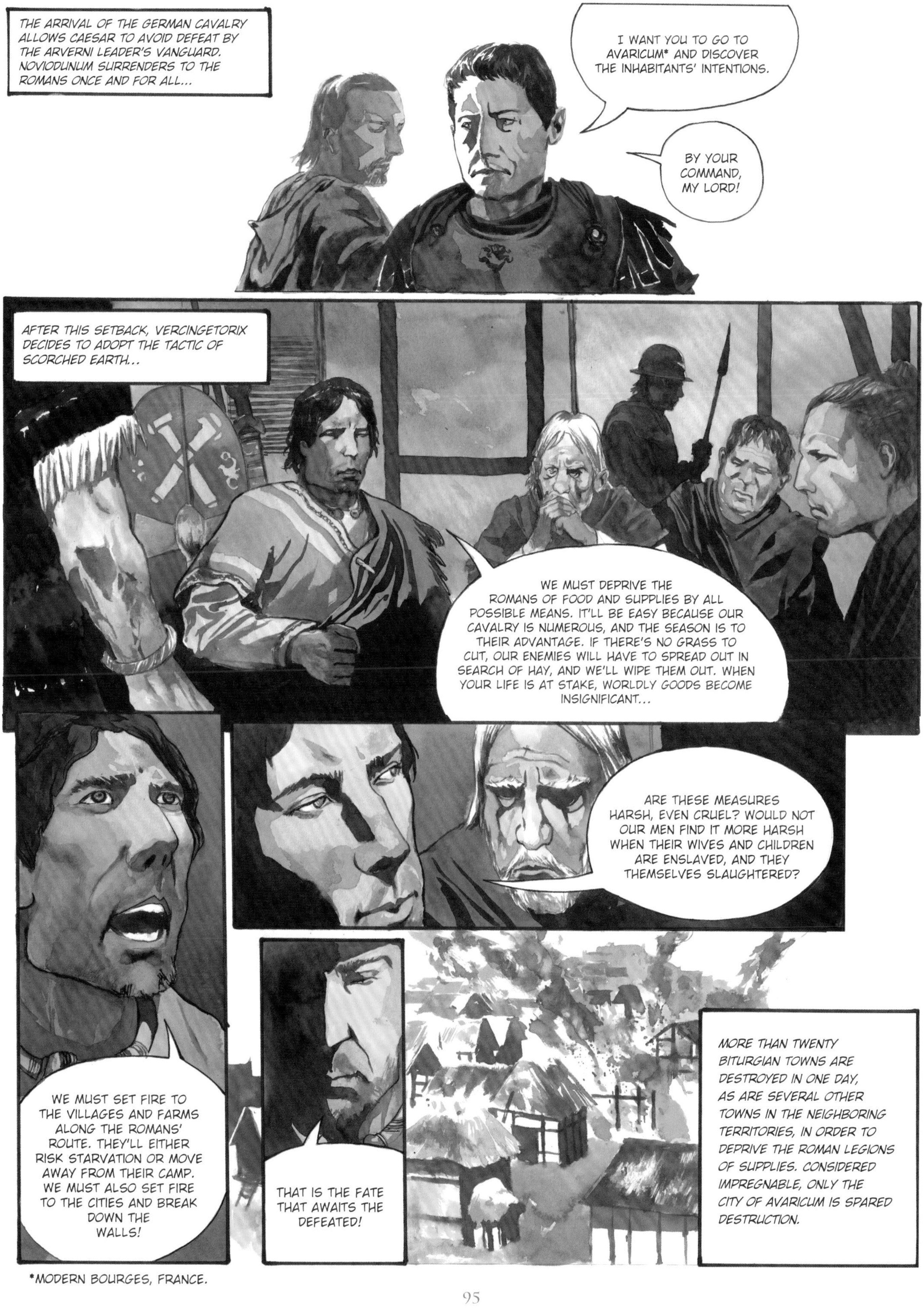
THE ARRIVAL OF THE GERMAN CAVALRY ALLOWS CAESAR TO AVOID DEFEAT BY THE ARVERNI LEADER'S VANGUARD. NOVIODUNUM SURRENDERS TO THE ROMANS ONCE AND FOR ALL...
I WANT YOU TO GO TO AVARICUM* AND DISCOVER THE INHABITANTS' INTENTIONS.
BY YOUR COMMAND, MY LORD!
AFTER THIS SETBACK, VERCINGETORIX DECIDES TO ADOPT THE TACTIC OF SCORCHED EARTH...
WE MUST DEPRIVE THE ROMANS OF FOOD AND SUPPLIES BY ALL POSSIBLE MEANS. IT'LL BE EASY BECAUSE OUR CAVALRY IS NUMEROUS, AND THE SEASON IS TO THEIR ADVANTAGE. IF THERE'S NO GRASS TO CUT, OUR ENEMIES WILL HAVE TO SPREAD OUT IN SEARCH OF HAY, AND WE'LL WIPE THEM OUT. WHEN YOUR LIFE IS AT STAKE, WORLDLY GOODS BECOME INSIGNIFICANT...
ARE THESE MEASURES HARSH, EVEN CRUEL? WOULD NOT OUR MEN FIND IT MORE HARSH WHEN THEIR WIVES AND CHILDREN ARE ENSLAVED, AND THEY THEMSELVES SLAUGHTERED?
WE MUST SET FIRE TO THE VILLAGES AND FARMS ALONG THE ROMANS' ROUTE. THEY'LL EITHER RISK STARVATION OR MOVE AWAY FROM THEIR CAMP. WE MUST ALSO SET FIRE TO THE CITIES AND BREAK DOWN THE WALLS!
THAT IS THE FATE THAT AWAITS THE DEFEATED!
MORE THAN TWENTY BITURGIAN TOWNS ARE DESTROYED IN ONE DAY, AS ARE SEVERAL OTHER TOWNS IN THE NEIGHBORING TERRITORIES, IN ORDER TO DEPRIVE THE ROMAN LEGIONS OF SUPPLIES. CONSIDERED IMPREGNABLE, ONLY THE CITY OF AVARICUM IS SPARED DESTRUCTION.

*MODERN BOURGES, FRANCE.

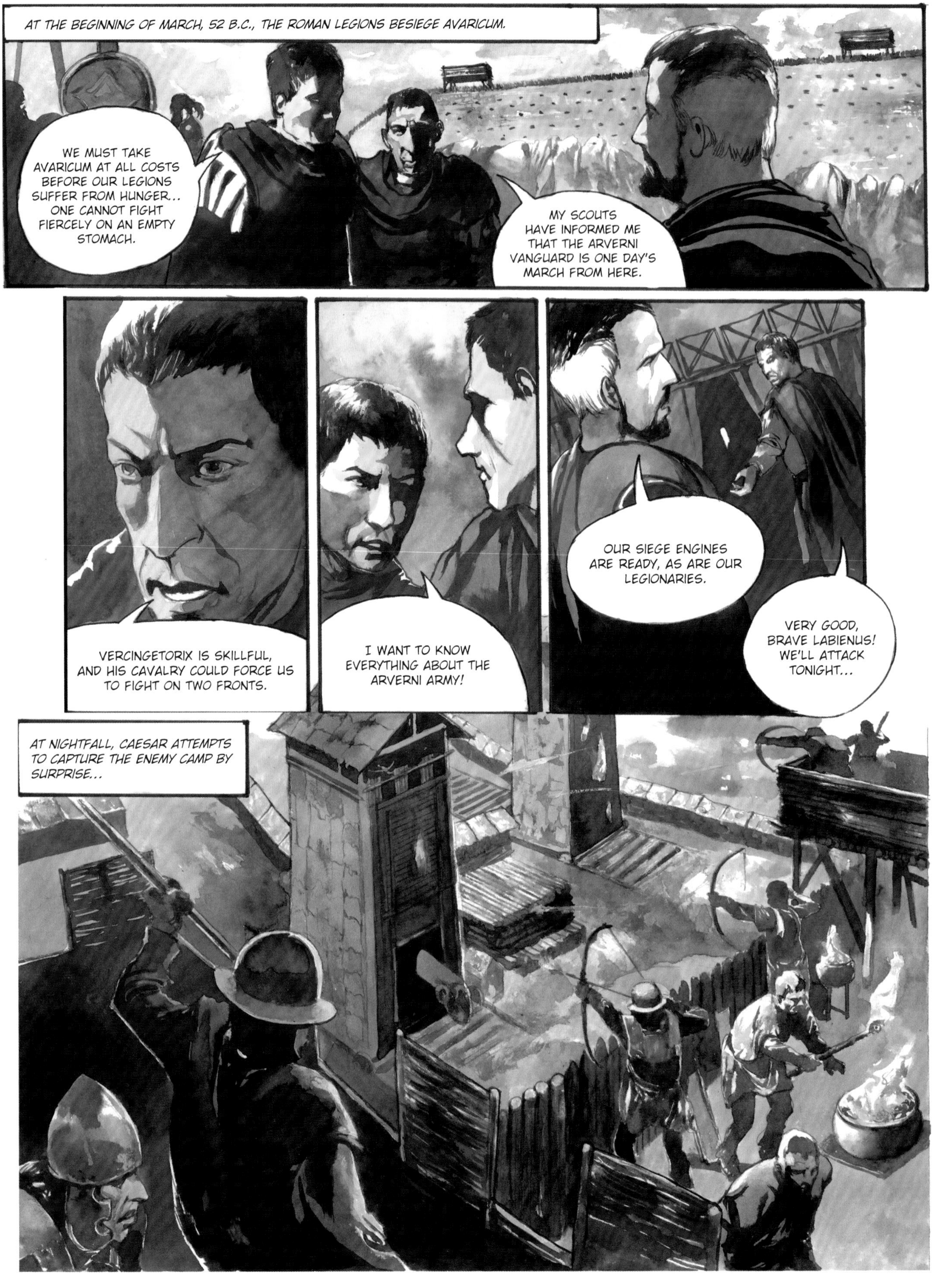
AT THE BEGINNING OF MARCH, 52 B.C., THE ROMAN LEGIONS BESIEGE AVARICUM.
WE MUST TAKE AVARICUM AT ALL COSTS BEFORE OUR LEGIONS SUFFER FROM HUNGER... ONE CANNOT FIGHT FIERCELY ON AN EMPTY STOMACH.
MY SCOUTS HAVE INFORMED ME THAT THE ARVERNI VANGUARD IS ONE DAY'S MARCH FROM HERE.
VERCINGETORIX IS SKILLFUL, AND HIS CAVALRY COULD FORCE US TO FIGHT ON TWO FRONTS.
I WANT TO KNOW EVERYTHING ABOUT THE ARVERNI ARMY!
OUR SIEGE ENGINES ARE READY, AS ARE OUR LEGIONARIES.
VERY GOOD, BRAVE LABIENUS! WE'LL ATTACK TONIGHT...
AT NIGHTFALL, CAESAR ATTEMPTS TO CAPTURE THE ENEMY CAMP BY SURPRISE...

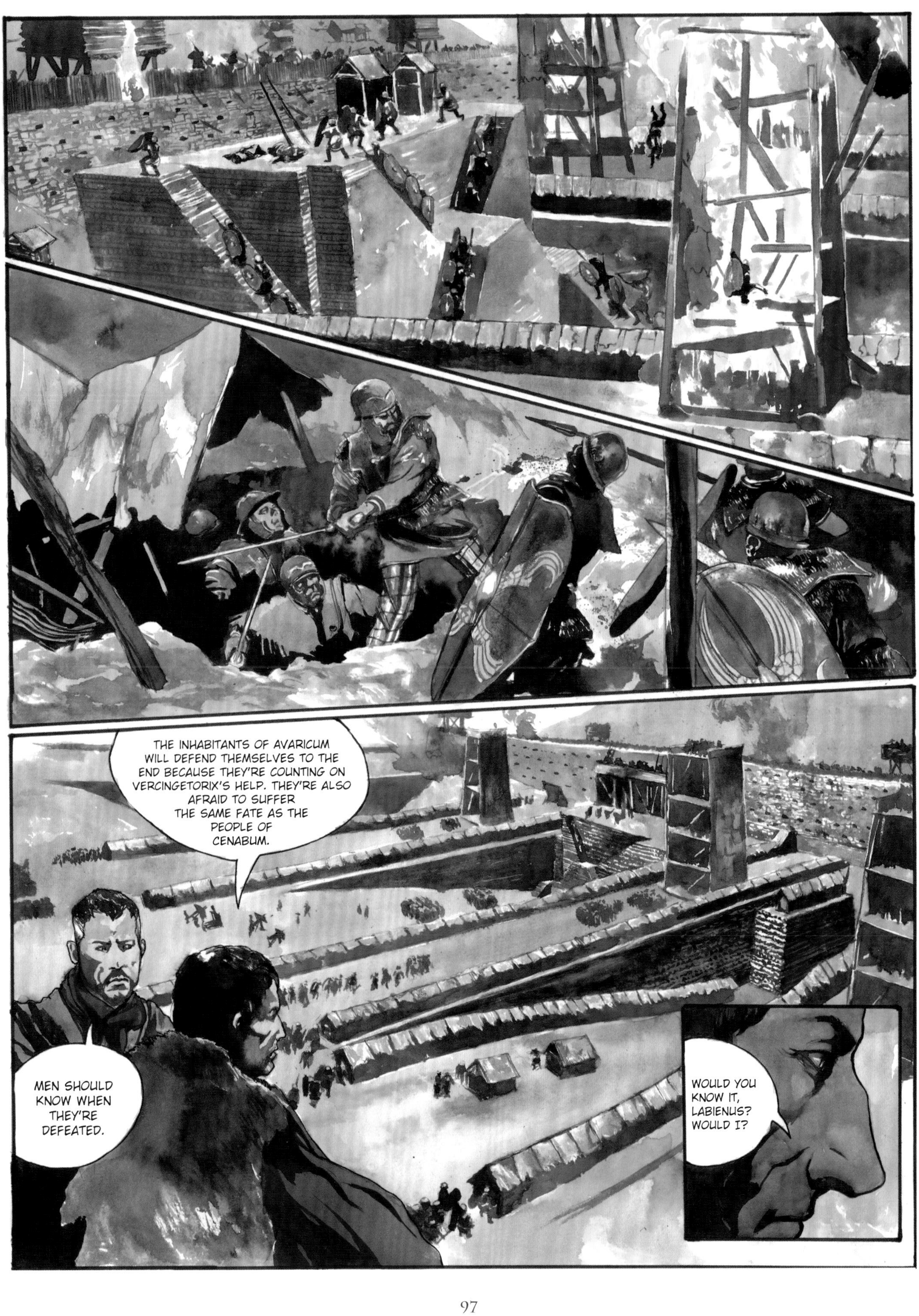
THE INHABITANTS OF AVARICUM WILL DEFEND THEMSELVES TO THE END BECAUSE THEY'RE COUNTING ON VERCINGETORIX'S HELP. THEY'RE ALSO AFRAID TO SUFFER THE SAME FATE AS THE PEOPLE OF CENABUM.
MEN SHOULD KNOW WHEN THEY'RE DEFEATED.
WOULD YOU KNOW IT, LABIENUS? WOULD I?

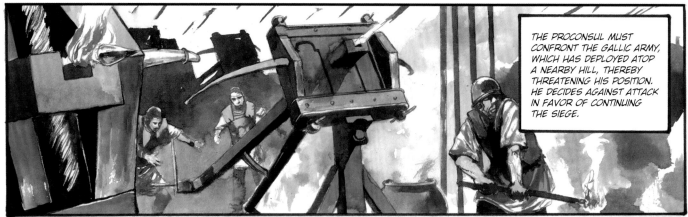

THE PROCONSUL MUST CONFRONT THE GALLIC ARMY, WHICH HAS DEPLOYED ATOP A NEARBY HILL, THEREBY THREATENING HIS POSITION. HE DECIDES AGAINST ATTACK IN FAVOR OF CONTINUING THE SIEGE.

ON THE OPPOSITE SIDE, VERCINGETORIX CARRIES OUT, ALONG WITH HIS CAVALRY AND LIGHT INFANTRY, THE DESTRUCTION OF ALL SUPPLY CONVOYS DESTINED FOR THE TWELVE ROMAN LEGIONS.

WE'VE CAPTURED ROMAN DESERTERS WHO CAN TELL US ABOUT THE STATE OF CAESAR'S CAMP.

OUR ARMY IS IN THE SAME DISTRESS AS WE ARE. WE'RE EXHAUSTED... THE SIEGE WORKS ARE WEARING US OUT.

OUR GENERAL HAS DECIDED TO ABANDON THE SIEGE WITHIN THREE DAYS IF WE DON'T OBTAIN RESULTS.

THANKS TO ME, WITHOUT COSTING YOU A DROP OF BLOOD, YOU'LL WITNESS A GREAT, VICTORIOUS ARMY WIPED OUT BY HUNGER. SOON, THEY WILL FLEE, SEEKING ASYLUM, BUT I'VE MADE CERTAIN THAT NO ONE WILL WELCOME THEM IN THEIR TERRITORY.

VERCINGETORIX IS A GREAT LEADER!

THE ROMAN LEGIONS ARE SOON SHORT ON SUPPLIES, WHILE HELP FROM THE AEDUI STILL HASN'T ARRIVED.

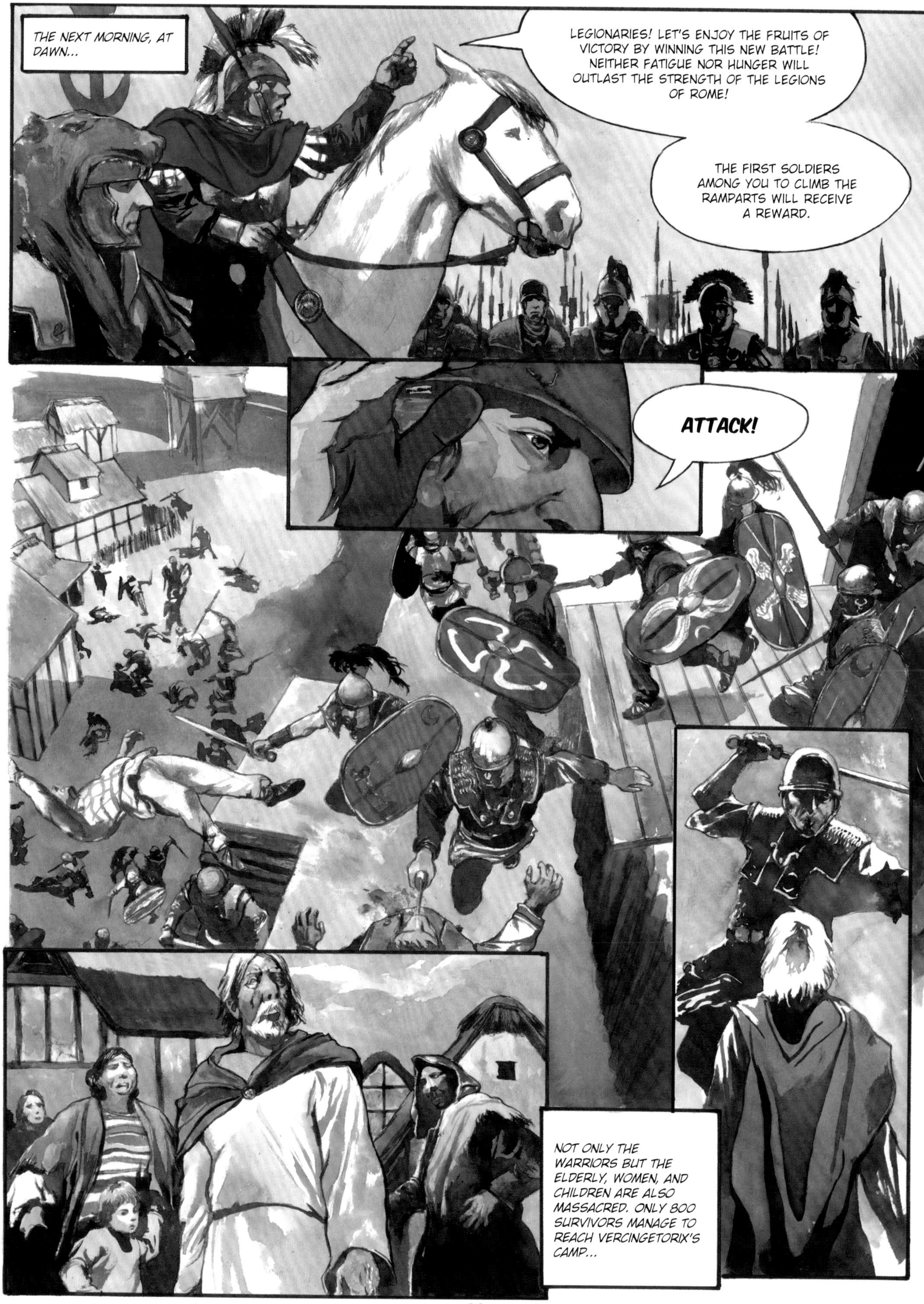
THE NEXT MORNING, AT DAWN...
LEGIONARIES! LET'S ENJOY THE FRUITS OF VICTORY BY WINNING THIS NEW BATTLE! NEITHER FATIGUE NOR HUNGER WILL OUTLAST THE STRENGTH OF THE LEGIONS OF ROME!
THE FIRST SOLDIERS AMONG YOU TO CLIMB THE RAMPARTS WILL RECEIVE A REWARD.
ATTACK!
NOT ONLY THE WARRIORS BUT THE ELDERLY, WOMEN, AND CHILDREN ARE ALSO MASSACRED. ONLY 800 SURVIVORS MANAGE TO REACH VERCINGETORIX'S CAMP...

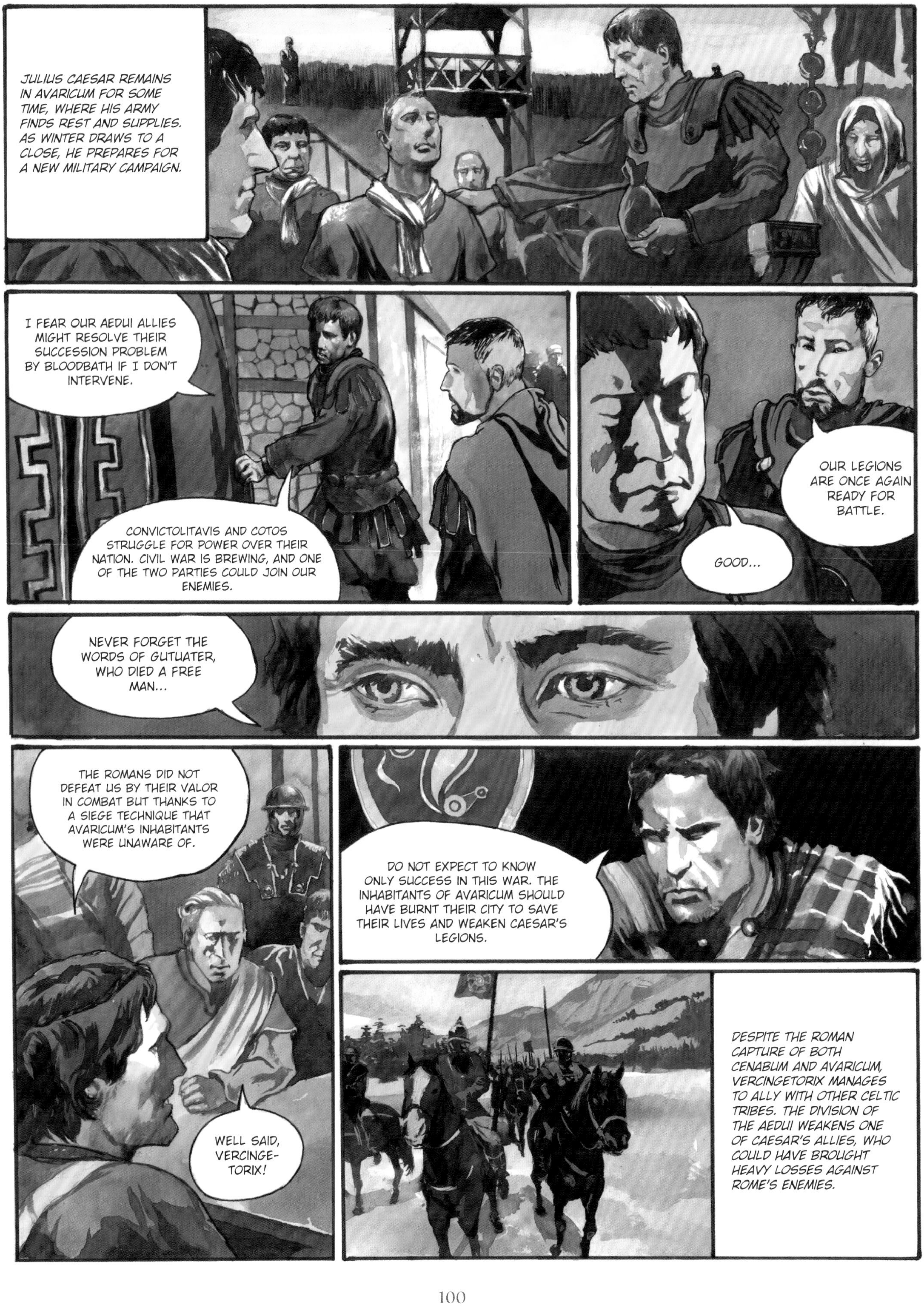
JULIUS CAESAR REMAINS IN AVARICUM FOR SOME TIME, WHERE HIS ARMY FINDS REST AND SUPPLIES. AS WINTER DRAWS TO A CLOSE, HE PREPARES FOR A NEW MILITARY CAMPAIGN.
I FEAR OUR AEDUI ALLIES MIGHT RESOLVE THEIR SUCCESSION PROBLEM BY BLOODBATH IF I DON'T INTERVENE.
CONVICTOLITAVIS AND COTOS STRUGGLE FOR POWER OVER THEIR NATION. CIVIL WAR IS BREWING, AND ONE OF THE TWO PARTIES COULD JOIN OUR ENEMIES.
OUR LEGIONS ARE ONCE AGAIN READY FOR BATTLE.
GOOD...
NEVER FORGET THE WORDS OF GUTUATER, WHO DIED A FREE MAN...
THE ROMANS DID NOT DEFEAT US BY THEIR VALOR IN COMBAT BUT THANKS TO A SIEGE TECHNIQUE THAT AVARICUM'S INHABITANTS WERE UNAWARE OF.
DO NOT EXPECT TO KNOW ONLY SUCCESS IN THIS WAR. THE INHABITANTS OF AVARICUM SHOULD HAVE BURNT THEIR CITY TO SAVE THEIR LIVES AND WEAKEN CAESAR'S LEGIONS.
WELL SAID, VERCINGETORIX!
DESPITE THE ROMAN CAPTURE OF BOTH CENABUM AND AVARICUM, VERCINGETORIX MANAGES TO ALLY WITH OTHER CELTIC TRIBES. THE DIVISION OF THE AEDUI WEAKENS ONE OF CAESAR'S ALLIES, WHO COULD HAVE BROUGHT HEAVY LOSSES AGAINST ROME'S ENEMIES.

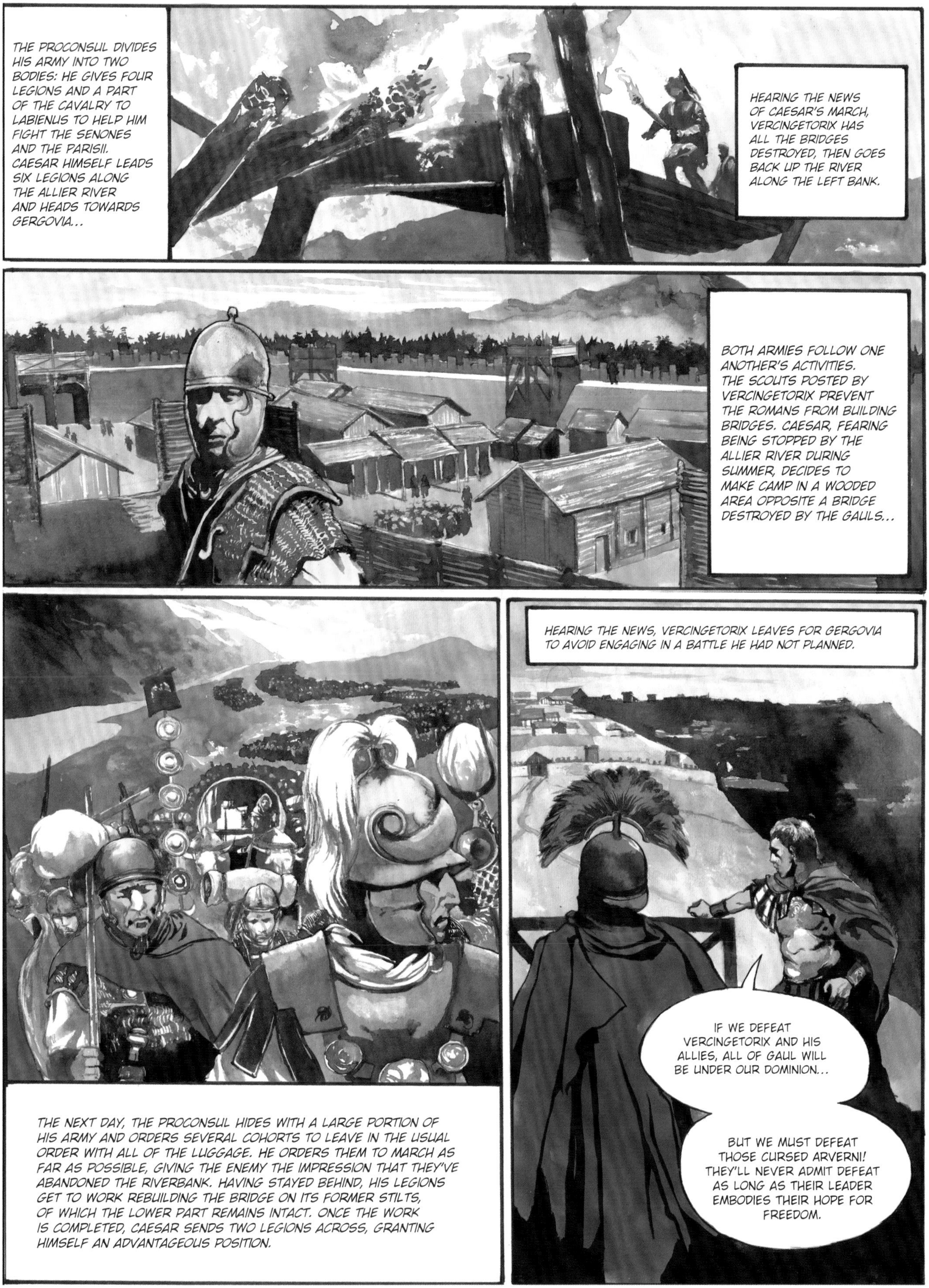
THE PROCONSUL DIVIDES HIS ARMY INTO TWO BODIES: HE GIVES FOUR LEGIONS AND A PART OF THE CAVALRY TO LABIENUS TO HELP HIM FIGHT THE SENONES AND THE PARISII. CAESAR HIMSELF LEADS SIX LEGIONS ALONG THE ALLIER RIVER AND HEADS TOWARDS GERGOVIA...
HEARING THE NEWS OF CAESAR'S MARCH, VERCINGETORIX HAS ALL THE BRIDGES DESTROYED, THEN GOES BACK UP THE RIVER ALONG THE LEFT BANK.
BOTH ARMIES FOLLOW ONE ANOTHER'S ACTIVITIES. THE SCOUTS POSTED BY VERCINGETORIX PREVENT THE ROMANS FROM BUILDING BRIDGES. CAESAR, FEARING BEING STOPPED BY THE ALLIER RIVER DURING SUMMER, DECIDES TO MAKE CAMP IN A WOODED AREA OPPOSITE A BRIDGE DESTROYED BY THE GAULS...
THE NEXT DAY, THE PROCONSUL HIDES WITH A LARGE PORTION OF HIS ARMY AND ORDERS SEVERAL COHORTS TO LEAVE IN THE USUAL ORDER WITH ALL OF THE LUGGAGE. HE ORDERS THEM TO MARCH AS FAR AS POSSIBLE, GIVING THE ENEMY THE IMPRESSION THAT THEY'VE ABANDONED THE RIVERBANK. HAVING STAYED BEHIND, HIS LEGIONS GET TO WORK REBUILDING THE BRIDGE ON ITS FORMER STILTS, OF WHICH THE LOWER PART REMAINS INTACT. ONCE THE WORK IS COMPLETED, CAESAR SENDS TWO LEGIONS ACROSS, GRANTING HIMSELF AN ADVANTAGEOUS POSITION.
HEARING THE NEWS, VERCINGETORIX LEAVES FOR GERGOVIA TO AVOID ENGAGING IN A BATTLE HE HAD NOT PLANNED.
IF WE DEFEAT VERCINGETORIX AND HIS ALLIES, ALL OF GAUL WILL BE UNDER OUR DOMINION...
BUT WE MUST DEFEAT THOSE CURSED ARVERNI! THEY'LL NEVER ADMIT DEFEAT AS LONG AS THEIR LEADER EMBODIES THEIR HOPE FOR FREEDOM.

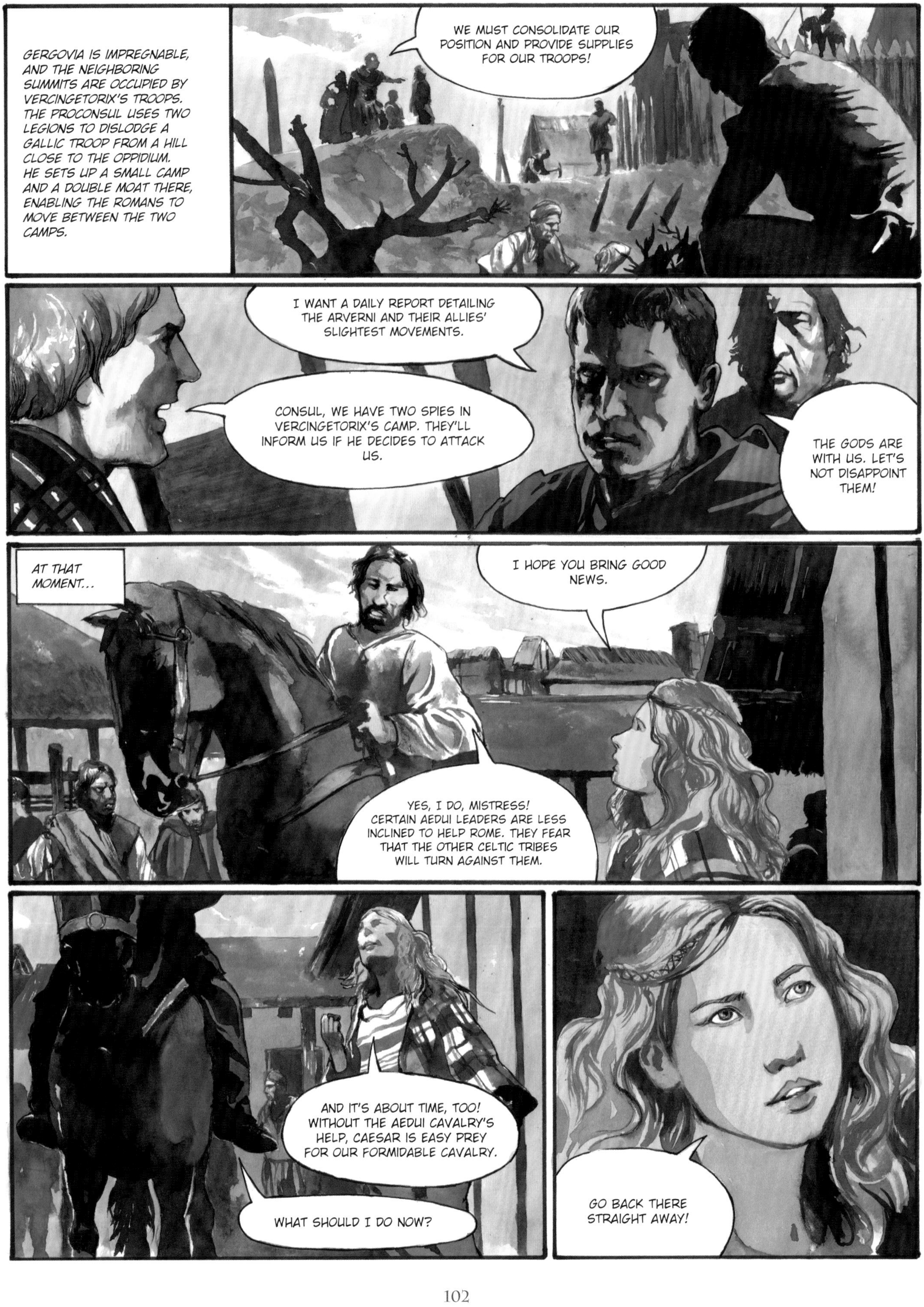
GERGOVIA IS IMPREGNABLE, AND THE NEIGHBORING SUMMITS ARE OCCUPIED BY VERCINGETORIX'S TROOPS. THE PROCONSUL USES TWO LEGIONS TO DISLODGE A GALLIC TROOP FROM A HILL CLOSE TO THE OPPIDIUM. HE SETS UP A SMALL CAMP AND A DOUBLE MOAT THERE, ENABLING THE ROMANS TO MOVE BETWEEN THE TWO CAMPS.
WE MUST CONSOLIDATE OUR POSITION AND PROVIDE SUPPLIES FOR OUR TROOPS!
I WANT A DAILY REPORT DETAILING THE ARVERNI AND THEIR ALLIES' SLIGHTEST MOVEMENTS.
CONSUL, WE HAVE TWO SPIES IN VERCINGETORIX'S CAMP. THEY'LL INFORM US IF HE DECIDES TO ATTACK US.
THE GODS ARE WITH US. LET'S NOT DISAPPOINT THEM!
AT THAT MOMENT...
I HOPE YOU BRING GOOD NEWS.
YES, I DO, MISTRESS! CERTAIN AEDUI LEADERS ARE LESS INCLINED TO HELP ROME. THEY FEAR THAT THE OTHER CELTIC TRIBES WILL TURN AGAINST THEM.
AND IT'S ABOUT TIME, TOO! WITHOUT THE AEDUI CAVALRY'S HELP, CAESAR IS EASY PREY FOR OUR FORMIDABLE CAVALRY.
WHAT SHOULD I DO NOW?
GO BACK THERE STRAIGHT AWAY!

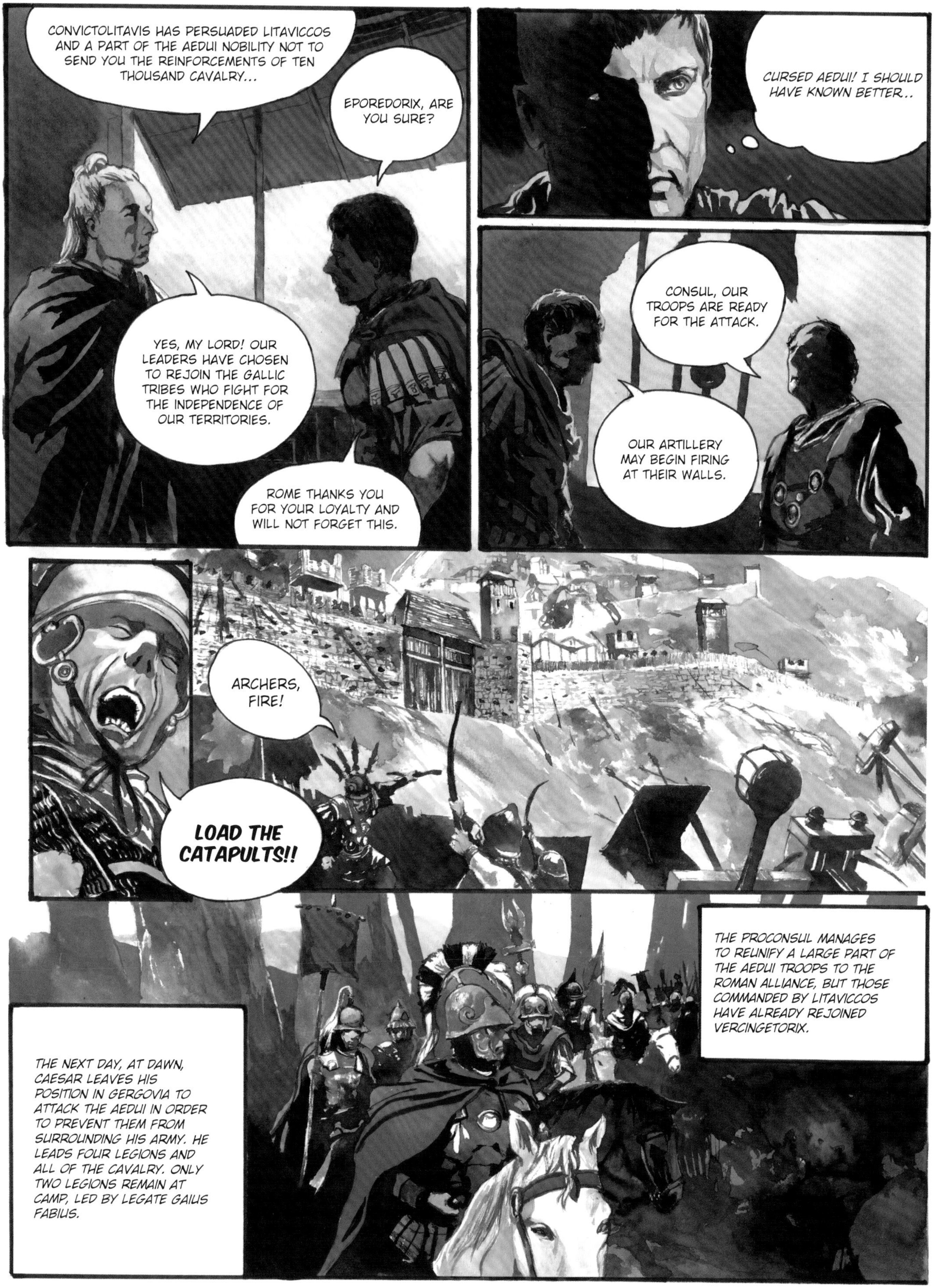
CONVICTOLITAVIS HAS PERSUADED LITAVICCOS AND A PART OF THE AEDUI NOBILITY NOT TO SEND YOU THE REINFORCEMENTS OF TEN THOUSAND CAVALRY...
EPOREDORIX, ARE YOU SURE?
YES, MY LORD! OUR LEADERS HAVE CHOSEN TO REJOIN THE GALLIC TRIBES WHO FIGHT FOR THE INDEPENDENCE OF OUR TERRITORIES.
ROME THANKS YOU FOR YOUR LOYALTY AND WILL NOT FORGET THIS.
CURSED AEDUI! I SHOULD HAVE KNOWN BETTER..
CONSUL, OUR TROOPS ARE READY FOR THE ATTACK.
OUR ARTILLERY MAY BEGIN FIRING AT THEIR WALLS.
ARCHERS, FIRE!
LOAD THE CATAPULTS!!
THE PROCONSUL MANAGES TO REUNIFY A LARGE PART OF THE AEDUI TROOPS TO THE ROMAN ALLIANCE, BUT THOSE COMMANDED BY LITAVICCOS HAVE ALREADY REJOINED VERCINGETORIX.
THE NEXT DAY, AT DAWN, CAESAR LEAVES HIS POSITION IN GERGOVIA TO ATTACK THE AEDUI IN ORDER TO PREVENT THEM FROM SURROUNDING HIS ARMY. HE LEADS FOUR LEGIONS AND ALL OF THE CAVALRY. ONLY TWO LEGIONS REMAIN AT CAMP, LED BY LEGATE GAIUS FABIUS.

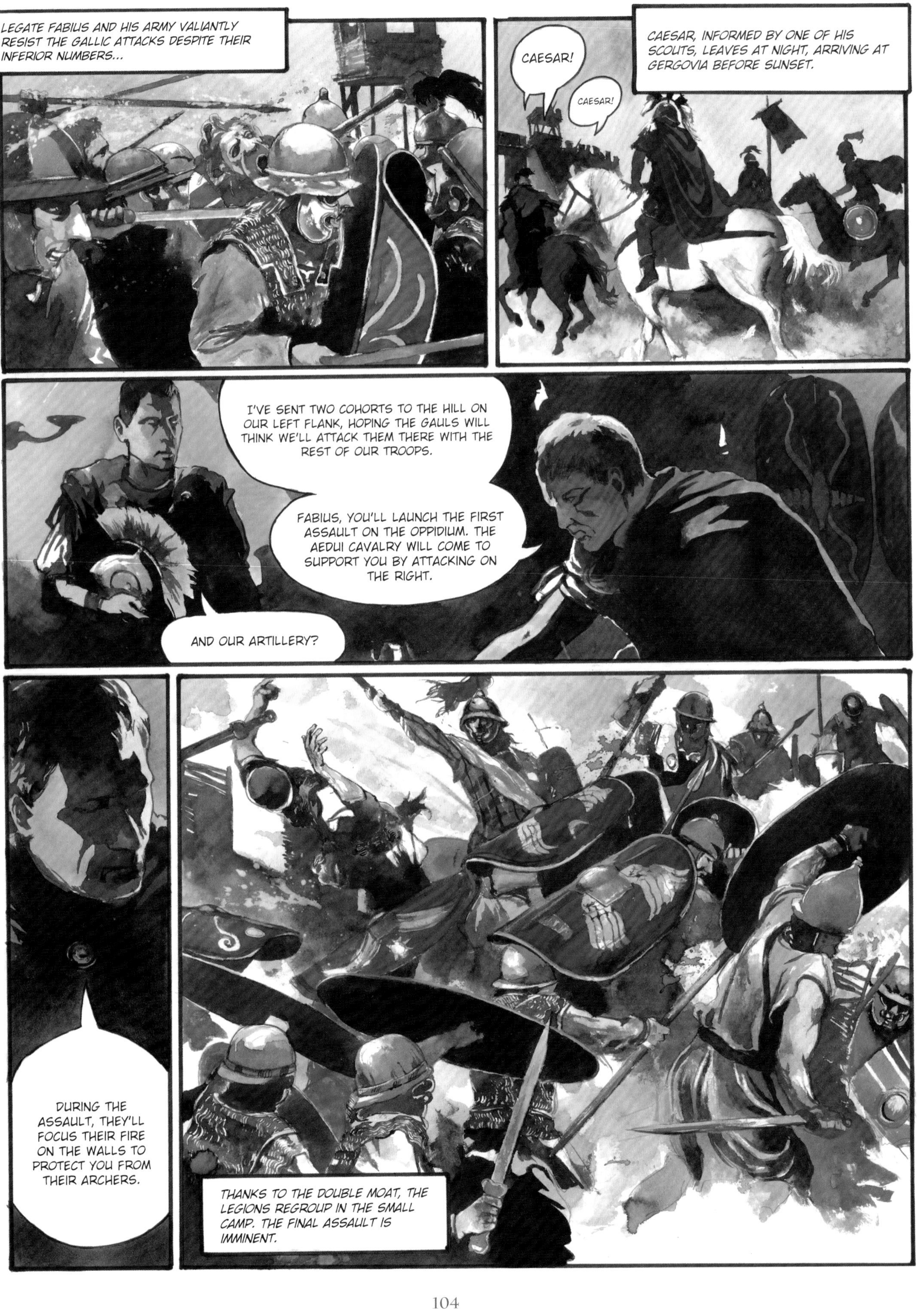

LEGATE FABIUS AND HIS ARMY VALIANTLY RESIST THE GALLIC ATTACKS DESPITE THEIR INFERIOR NUMBERS...
CAESAR!
CAESAR!
CAESAR, INFORMED BY ONE OF HIS SCOUTS, LEAVES AT NIGHT, ARRIVING AT GERGOVIA BEFORE SUNSET.
I'VE SENT TWO COHORTS TO THE HILL ON OUR LEFT FLANK, HOPING THE GAULS WILL THINK WE'LL ATTACK THEM THERE WITH THE REST OF OUR TROOPS.
FABIUS, YOU'LL LAUNCH THE FIRST ASSAULT ON THE OPPIDIUM. THE AEDUI CAVALRY WILL COME TO SUPPORT YOU BY ATTACKING ON THE RIGHT.
AND OUR ARTILLERY?
DURING THE ASSAULT, THEY'LL FOCUS THEIR FIRE ON THE WALLS TO PROTECT YOU FROM THEIR ARCHERS.
THANKS TO THE DOUBLE MOAT, THE LEGIONS REGROUP IN THE SMALL CAMP. THE FINAL ASSAULT IS IMMINENT.

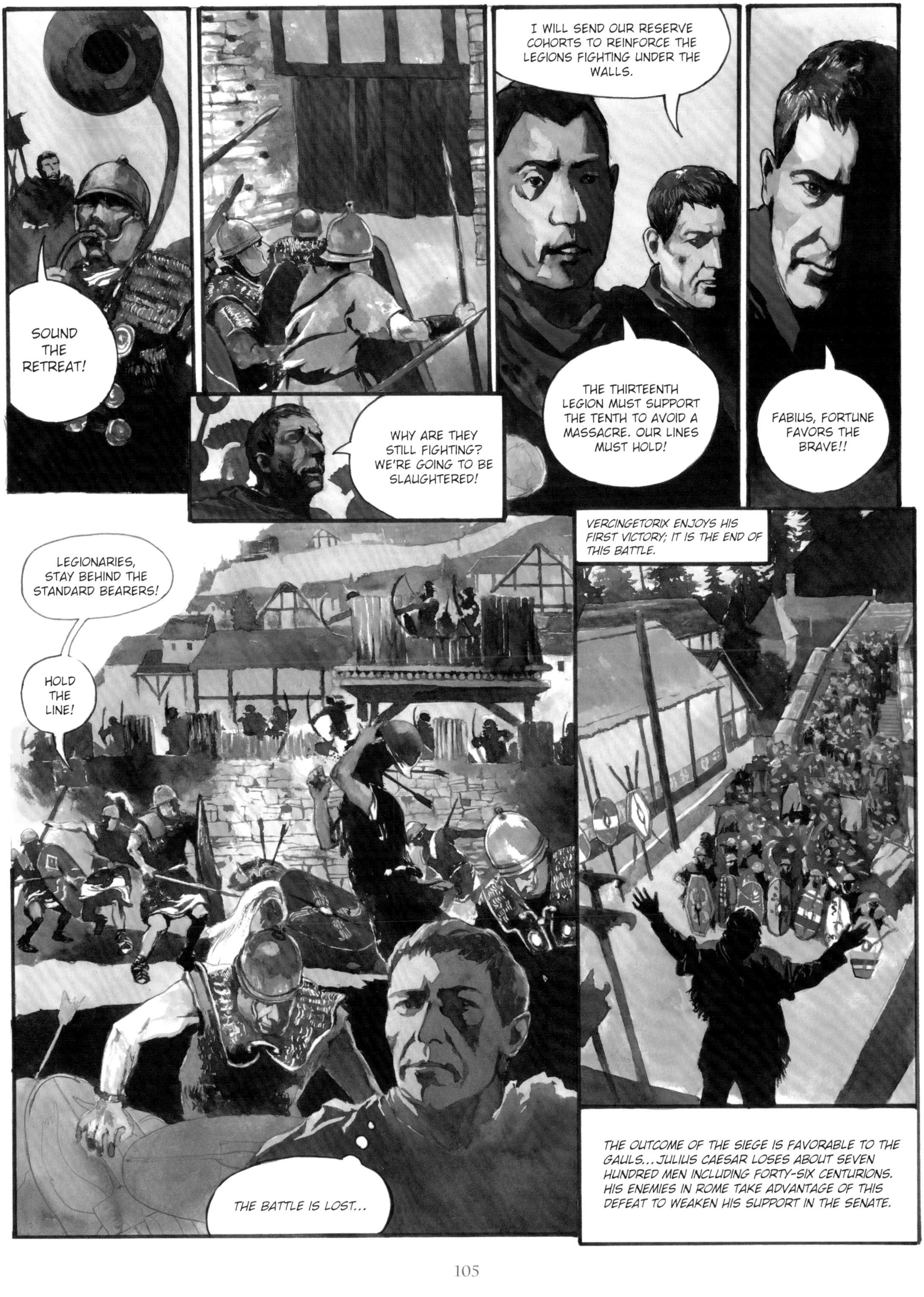
SOUND THE RETREAT!
WHY ARE THEY STILL FIGHTING? WE'RE GOING TO BE SLAUGHTERED!
I WILL SEND OUR RESERVE COHORTS TO REINFORCE THE LEGIONS FIGHTING UNDER THE WALLS.
THE THIRTEENTH LEGION MUST SUPPORT THE TENTH TO AVOID A MASSACRE. OUR LINES MUST HOLD!
FABIUS, FORTUNE FAVORS THE BRAVE!!
LEGIONARIES, STAY BEHIND THE STANDARD BEARERS!
HOLD THE LINE!
THE BATTLE IS LOST...
VERCINGETORIX ENJOYS HIS FIRST VICTORY; IT IS THE END OF THIS BATTLE.
THE OUTCOME OF THE SIEGE IS FAVORABLE TO THE GAULS... JULIUS CAESAR LOSES ABOUT SEVEN HUNDRED MEN INCLUDING FORTY-SIX CENTURIONS. HIS ENEMIES IN ROME TAKE ADVANTAGE OF THIS DEFEAT TO WEAKEN HIS SUPPORT IN THE SENATE.

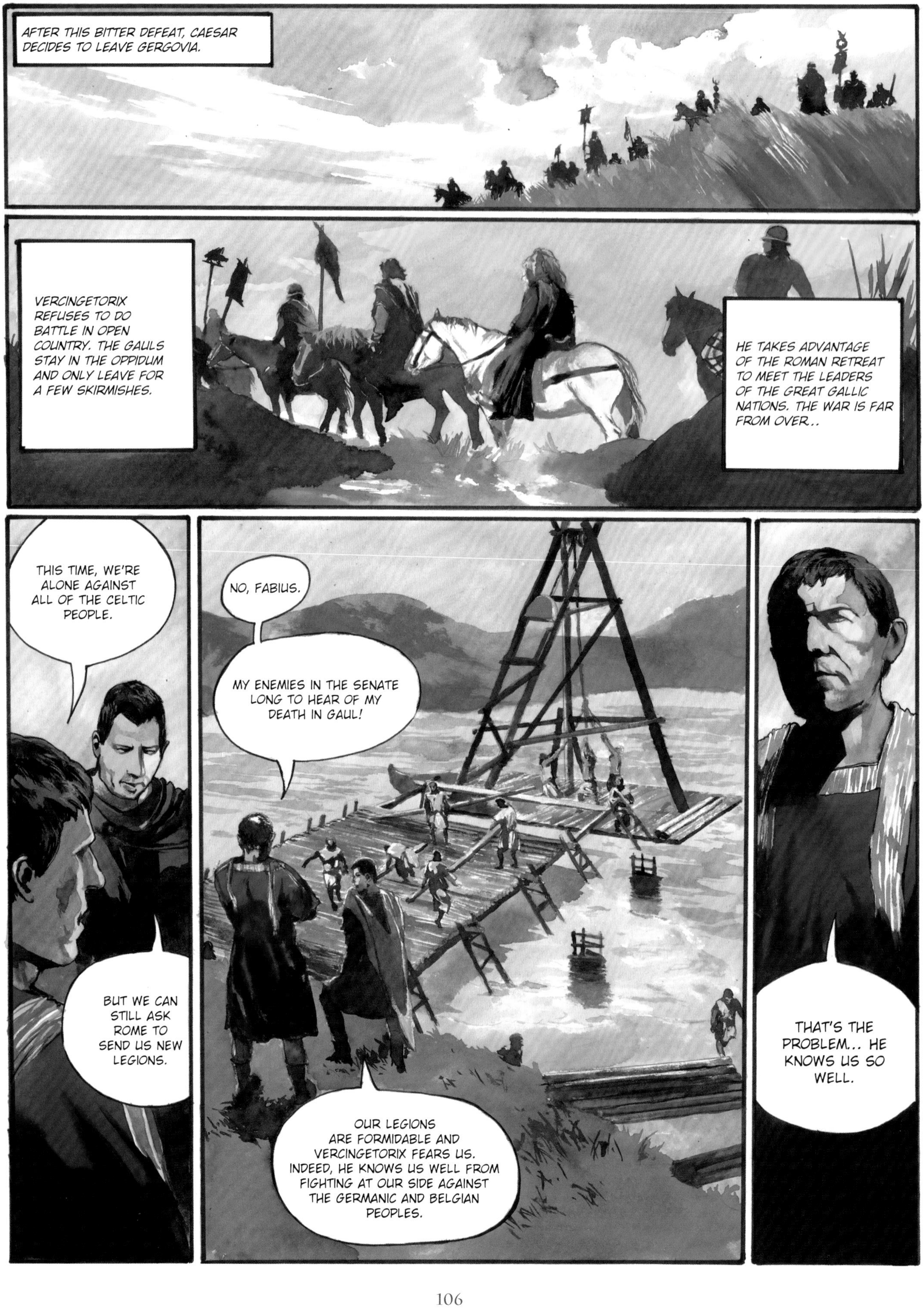
AFTER THIS BITTER DEFEAT, CAESAR DECIDES TO LEAVE GERGOVIA.
VERCINGETORIX REFUSES TO DO BATTLE IN OPEN COUNTRY. THE GAULS STAY IN THE OPPIDUM AND ONLY LEAVE FOR A FEW SKIRMISHES.
HE TAKES ADVANTAGE OF THE ROMAN RETREAT TO MEET THE LEADERS OF THE GREAT GALLIC NATIONS. THE WAR IS FAR FROM OVER..
THIS TIME, WE'RE ALONE AGAINST ALL OF THE CELTIC PEOPLE.
BUT WE CAN STILL ASK ROME TO SEND US NEW LEGIONS.
NO, FABIUS.
MY ENEMIES IN THE SENATE LONG TO HEAR OF MY DEATH IN GAUL!
OUR LEGIONS ARE FORMIDABLE AND VERCINGETORIX FEARS US. INDEED, HE KNOWS US WELL FROM FIGHTING AT OUR SIDE AGAINST THE GERMANIC AND BELGIAN PEOPLES.
THAT'S THE PROBLEM... HE KNOWS US SO WELL.

AT THE SAME TIME, NOT FAR FROM LUTETIA...

CAMULOGENE HAS POSTED HIS TROOPS ALONG THE SEINE... HE'S BLOCKING THE ROAD TO LUTETIA.

WE MUST AVOID FIGHTING IN THE MARSH, WHERE WE RISK ANNIHILATION. WE MUST CHANGE COURSE!

WHAT ARE YOUR ORDERS, LEGATE LABIENUS?

TO METLOSEDUM!

UNABLE TO TRAVERSE THE MARSH SURROUNDING THE SEINE, THE ROMANS SEIZE THE SENONIAN CITY OF METLODSEDUM, THEN CROSS THE RIVER SAFELY.

BLOODY ROMAN SWINE!

THE LEGIONS HAVE MANAGED TO CROSS THE SEINE. WE MUST DESTROY LUTETIA AND THE REMAINING BRIDGES!

THIS IS THE MOMENT TO STRIKE!

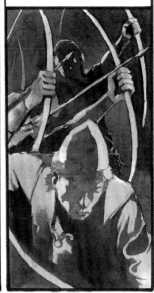

LABIENUS FINDS HIMSELF CUT OFF FROM HIS LUGGAGE AND RESERVE TROOPS. MOREOVER, THE BELLOVACI, ON THE VERGE OF REVOLT, ARE BECOMING A REAL THREAT TO THE ROMAN ARMIES.

THE LEGATE ATTEMPTS A RETREAT IN AGEDINCUM, CROSSING THE RIVER AT NIGHT BY SMALL BOATS, BUT THE GAULS ATTEMPT TO PREVENT HIM FROM REACHING THE OPPOSITE BANK...

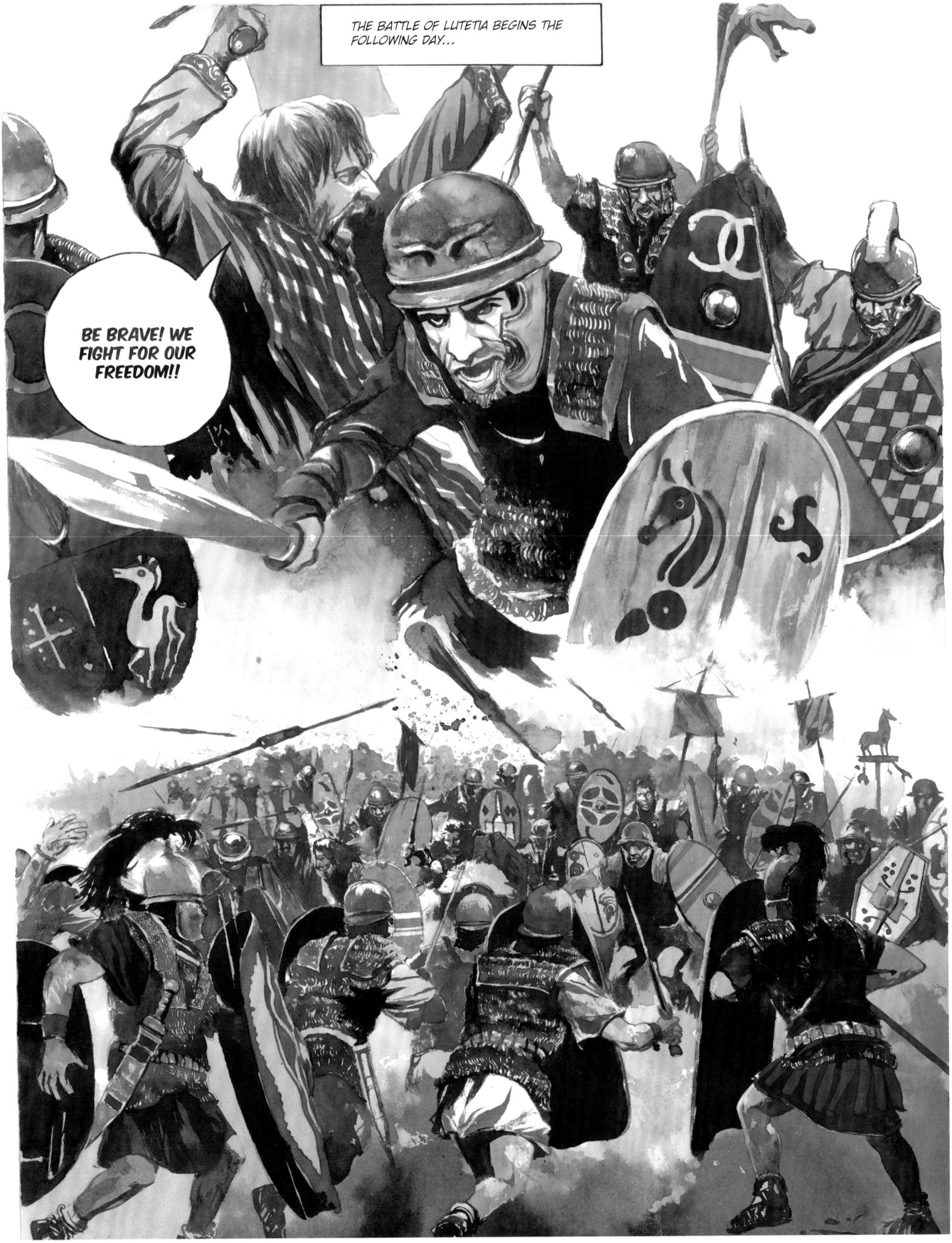
THE BATTLE OF LUTETIA BEGINS THE FOLLOWING DAY...
BE BRAVE! WE FIGHT FOR OUR FREEDOM!!

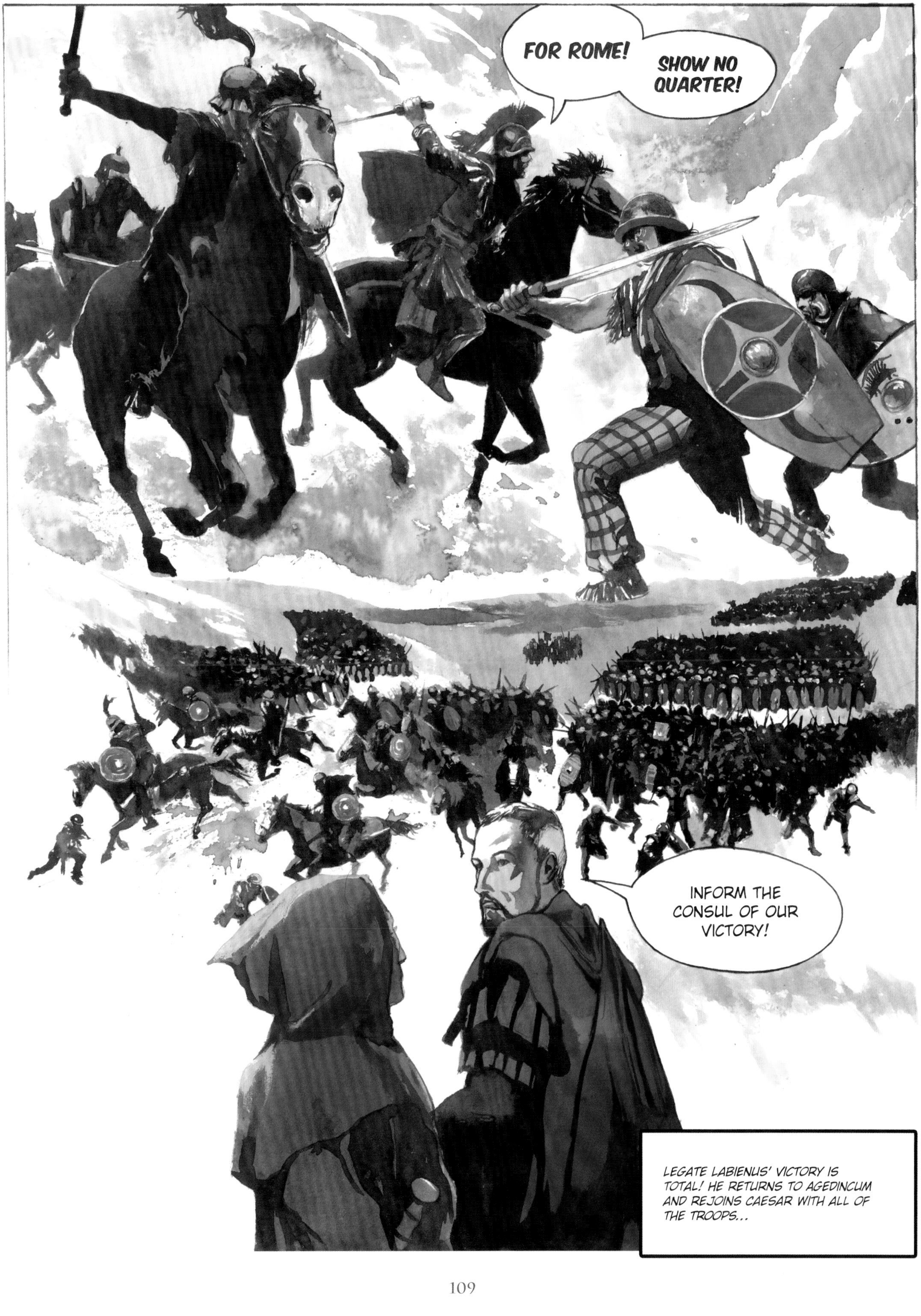
FOR ROME!
SHOW NO QUARTER!
INFORM THE CONSUL OF OUR VICTORY!
LEGATE LABIENUS' VICTORY IS TOTAL! HE RETURNS TO AGEDINCUM AND REJOINS CAESAR WITH ALL OF THE TROOPS...

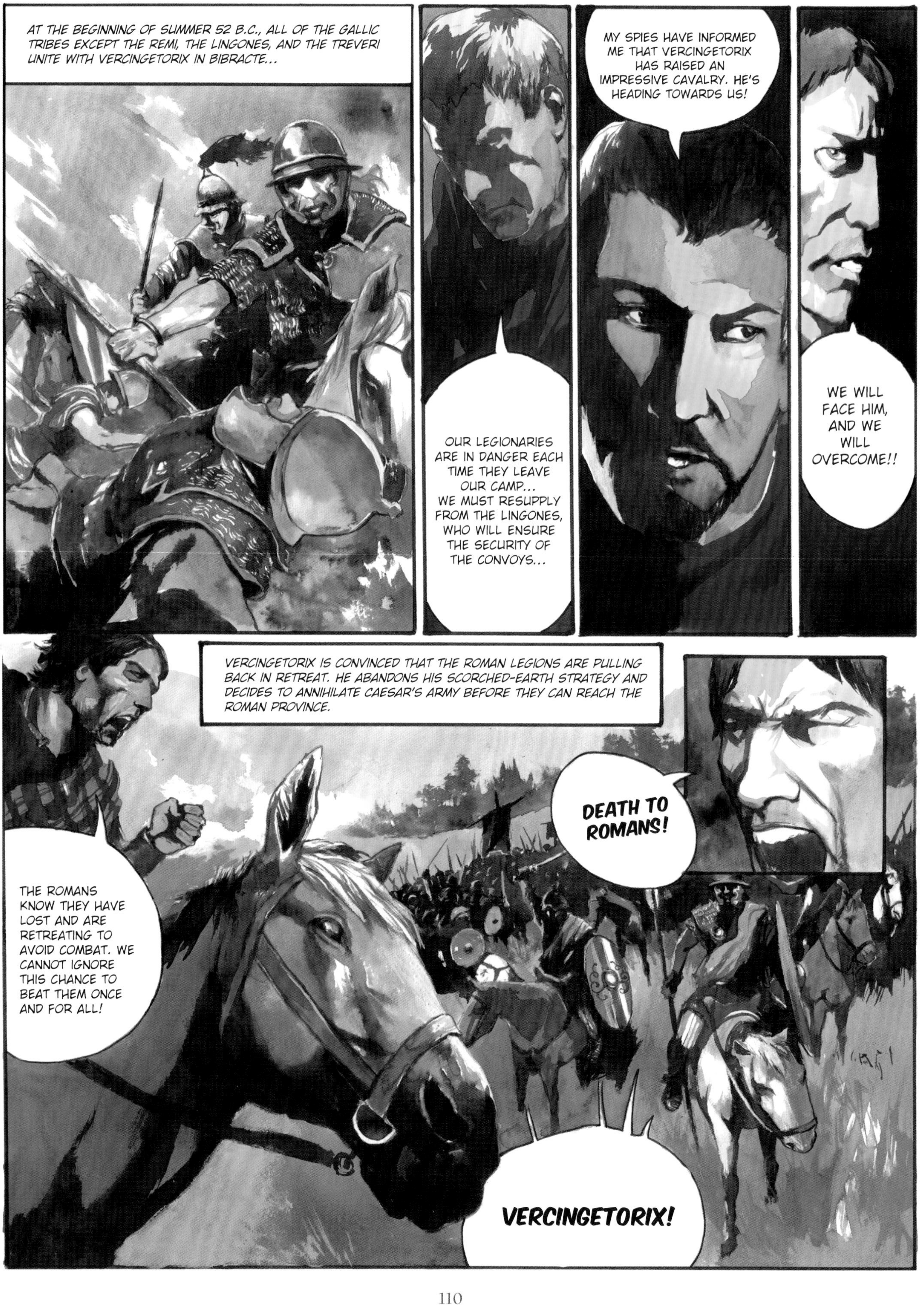

AT THE BEGINNING OF SUMMER 52 B.C., ALL OF THE GALLIC TRIBES EXCEPT THE REMI, THE LINGONES, AND THE TREVERI UNITE WITH VERCINGETORIX IN BIBRACTE...
OUR LEGIONARIES ARE IN DANGER EACH TIME THEY LEAVE OUR CAMP... WE MUST RESUPPLY FROM THE LINGONES, WHO WILL ENSURE THE SECURITY OF THE CONVOYS...
MY SPIES HAVE INFORMED ME THAT VERCINGETORIX HAS RAISED AN IMPRESSIVE CAVALRY. HE'S HEADING TOWARDS US!
WE WILL FACE HIM, AND WE WILL OVERCOME!!
VERCINGETORIX IS CONVINCED THAT THE ROMAN LEGIONS ARE PULLING BACK IN RETREAT. HE ABANDONS HIS SCORCHED-EARTH STRATEGY AND DECIDES TO ANNIHILATE CAESAR'S ARMY BEFORE THEY CAN REACH THE ROMAN PROVINCE.
THE ROMANS KNOW THEY HAVE LOST AND ARE RETREATING TO AVOID COMBAT. WE CANNOT IGNORE THIS CHANCE TO BEAT THEM ONCE AND FOR ALL!
DEATH TO ROMANS!
VERCINGETORIX!

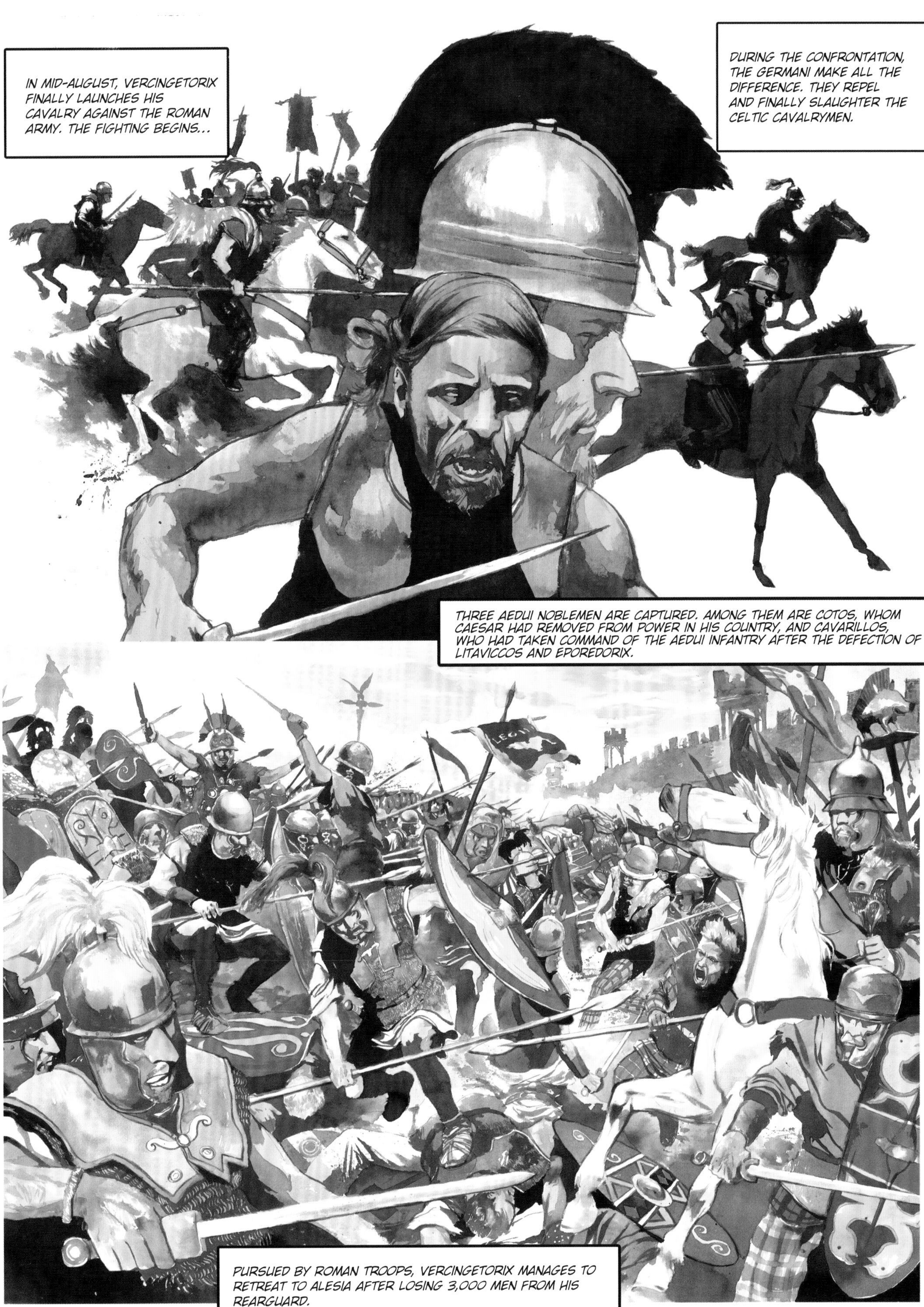
IN MID-AUGUST, VERCINGETORIX FINALLY LAUNCHES HIS CAVALRY AGAINST THE ROMAN ARMY. THE FIGHTING BEGINS...
DURING THE CONFRONTATION, THE GERMANI MAKE ALL THE DIFFERENCE. THEY REPEL AND FINALLY SLAUGHTER THE CELTIC CAVALRYMEN.
THREE AEDUI NOBLEMEN ARE CAPTURED. AMONG THEM ARE COTOS, WHOM CAESAR HAD REMOVED FROM POWER IN HIS COUNTRY, AND CAVARILLOS, WHO HAD TAKEN COMMAND OF THE AEDUI INFANTRY AFTER THE DEFECTION OF LITAVICCOS AND EPOREDORIX.
PURSUED BY ROMAN TROOPS, VERCINGETORIX MANAGES TO RETREAT TO ALESIA AFTER LOSING 3,000 MEN FROM HIS REARGUARD.

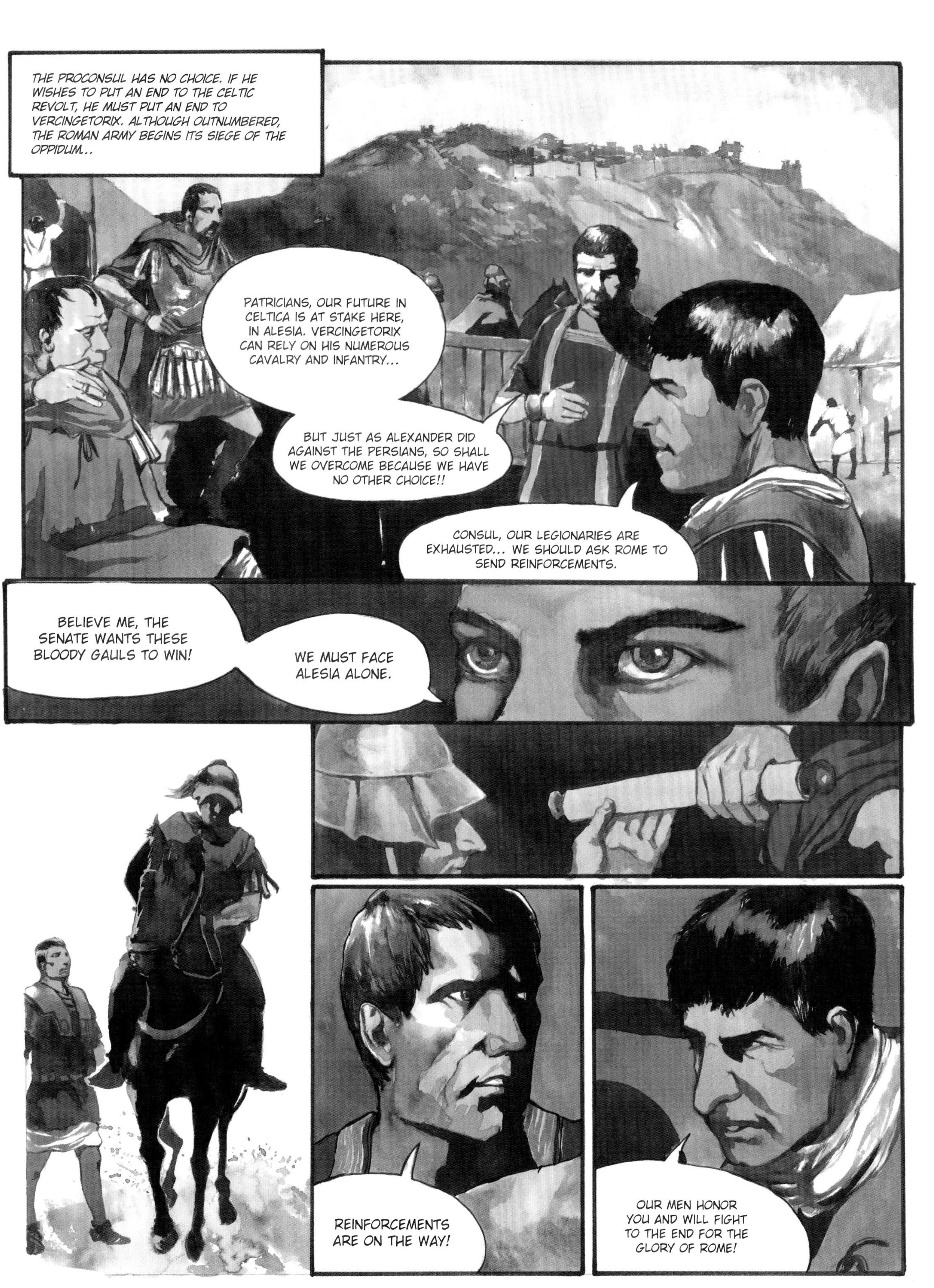

THE PROCONSUL HAS NO CHOICE. IF HE WISHES TO PUT AN END TO THE CELTIC REVOLT, HE MUST PUT AN END TO VERCINGETORIX. ALTHOUGH OUTNUMBERED, THE ROMAN ARMY BEGINS ITS SIEGE OF THE OPPIDUM...
PATRICIANS, OUR FUTURE IN CELTICA IS AT STAKE HERE, IN ALESIA. VERCINGETORIX CAN RELY ON HIS NUMEROUS CAVALRY AND INFANTRY...
BUT JUST AS ALEXANDER DID AGAINST THE PERSIANS, SO SHALL WE OVERCOME BECAUSE WE HAVE NO OTHER CHOICE!!
CONSUL, OUR LEGIONARIES ARE EXHAUSTED... WE SHOULD ASK ROME TO SEND REINFORCEMENTS.
BELIEVE ME, THE SENATE WANTS THESE BLOODY GAULS TO WIN!
WE MUST FACE ALESIA ALONE.
REINFORCEMENTS ARE ON THE WAY!
OUR MEN HONOR YOU AND WILL FIGHT TO THE END FOR THE GLORY OF ROME!

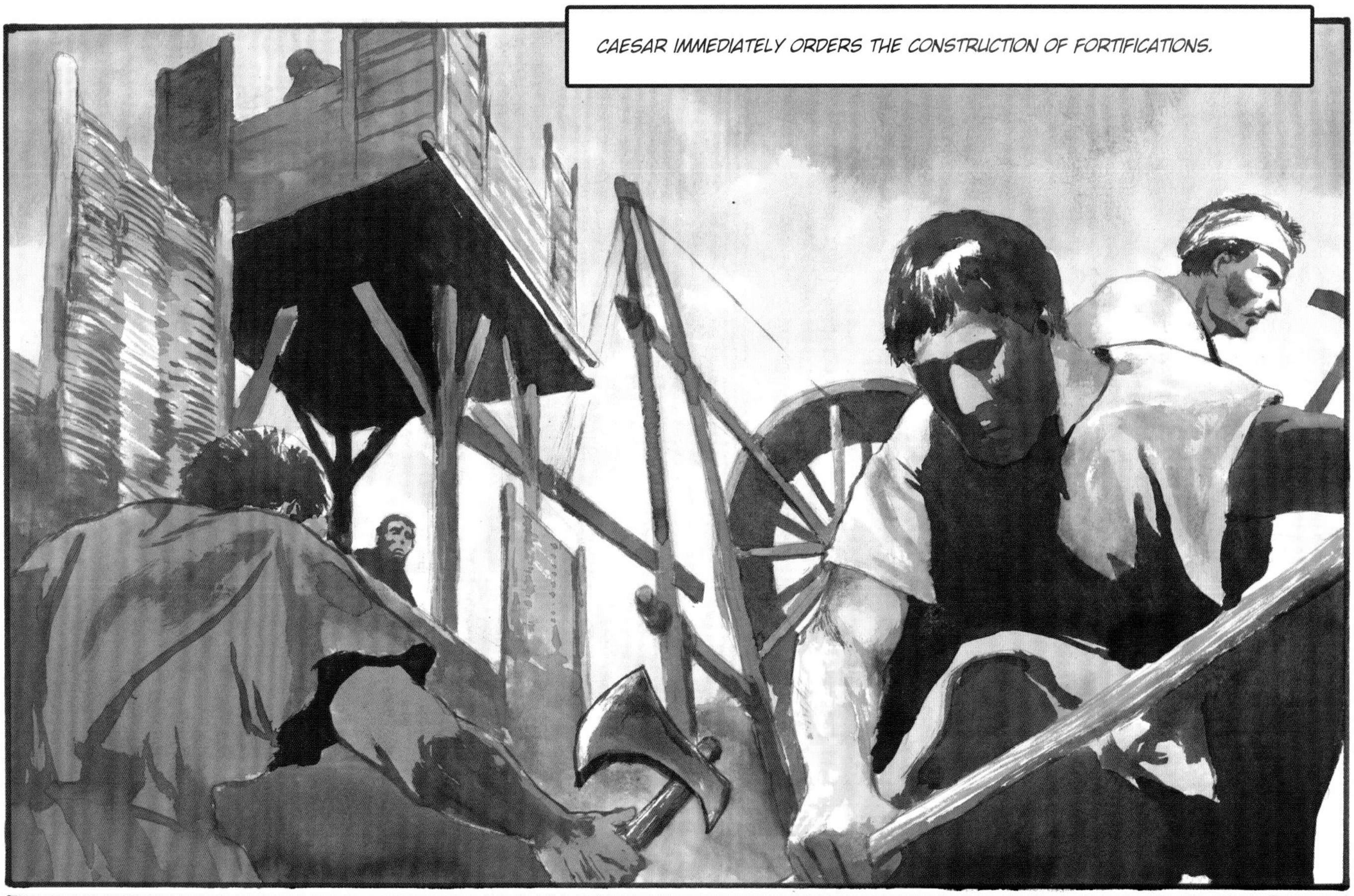
CAESAR IMMEDIATELY ORDERS THE CONSTRUCTION OF FORTIFICATIONS.

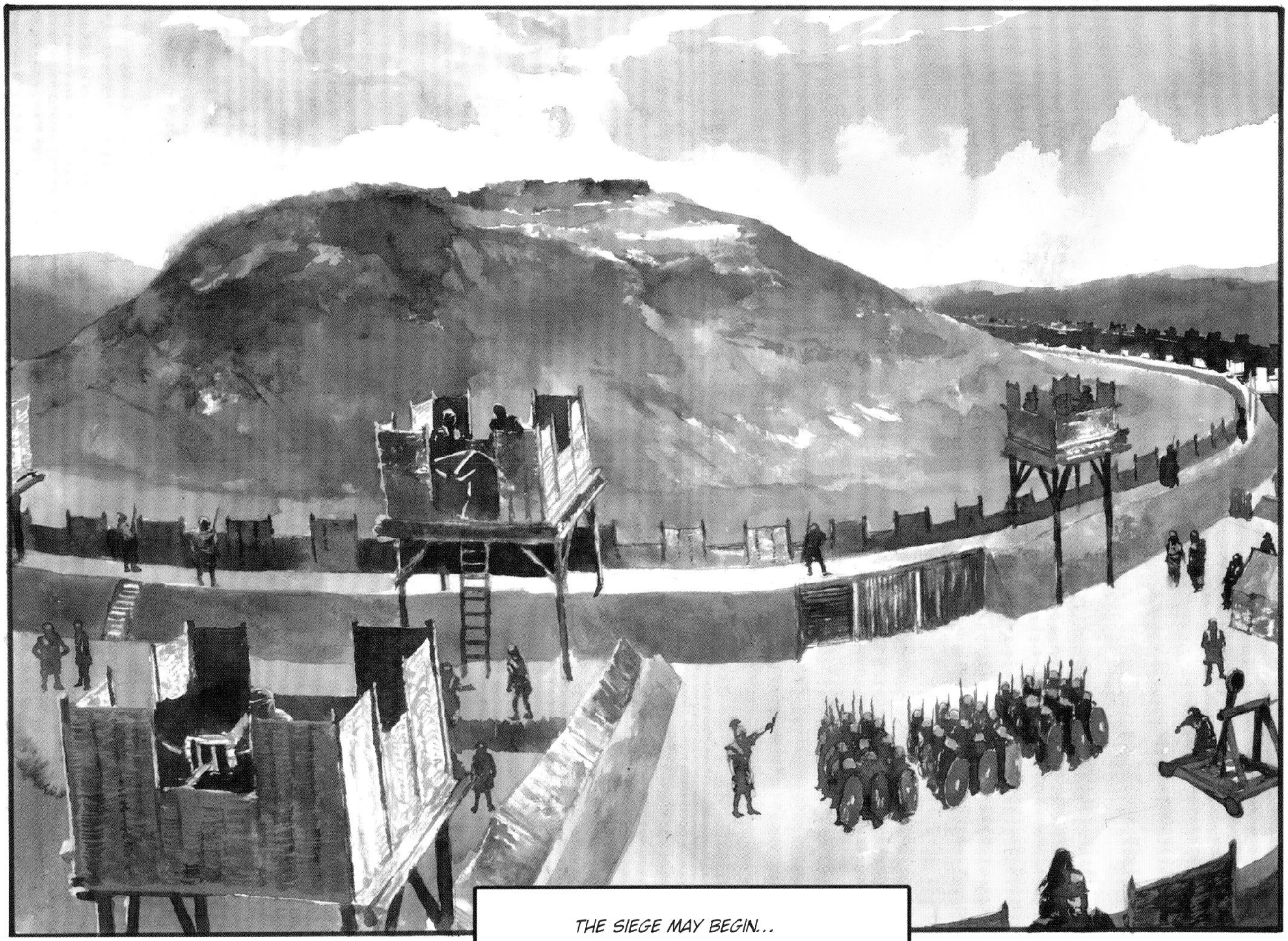
THE SIEGE MAY BEGIN...

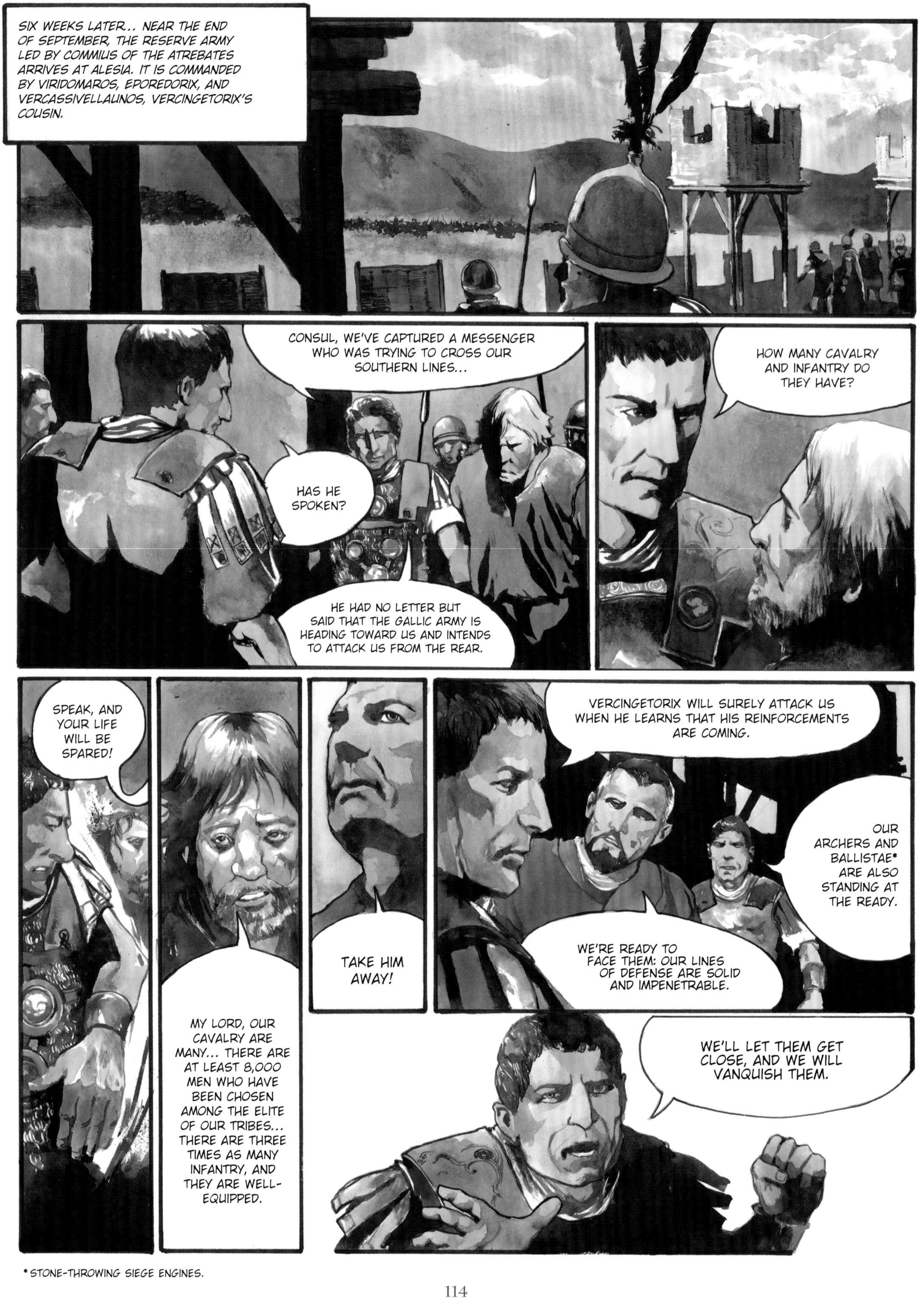
SIX WEEKS LATER… NEAR THE END OF SEPTEMBER, THE RESERVE ARMY LED BY COMMIUS OF THE ATREBATES ARRIVES AT ALESIA. IT IS COMMANDED BY VIRIDOMAROS, EPOREDORIX, AND VERCASSIVELLAUNOS, VERCINGETORIX'S COUSIN.
CONSUL, WE'VE CAPTURED A MESSENGER WHO WAS TRYING TO CROSS OUR SOUTHERN LINES…
HAS HE SPOKEN?
HE HAD NO LETTER BUT SAID THAT THE GALLIC ARMY IS HEADING TOWARD US AND INTENDS TO ATTACK US FROM THE REAR.
HOW MANY CAVALRY AND INFANTRY DO THEY HAVE?
SPEAK, AND YOUR LIFE WILL BE SPARED!
MY LORD, OUR CAVALRY ARE MANY… THERE ARE AT LEAST 8,000 MEN WHO HAVE BEEN CHOSEN AMONG THE ELITE OF OUR TRIBES… THERE ARE THREE TIMES AS MANY INFANTRY, AND THEY ARE WELL-EQUIPPED.
TAKE HIM AWAY!
VERCINGETORIX WILL SURELY ATTACK US WHEN HE LEARNS THAT HIS REINFORCEMENTS ARE COMING.
WE'RE READY TO FACE THEM: OUR LINES OF DEFENSE ARE SOLID AND IMPENETRABLE.
OUR ARCHERS AND BALLISTAE* ARE ALSO STANDING AT THE READY.
WE'LL LET THEM GET CLOSE, AND WE WILL VANQUISH THEM.

* STONE-THROWING SIEGE ENGINES.

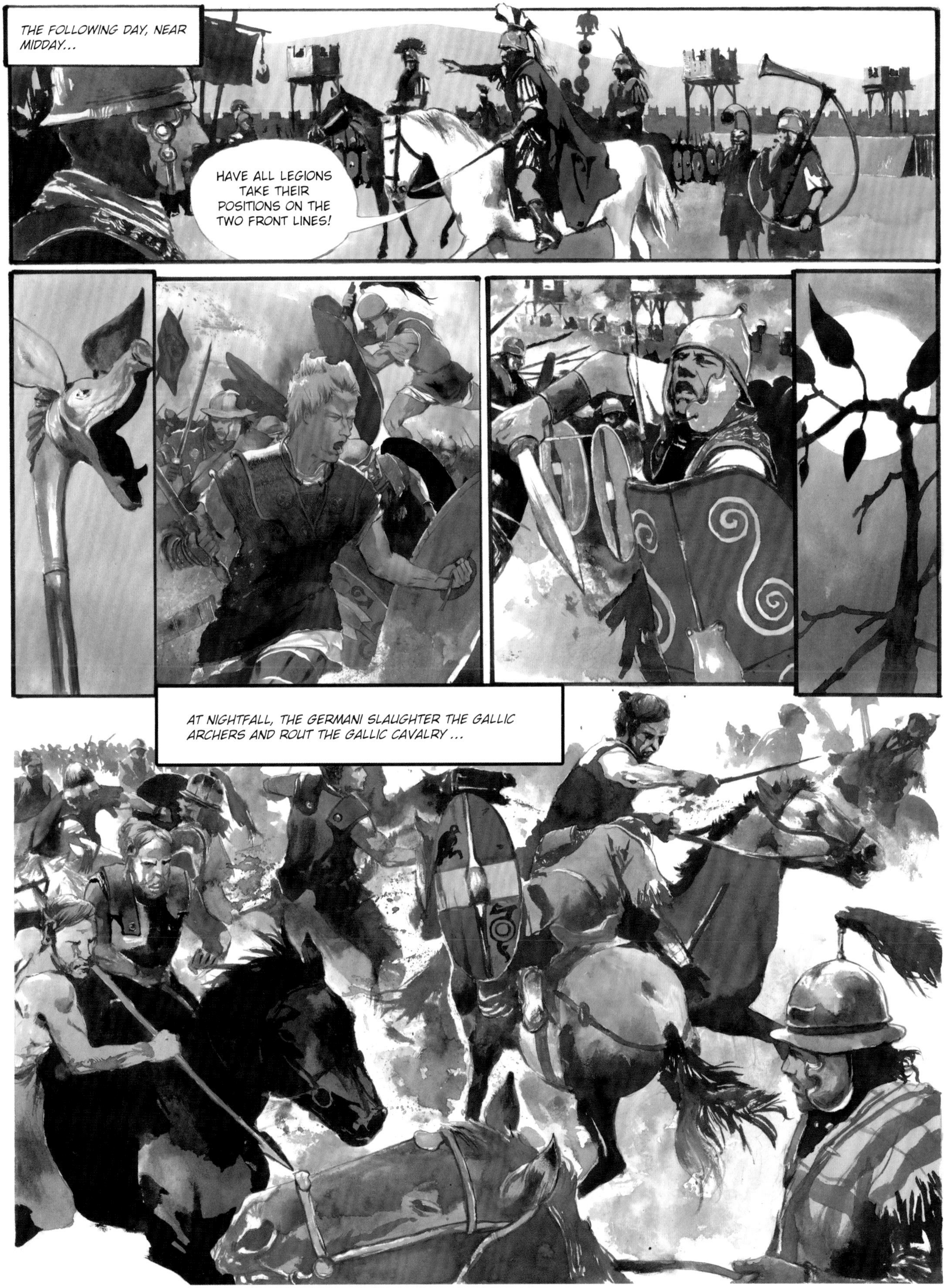
THE FOLLOWING DAY, NEAR MIDDAY...
HAVE ALL LEGIONS TAKE THEIR POSITIONS ON THE TWO FRONT LINES!
AT NIGHTFALL, THE GERMANI SLAUGHTER THE GALLIC ARCHERS AND ROUT THE GALLIC CAVALRY ...

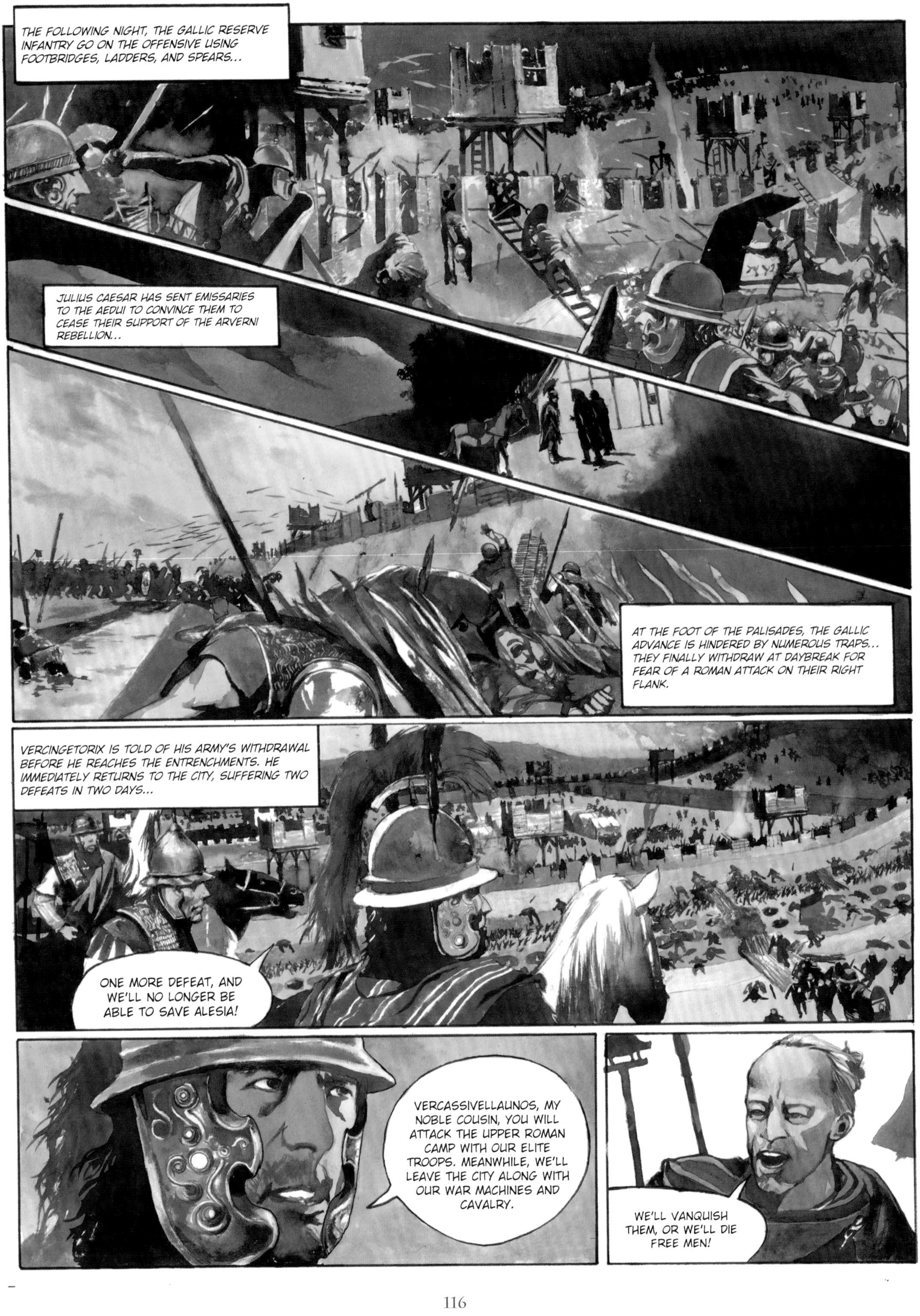
THE FOLLOWING NIGHT, THE GALLIC RESERVE INFANTRY GO ON THE OFFENSIVE USING FOOTBRIDGES, LADDERS, AND SPEARS...
JULIUS CAESAR HAS SENT EMISSARIES TO THE AEDUI TO CONVINCE THEM TO CEASE THEIR SUPPORT OF THE ARVERNI REBELLION...
AT THE FOOT OF THE PALISADES, THE GALLIC ADVANCE IS HINDERED BY NUMEROUS TRAPS... THEY FINALLY WITHDRAW AT DAYBREAK FOR FEAR OF A ROMAN ATTACK ON THEIR RIGHT FLANK.
VERCINGETORIX IS TOLD OF HIS ARMY'S WITHDRAWAL BEFORE HE REACHES THE ENTRENCHMENTS. HE IMMEDIATELY RETURNS TO THE CITY, SUFFERING TWO DEFEATS IN TWO DAYS...
ONE MORE DEFEAT, AND WE'LL NO LONGER BE ABLE TO SAVE ALESIA!
VERCASSIVELLAUNOS, MY NOBLE COUSIN, YOU WILL ATTACK THE UPPER ROMAN CAMP WITH OUR ELITE TROOPS. MEANWHILE, WE'LL LEAVE THE CITY ALONG WITH OUR WAR MACHINES AND CAVALRY.
WE'LL VANQUISH THEM, OR WE'LL DIE FREE MEN!

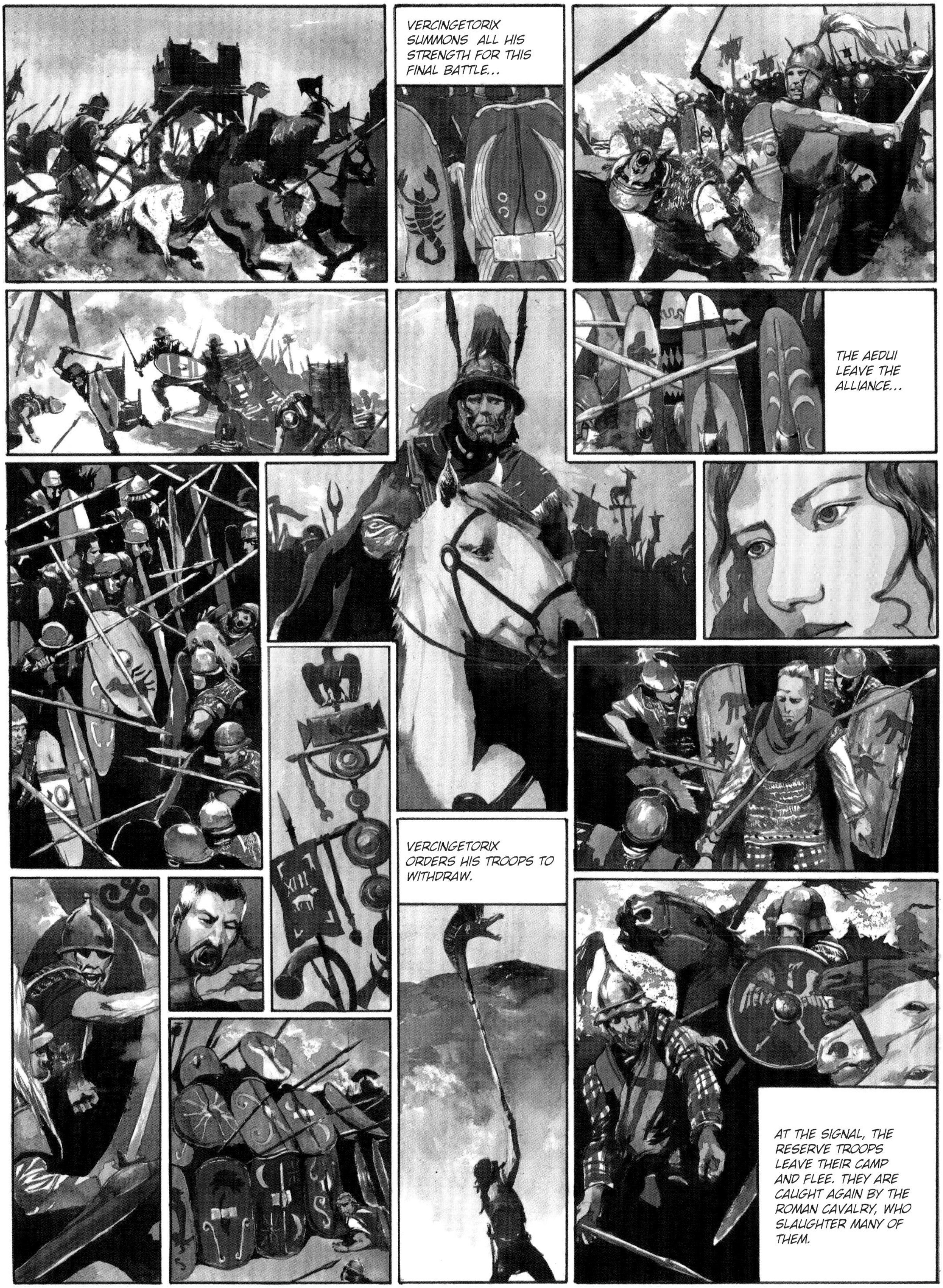
VERCINGETORIX SUMMONS ALL HIS STRENGTH FOR THIS FINAL BATTLE...
THE AEDUI LEAVE THE ALLIANCE...
VERCINGETORIX ORDERS HIS TROOPS TO WITHDRAW.
AT THE SIGNAL, THE RESERVE TROOPS LEAVE THEIR CAMP AND FLEE. THEY ARE CAUGHT AGAIN BY THE ROMAN CAVALRY, WHO SLAUGHTER MANY OF THEM.

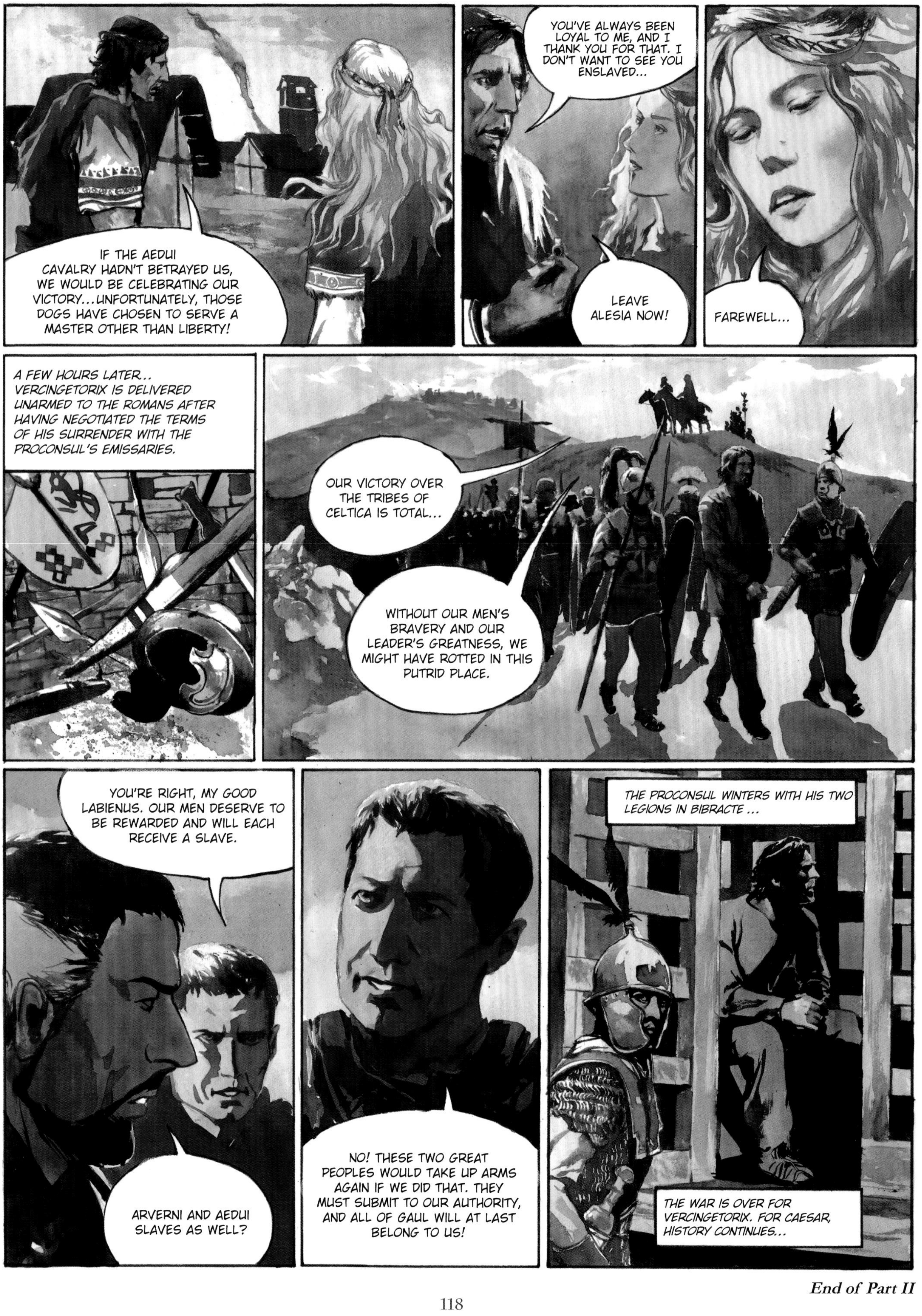
IF THE AEDUI CAVALRY HADN'T BETRAYED US, WE WOULD BE CELEBRATING OUR VICTORY...UNFORTUNATELY, THOSE DOGS HAVE CHOSEN TO SERVE A MASTER OTHER THAN LIBERTY!
YOU'VE ALWAYS BEEN LOYAL TO ME, AND I THANK YOU FOR THAT. I DON'T WANT TO SEE YOU ENSLAVED...
LEAVE ALESIA NOW!
FAREWELL...
A FEW HOURS LATER.. VERCINGETORIX IS DELIVERED UNARMED TO THE ROMANS AFTER HAVING NEGOTIATED THE TERMS OF HIS SURRENDER WITH THE PROCONSUL'S EMISSARIES.
OUR VICTORY OVER THE TRIBES OF CELTICA IS TOTAL...
WITHOUT OUR MEN'S BRAVERY AND OUR LEADER'S GREATNESS, WE MIGHT HAVE ROTTED IN THIS PUTRID PLACE.
YOU'RE RIGHT, MY GOOD LABIENUS. OUR MEN DESERVE TO BE REWARDED AND WILL EACH RECEIVE A SLAVE.
ARVERNI AND AEDUI SLAVES AS WELL?
NO! THESE TWO GREAT PEOPLES WOULD TAKE UP ARMS AGAIN IF WE DID THAT. THEY MUST SUBMIT TO OUR AUTHORITY, AND ALL OF GAUL WILL AT LAST BELONG TO US!
THE PROCONSUL WINTERS WITH HIS TWO LEGIONS IN BIBRACTE ...
THE WAR IS OVER FOR VERCINGETORIX. FOR CAESAR, HISTORY CONTINUES...

*End of Part II*

This graphic novel takes place during the conquest of "Celtic" Gaul by Julius Caesar's legions from 58 to 50 B.C. Our story is based on the Commentaries on the Gallic War, Caesar's first-hand account of the Gallic War while he was leading it, published in Rome just after the end of his proconsulate for his own glory and propaganda. The historical background of this story mainly refers to this book, but we have also used the latest research carried out on this subject so as to be closer to historical reality. However, we chose to focus on the political path of six personalities who lived through this troubled period, namely Julius Caesar, Vercingetorix, an Aedui spy working for the Romans, a fanatical druid who preaches all-out war against the invaders, an Arverni chief fighting under Vercingetorix's command, and a Roman general close to the senatorial party which obeys Caesar but does not share his ambitions.

Moreover, we described the special relationship between Caesar and Vercingetorix. First friends and allies, their relationship deteriorates until finally, they become fierce rivals, fighting for the same ideal of supreme power. Victory or death is the only possible outcome. Thus, we used the historical background described by Caesar as a basis for individual stories that interweave and contribute to the fundamental change in the Roman Empire and even to the approaching end of the republic.

Spying, subversion, political alliance, strategy, and propaganda serve a man and his cause: Caesar and Rome.

This graphic novel, blending fiction and reality, myth and legend, allows the reliving of an extraordinary adventure led by a man who made his mark on human history.

# FREELY ADAPTED FROM JULIUS CAESAR'S BOOK

We have used the edition of *Commentaries on the Gallic War* by Julius Caesar, translated into French by L.A. Constans and published by the French publishing house Gallimard in 1981. We have respected the chronology used in this edition.

## SYNOPSIS

Julius Caesar quickly leaves for his post in Gaul when his consulship ends. He stays in his provinces during his governorship so as to avoid prosecution in Italy. In winter, he returns to Cisalpine Gaul, where he meets his supporters. Each year, he makes sure that he has the support of some magistrates elected in Rome. He exchanges coded messages with Balbus, his secretary in charge of the management of his affairs in Italy.

As early as March of 58 B.C., he takes advantage of the migration of the Helvetians and their allies to start the conquest of Celtic Gaul. Of course, this military campaign is motivated not only by his political ambitions but also by economic interests. Indeed, the Romans do business with some Gallic nations, such as the Aedui and the Arverni.

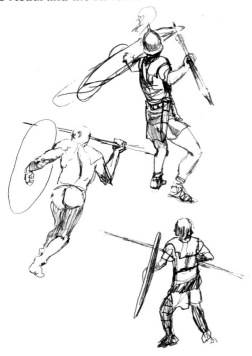

In Rome, the conservatives have reservations about the war he leads in lands owned by long-standing allies. Cato - who is scandalized by Caesar's confrontation with the German Ariovistus, considered to be "the Roman people's friend," claims that Caesar must pay for his treason and be handed over to the Germans. Caesar's total victory over Ariovistus enables him to become an essential leader in Celtic affairs.

Belgium and a part of the Atlantic coast are conquered in 57 B.C. The Belgian enemy is annihilated - no longer a threat to Rome nor to its Gaulish neighbors. Despite their victories over the Nantuates, the Veragri, and the Seduni, as well as the capture of the Great St. Bernard Pass, Galba's legions must withdraw and return to the country of the Allobroges for winter.

In 56 B.C. Lucius Domitius Ahenobarbus, the candidate for the consulship, supported by Cato and Cicero, proposes that Caesar be deposed and replaced. Caesar, Crassus, and Pompey hold a conference in Lucca, gathering all the senators who support them. The three political partners renew their alliance and divide several provinces among themselves. Thanks to Caesar's support, Pompey and Crassus win the elections and are re-elected for a second consulship the following year. As he has obligations to Pompey, Cicero yields and accepts the extension of Caesar's government for another five years. During this period, the Roman legions lead a campaign against the Armoricans and the Venetian fleet, and another against the Aquitanians. Celtic Gaul gradually becomes a Roman province. During his second term in 55 B.C. Caesar crosses the channel and starts an incursion into Brittany, a land unknown to the Romans at the time. He makes a show of force in Germanic territory, fighting against the Sicambri, the Tencteri, and the Usipii across the Rhine. The following year, he prepares another expedition to Brittany. But in winter, the situation in Gaul deteriorates, leading to widespread revolt in conquered territories, which soon becomes uncontrollable.

At the end of their consulship in 54 B.C., Crassus goes to Asia pursuing military glory while Pompey governs Hispania and Africa from Rome, preferring to send his legates there. Pompey lends two of his four legions to Caesar, who needs reinforcements.

In 53 B.C., Crassus, his son Publius, and most of his army are annihilated by the Parthians at Carrhae. The same year, Julia, Caesar's daughter, Pompey's wife, dies. The alliance of the triumvirate is irrevocably dissolved. Another incursion in Germanic territory aims at punishing the Barbarians who support the revolting Gallic tribes and preventing Ambiorix, Prince of the Eburones, from invading the Celtic territory.

52 B.C. is a crucial year for Vercingetorix! Indeed, the Gallic revolt spreads under the leadership of the Arverni, and Rome is in such disarray that Pompey is made sole Consul with the consent of the Conservatives. He is now their defender. Meanwhile, Julius Caesar wins a resounding victory thanks to his siege at the Battle of Alesia, forcing Vercingetorix's surrender.

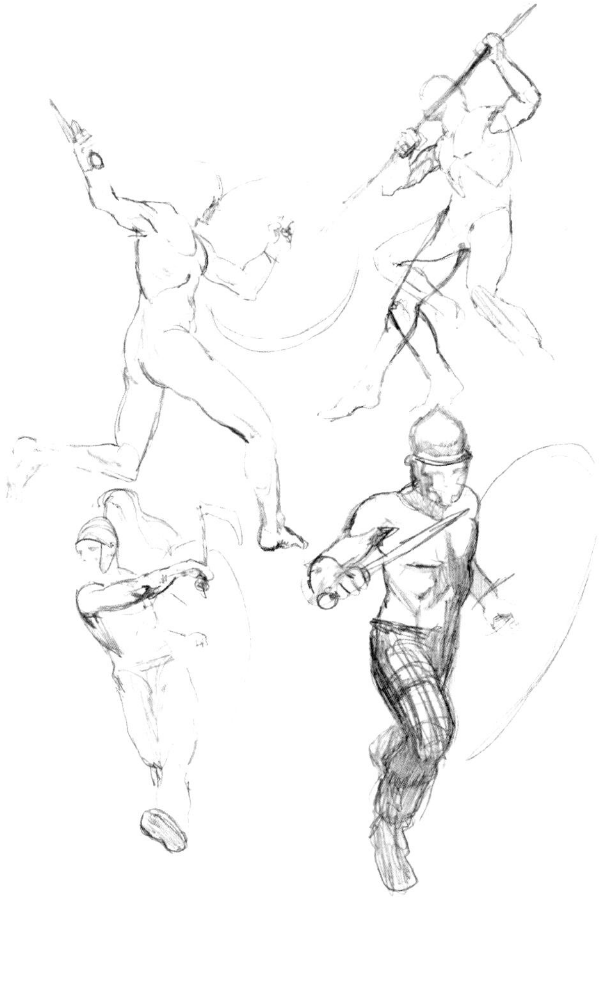

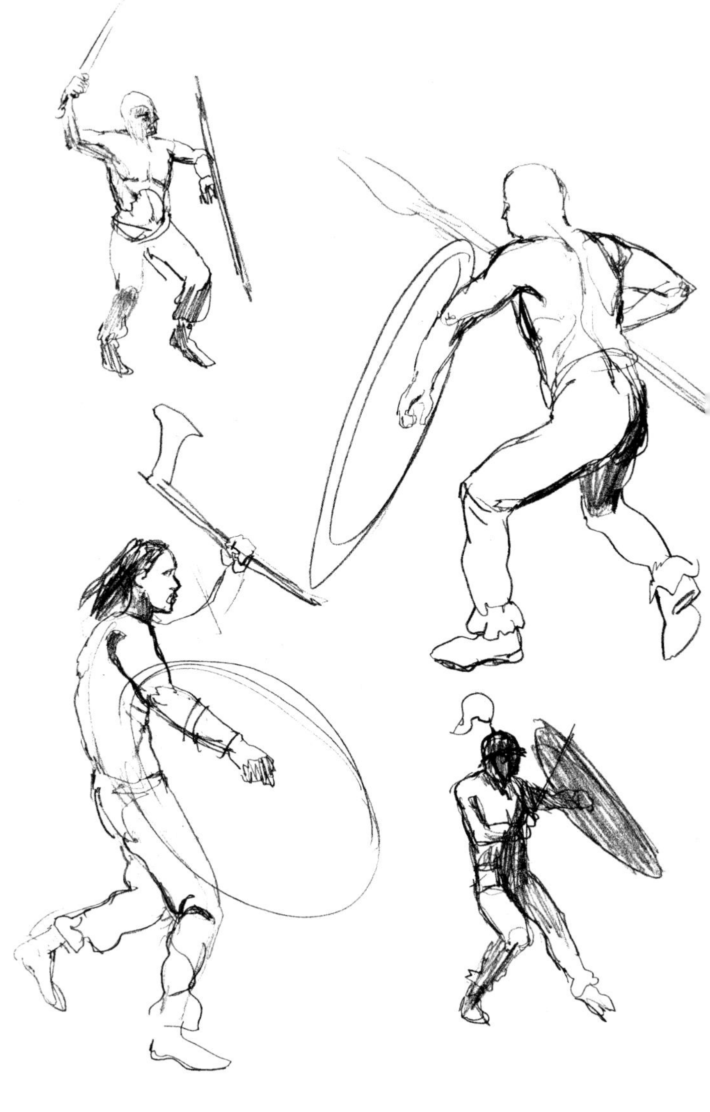

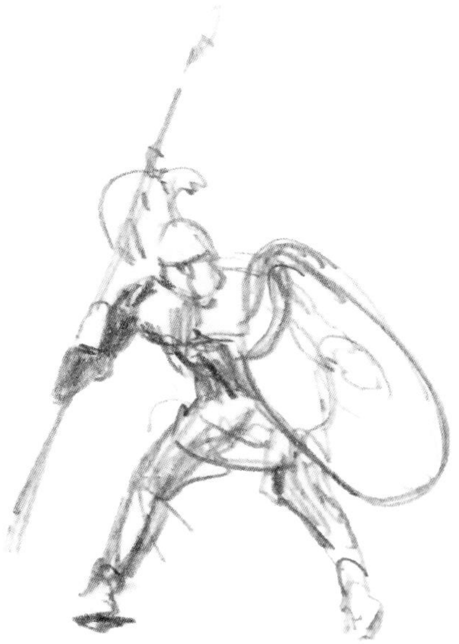

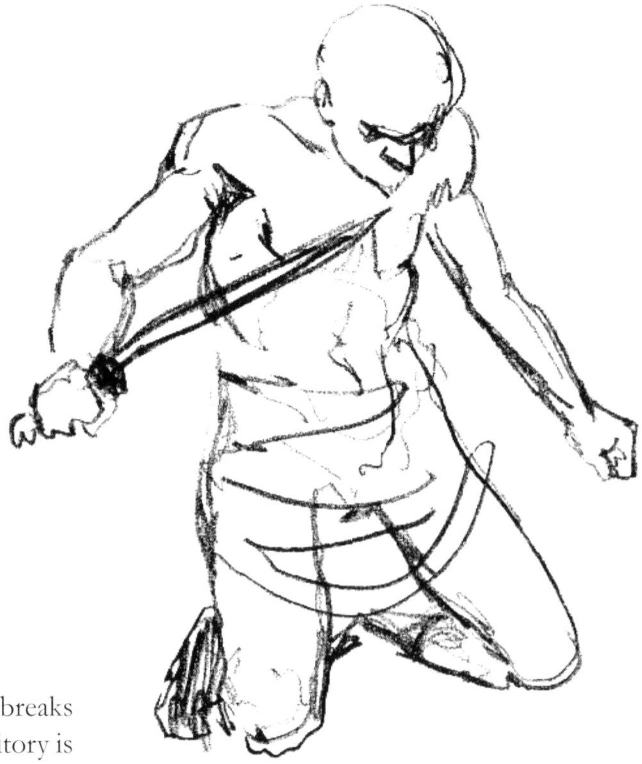

The following year, after overcoming the last outbreaks of war, Caesar asserts that the entire Gallic territory is effectively conquered. Now that his term as governor has finished, he intends to win the Roman people's support in order to return to Rome. He responds to the criticisms that have been made of his conduct during the war by publishing *Commentaries on the Gallic War*.

The Conservative senators do all they can to prevent his candidacy. In 50 B.C. Caesar, managing his affairs from Cisalpine Gaul ensures that Mark Antony is elected tribune of the Plebeians for the next term of office. The Conservatives react and make contact with Labienus, Caesar's best general. At the end of the year, the first confrontations remain legal and take place at the Senate. The Plebeian Tribune Curio proposes that Pompey and Caesar's armies be simultaneously disbanded, which the Roman consuls oppose. The march on Rome soon becomes inevitable...

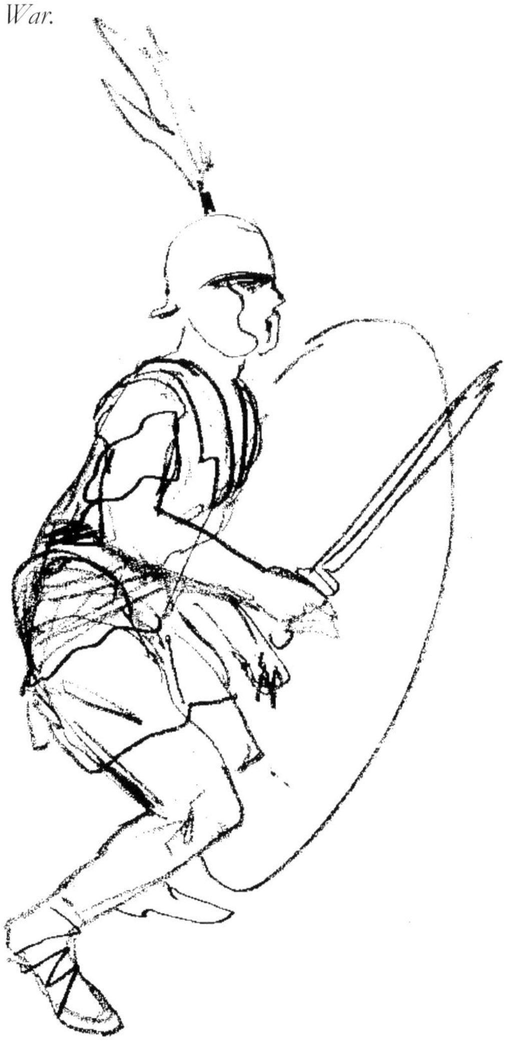

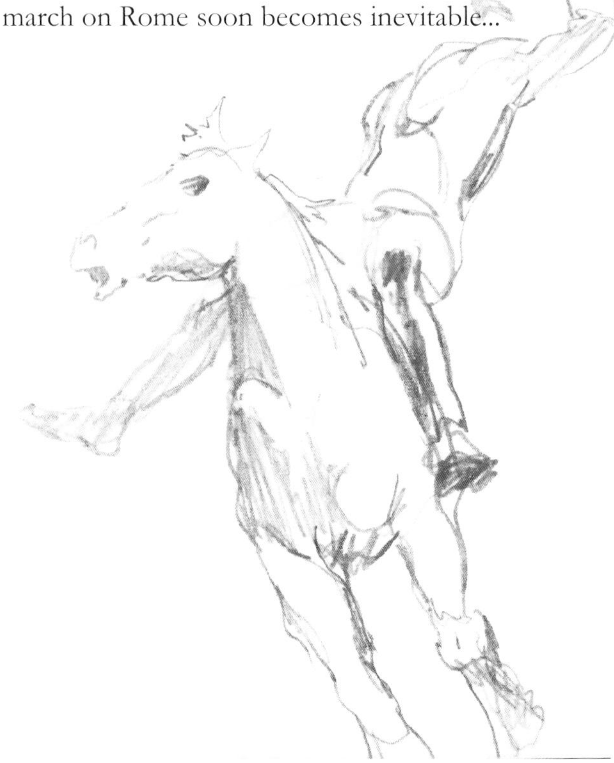

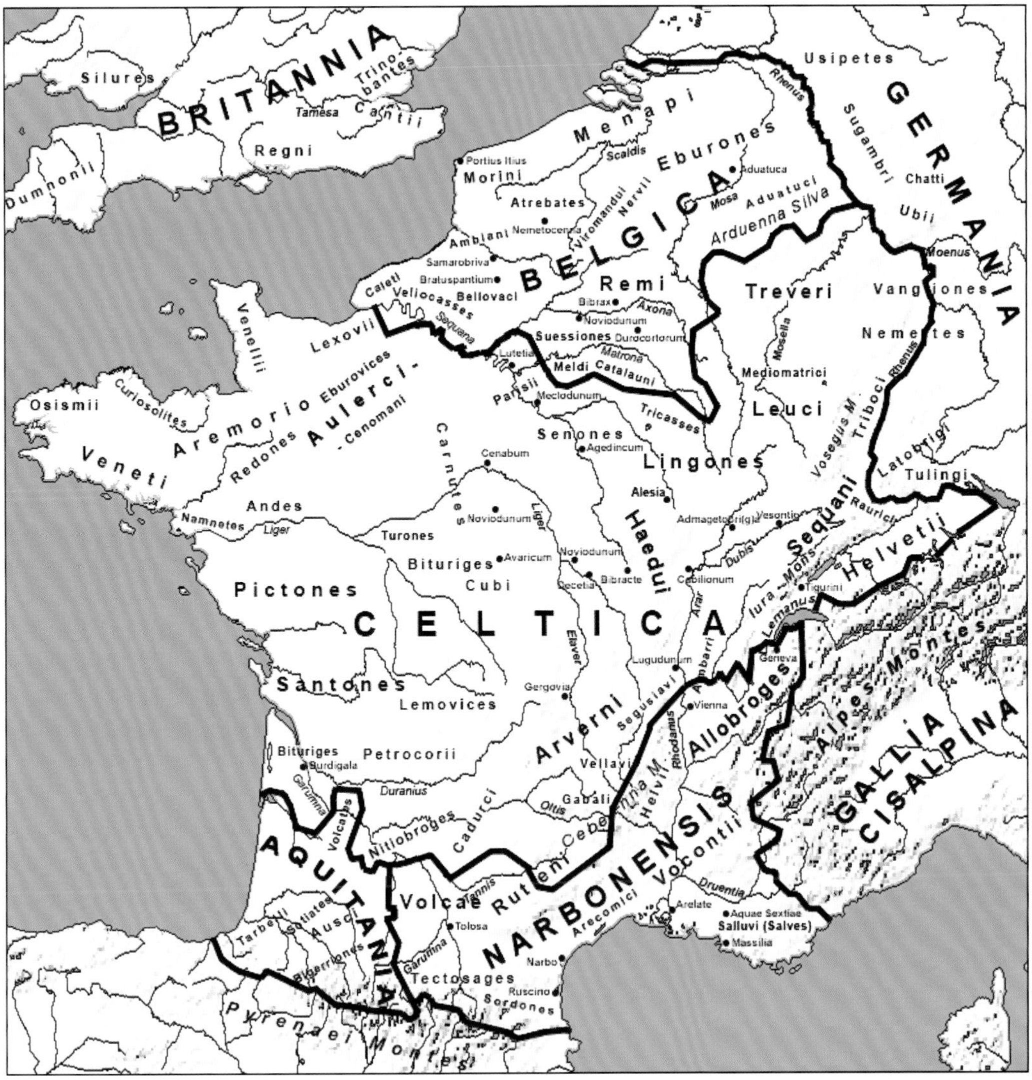
BRITANNIA
Silures
Trinobantes
Tamesa
Cantii
Regni
Dumnonii
GERMANIA
Usipetes
Rhenus
Sugambri
Chatti
Ubii
Moenus
Vangiones
Nemetes
Menapi
Portius Itius
Morini
Atrebates
Scaldis
Eburones
Aduatuca
Aduatuci
Mosa
Arduenna Silva
Nervii
Viromandui
BELGICA
Ambiani
Samarobriva
Bratuspantium
Bellovaci
Caleti
Veliocasses
Sequana
Remi
Bibrax
Axona
Noviodunum
Suessiones
Durocortorum
Treveri
Mosella
Mediomatrici
Leuci
Triboci
Lexovii
Venellii
Lutetia
Matrona
Meldi
Catalauni
Parisii
Metlodunum
Tricasses
Senones
Agedincum
Lingones
Latobrigi
Tulingi
Vosegus M.
Osismii
Curiosolites
Aremorio
Eburovices
Aulerci
Cenomani
Redones
Veneti
Carnutes
Cenabum
Noviodunum
Liger
Andes
Namnetes
Turones
Alesia
Haedui
Admagetobriga
Vesontio
Sequani
Rauraci
Helvetii
Bituriges
Avaricum
Cubi
Noviodunum
Decetia
Bibracte
Cabilionum
Pictones
Iura Mons
Lemanus
Tigurini
CELTICA
Elaver
Arar
Lugudunum
Geneva
Alpes Montes
Santones
Gergovia
Lemovices
Segusiavi
Vienna
Allobroges
Arverni
Bituriges
Burdigala
Petrocorii
Vellavi
GALLIA CISALPINA
Garumna
Duranius
Gabali
Olt is
Helvii
Rhodanus
Nitiobroges
Cadurci
Cebenna M.
Vocontii
AQUITANIA
NARBONENSIS
Volcae
Ruteni
Druentia
Arelate
Aquae Sextiae
Salluvi (Salves)
Massilia
Tolosa
Arecomici
Tarbelli
Ausci
Tectosages
Narbo
Ruscino
Sordones
Pyrenaei Montes

GALLIC TRIBES, 1ST CENTURY B.C. (FEITSCHERG ©2005)

## Cisalpine and Narbonensian Gaul

Caesar is a proconsul in these two Roman provinces where two legates represent him when absent. He stays there when he is not at war and avoids going to Rome for fear of being arrested by his enemies. This long-lasting exile enables him to keep a faithful army and thus control rich and powerful provinces. Part of our story -- essentially Part Two -- takes place in Cisalpine Gaul.

## Celtic Gaul, Brittania, and Belgium

During their numerous military campaigns, Julius Caesar and his generals fight against hundreds of Celtic tribes to subject them, destroy cities, and enslave thousands of men and women. Caesar fails to conquer the territories controlled by the Germans as well as Brittania (Great Britain). However, the whole territory of Celtic Gaul is annexed to the Roman Empire after the victory at Alesia, enabling Caesar to return triumphantly to Rome.

## The Forest of the Carnutes

This forest is an essential place of spirituality for the Druids, who incite their people to rebel against the Romans. Druid Gutuater, who appears right from the beginning of our story, will finally convince the peoples of Celtic Gaul to unite against the Roman invader.

# THE CHARACTERS OF OUR STORY

## Julius Caesar

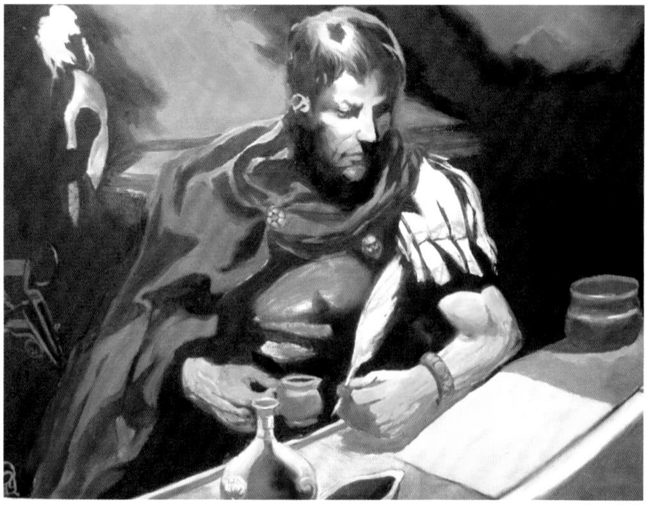

He is the main protagonist and the narrator of the story. This character appears very quickly in the story to give it depth and also to unveil his psychology. We have sometimes used "real" dialogue, that is to say, the ones reported by Caesar in his book.

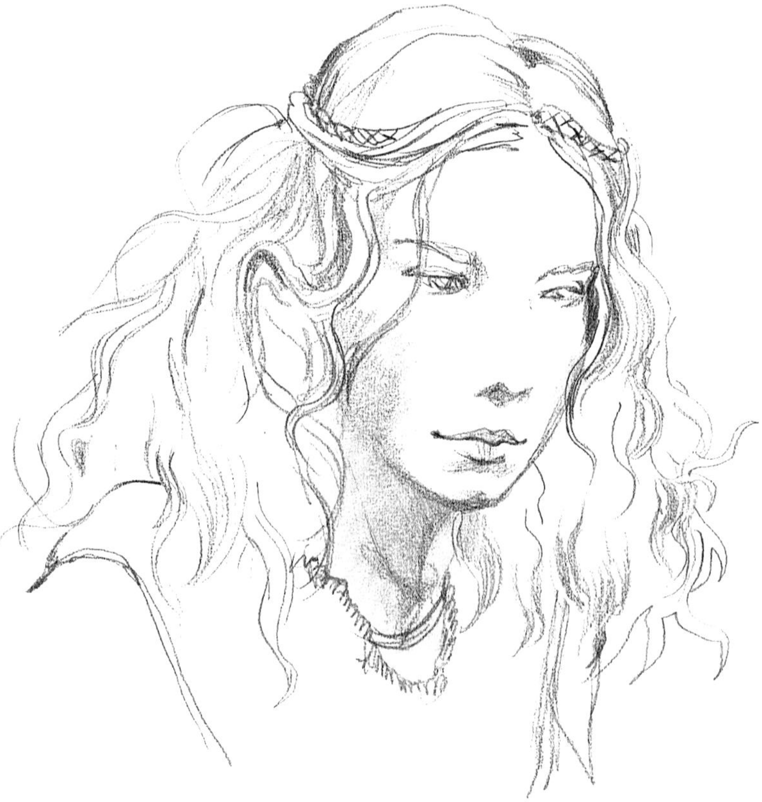

## Titus Labienus

First a tribune of the Plebeians, he then becomes one of Caesar's legates and generals. The Gauls consider him to be the most dangerous Roman during this war of conquest.

## Marc Antony

He is also one of Caesar's great generals. He becomes his most faithful ally, contrary to Labienus, who ultimately sides with Pompey. He is entirely dedicated to his master and mentor.

## Petrus Volusenus (a fictitious character)

Waging war with Caesar as early as the first military campaign in Celtic Gaul, this general is close to the senatorial party and distrusts his proconsul. He does not hesitate to inform the senators who plot against the friends of the Julii in Rome. He partakes in all the battles, braving death for Rome's eternal glory. He finally sides with Titus Labienus in Pompey's camp when Caesar decides to seize power with his army.

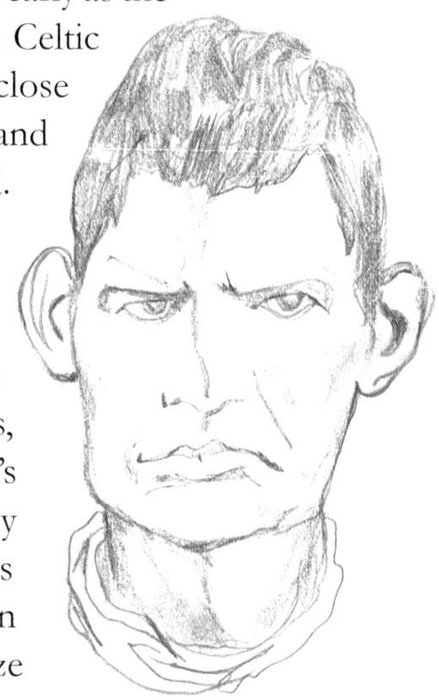

## Eponine (a fictitious character)

This Aedui spy is the daughter of an Aedui chief who was murdered by a Sequani mercenary, an enemy of Rome working for Orgetorix. Antony hired her to conduct intelligence operations in the tribes that have not yet been subjugated. She works with two men who obey her and are ready to risk their lives to help her. They are experienced warriors. She is fascinated by Rome but loves a Gallic chief, although she is supposed to seduce him. Before dying, she makes peace with her family during her brother's funeral. He died as a soldier working in the contingent of the Roman allies.

# Vercingetorix

He was with Caesar during much of the war and may have been with him as early as the beginning of the Gallic War. By virtue of his high rank, he was part of Caesar's circle. The Roman leader was also his mentor. During our story, his desertion, which Caesar is unable to explain to the Senate, is seen as great treason. Vercingetorix applies the Roman strategies and organizes his army in accordance with the principles he was taught by Caesar. Let us not forget that the Arverni were part of the alliance with the Romans and that Vercingetorix, their leader, was expected to hold a high position in the republic. During the revolt of 52 B.C., he becomes the leader of all the Gallic tribes. From that moment, Caesar considers him a personal enemy and fights him unceasingly until the battle of Alesia, where he has to surrender to avoid a massacre. During the revolt, Vercingetorix applies the tactics he learned from Caesar and gathers his soldiers in legions. In this story, we have explored the special relationship (according to Dion Cassius or Suetonius, it was almost a filial link) between these two men, who are very much alike. We have also shown the different aspects of each culture as well as the refinement of the Gallic society and what it brought to the Romans.

## Aupex the Younger (fictitious character)

An Arverni chief who fights under Vercingetorix's command. He prefers to flee rather than surrender to the Romans. Nevertheless, he spies for Gutuater the Carnute and has no hesitation about betraying his camp when he chooses to join the unsubmitted tribes.

## Gutuater the Carnute (fictitious character)

Druid Gutuater is a fanatic who preaches all-out war against the invaders. He is one of Rome's most wanted enemies. He appears at the beginning of our story.

# The Romans

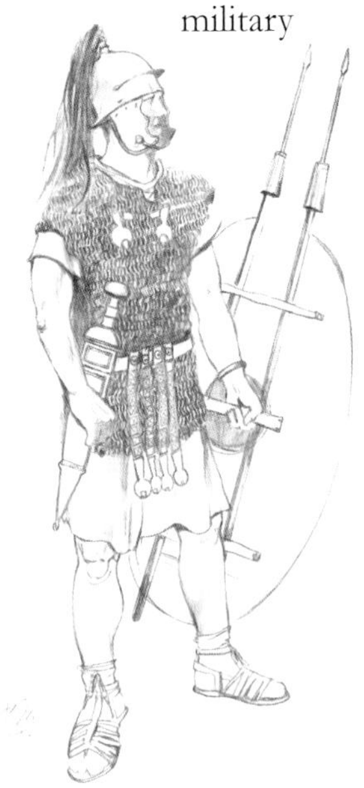

In the first century B.C., the Roman armament and military equipment were still broadly similar to the Celtic ones. The Celtic coats of mail (lorica hamata) and Montefortino and Coolus bronze helmets had become widespread. The legionaries wore different helmets (see illustrations 1, 2, 5, and 6) from the simple skullcap fastened with a thong to the more imposing helmet fitted with large angular cheek pieces or projecting ear guards.

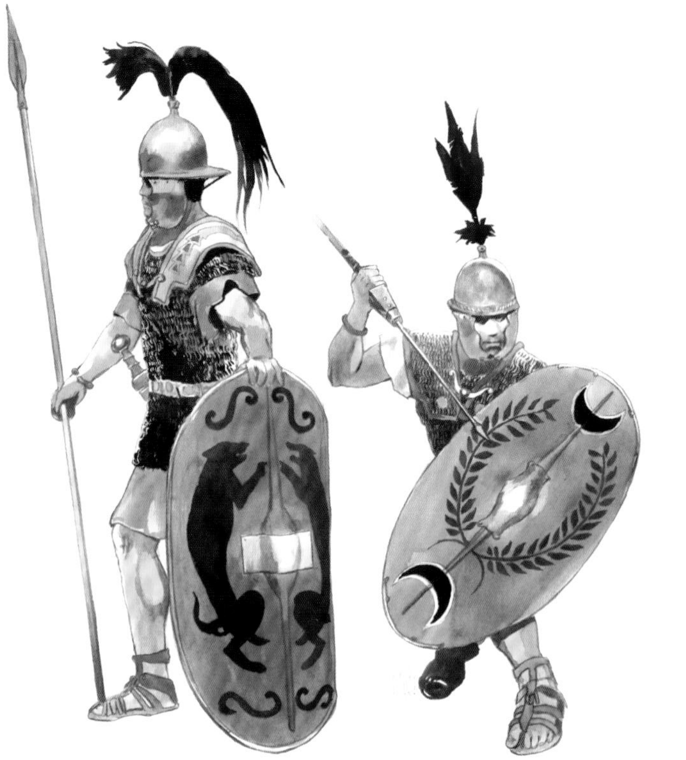

Let us note that equipment is our subject matter since the notion of uniforms barely existed in Roman times. In fact, the army's equipment was rather heterogeneous, varying from the slingers' leather or metal protections to the elite legionaries' heavy armored protections. There were numerous differences, for it seemed that each cohort of centurion took their own approach to the decoration of their equipment.

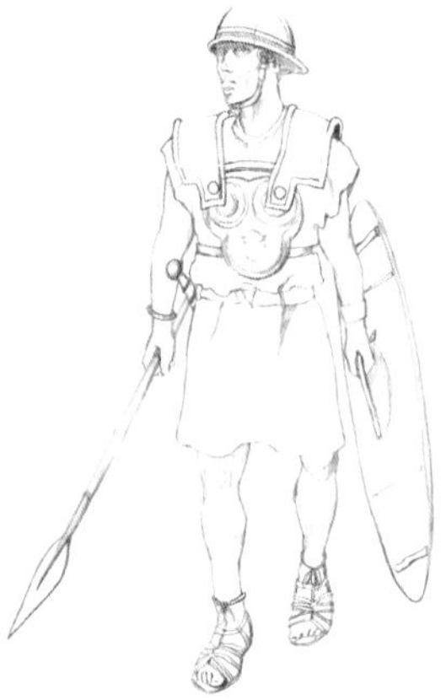

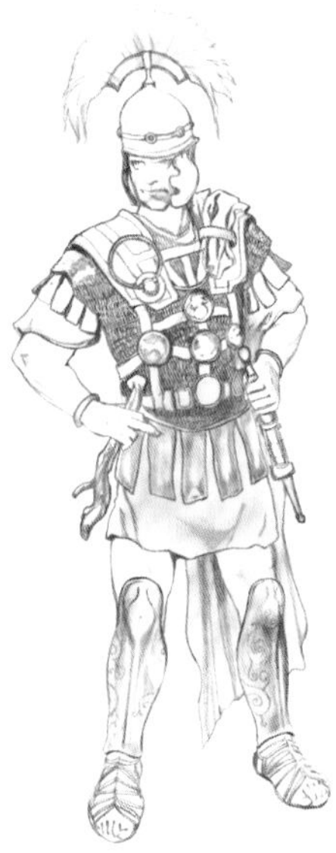

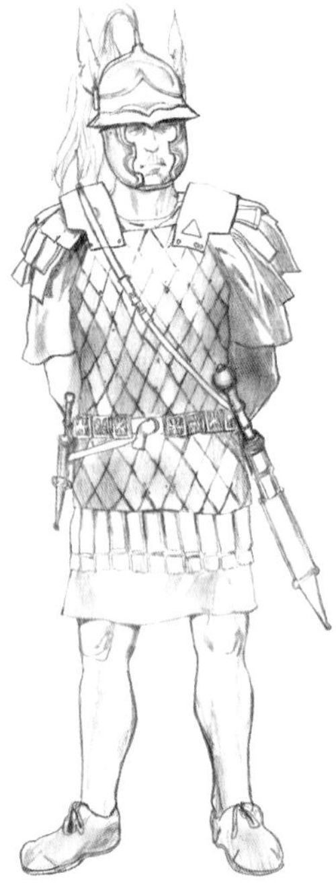

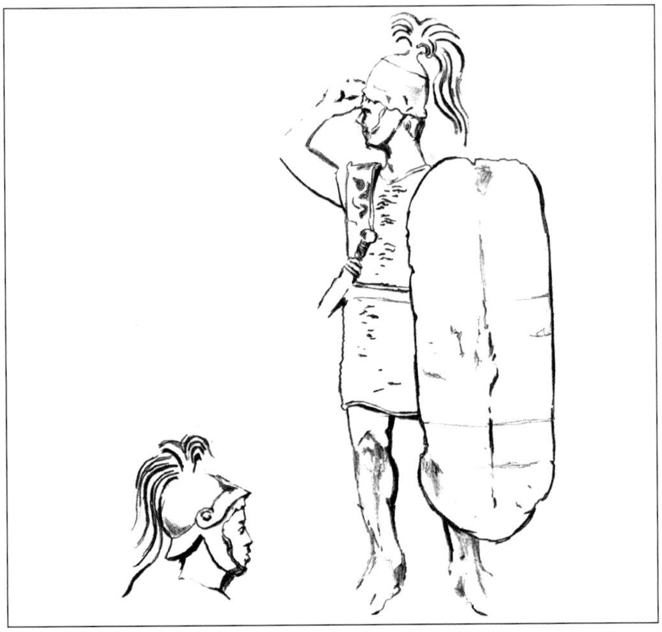

This bas-relief represents a Roman soldier wearing a coat of mail, an oval shield, and a slightly hellenized crest helmet whose features are shown with more precision on the centurion's head.

Indeed, the numerous simplified representations of the Roman uniform that have been made in the past have contributed to misrepresenting it as a unique "official" uniform. This simplification has its origins in the way the Romans themselves stylized their representations on the bas-reliefs. Their reference to Greece and its legendary past accounts for the graphic Hellenization of the soldiers. Referring to the Arch of Constantine or Trajan's Column, the neo-classical painters and sculptors have, in turn, copied and faithfully reproduced the sources they had at their disposal, contributing to the creation of a sort of "fictitious" Roman equipped with a helmet and armor which were historically inaccurate. Archaeological research has proven that Roman equipment has evolved over the centuries along with the resources and the battle skills. Hollywood filmmakers preferred to ignore this and kept the 19th-century model, thus contributing, in turn, to an oversimplified image of the Romans and the Gauls. They have done the same with Vikings.

Illustration representing a stylized Roman, very similar to the bas-reliefs.

In Caesar's time, shields were not square-shaped but oval, and the laminated or laminar armor (lorica segmentata or segmented plates) did not exist yet since it was created after Augustus' imperial reform. Clearly, the image of the typical legionary is not based in reality. However, it has been gradually changing over the last few years as we can notice in documentaries, quality historical reenactments, and even in big-budget movies with historical pageants (although the representation of the typical imperial Gaul often remains unchanged).

Comparatively, the quality of the representation of Gauls is not better, a mistake that is partly due to Romans who also characterized them as being close to the popular imagery of the Barbarian of the time and to reinforce their propaganda. Yet, Celtic nations were refined and adapted to the Greco-Roman way of life. Indeed, Celtic noblemen were close-shaven and had neat, short hair, and their hairstyle could even be sophisticated. They often had a beard but rarely grew a mustache. The misleading representation of the Gauls, which also spread in the 19th century, added an Attic helmet of Roman origin and an armor dating from another age from Gallic folklore...

## The Gauls

The Celtic nations' equipment has common origins. The Celts prided themselves on being at the cutting edge of metalworking. The coats of mail and iron helmets provided a better protection for the Celtic combatants. Their swords were long and straight, and their flat shields usually smaller than those of the Romans. But there are few differences between the 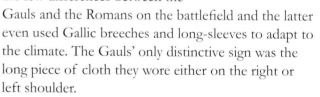 Gauls and the Romans on the battlefield and the latter even used Gallic breeches and long-sleeves to adapt to the climate. The Gauls' only distinctive sign was the long piece of cloth they wore either on the right or left shoulder.

# CAESAR'S NINE-YEAR CAMPAIGN IN A FEW DATES

**59 B.C.: Gaius Julius Caesar and Marcus Calpurnius Bibulus' Consulship**
- Thanks to the *Lex Vatinia*, Caesar is appointed to govern Cisalpine Gaul (northern Italy) and Illyricum (southeastern Europe), giving him command of three legions. The term of his governorship is set at five years.
- After a *Senatus Consulte*, Transalpine Gaul (southern France) is added, giving him command of another legion.

**58 B.C.: Lucius Calpurnius Piso Caesoninus and Aulus Gabinus' Consulship**
- Beginning of the migration of the Helvetians and the Boii towards western Celtic Gaul under the command of Divico (leader of the Gaul tribe of Tigurini).
- Caesar repels them in Genua (Genoa), then pursues them when the Aedui ask him for help. He defeats them for the first time on the banks of the river Saône {east of France).
- Overwhelming victory of Caesar and Labienus near Bibracte (the capital of the Aedui).
- The Helvetians are sent back to their land while the Boii, who are forced to stay in the region, become the Aedui's new vassals.
- Beginning of the military campaign against the Germans: failure of the embassies and of the meetings between Caesar and Ariovistus.
- Victory of Caesar's legions in the Alsace Plain. Ariovistus flees toward Germania.

**57 B.C.: Publius Cornelius Lentulus Spinther and Quintus Caecilius Metellus Nepos' consulship**
- Beginning of the war against the Belgians.
- Caesar's first victory over the Suessiones and the Bellovaci who surrender.
- Second victory of Caesar and Labienus over the Nervii, the Atrebates, and the Viromandui, who also surrender.
- Publius Crassus conquers the peoples of Armorica and the Atlantic.
- Battle of Octodurus in the Alps.

**56 B.C.: Gnaeus Cornelius Lentulus Marcellinus and Lucius Marcius Philippus's consulship**
- Beginning of the Battle of Morbihan against the Veneti after the revolt of Gaulish tribes against Publius Crassus.
- Naval victory of Decimus Junius Brutus Albinus over the Veneti: the Armoricans are now conquered.

- Quintus Titurius Sabinus conquers the Venelli and their allies led by Viridorix.
- Publius Crassus defeats the Aquitani, and then he imposes Roman rule in this region.

**55 B.C.: Marcus Licinius Crassus and Gnaeus Pompeius Magnus's Consulship**
- Victory over the Usipii and the Tencteri, Germanic peoples.
- Caesar crosses over the Rhine: it is the first time a Roman general ventures into Germany.
- First military expeditions in Brittany.
- Labienus' victorious campaign over the Morini and the Menapii in Belgium.
- Extension of Caesar's governorship for another five years.

**54 B.C. : Appius Claudius Pulcher and Lucius Domitius Ahenobarbus' Consulship**
- Second expedition in Brittany: Caesar's victory over the Britonic coalition led by Cassivellaunos Appius Claudius Pulcher and Lucius Domitius Ahenobarbus.
- Major uprising in Gaul (the Eburones, led by Ambiorix and Catuvolcos, were more particularly involved in the revolt).
- Massacre of a Roman legion under the command of Quintus Titurius Sabinus and Lucius Aurunculeius by Ambiorix. A legion commanded by Quintus Tullius Cicero is besieged by the Nervii, who are lated defeated by Caesar.
- Titus Labienus is also trapped by the Treveri. He manages to repel them without Caesar's help by killing their leader, Indutiomaros.

**53 av. B.C.: Marcus Valerius Messalla Rufus and Gnaeus Domitius Calvinus Consulship**
- Caesar and Labienus put an end to the uprisings in northern Gaul.
- Caesar's second crossing over the Rhine.
- The Eburones are exterminated by the Romans. Ambiorix manages to flee.

**52 B.C.: Gnaeus Pompeius Magnus and Quintus Caecilius Metellus Pius Scipio Nasica's Consulship**
- The Romans are massacred by the Carnutes in Cenabum.
- Beginning of the revolt uniting a part of the Gaulish peoples led by Vercingetorix.
- After several defeats, the Arverni practice the scorched earth policy.
- Caesar besieges, captures, and destroys Avaricum.

- Battle and siege of Gergovia. The Aedui treason causes Caesar's retreat and defeat.
- Labienus' victory over the Senones and the Parisii.
- Vercingetorix is defeated and withdraws to Alesia.
-In Alesia, the relief army and the besieged Gauls are defeated. Vercingetorix surrenders to Caesar.

**51 B.C.: Servius Sulpicius Rufus and Marcus Claudius Marcellus's Consulship**

- Caesar's victory over the Bituriges and the Bellovaci, commanded by the Atrebates Leader Commius. Gaius Caninius and Gaius Fabius beat the Pictones.

- Caninius crushes the Cadurci near Uxelodunum.
-Uxellodunum is besieged but resists the Romans. After Caesar's arrival, the subjugated inhabitants are mutilated as a deterrent.
-Labienus' overwhelming victory over the Treveri: the last revolts are subdued.

# SELECTED BIBLIOGRAPHY

**English**
Peter Connelly & MacDonald, *The Roman Army*, Phoebus, 1975.
Ross Cowan & Adam Hook, *Roman Battle Tactics 109 BC/ AD 313*, Osprey Publishing, 2007.
Ross Cowan & Angus McBride, *Roman Legionary 68 BC/AD 69*, Osprey Publishing, 2003.
Peter Connolly & Andrew Solway, *Ancient Rome*, Oxford, 2001.
Peter Wilcox et Angus McBride, *Rome's Ennemies, Gallic & British Celts*, Osprey Publishing, 1985.

**Francais (French)**
Christian Goudineau, *Le Dossier Vercingétorix*, Actes sud, 2001.
Christian Goudineau, *César et la Gaule*, Seuil histoire, 2000.
Christian-J. Guyonvarc'h et Françoise Le Roux, *Les Druides*, Ouest-France, 2000.
Robert Etienne, *Jules César*, Fayard, 1997.
Jacques Harmand, *Vercingétorix*, Fayard, 1996.
Paul-Marie Duval, *La Gaule pendant la paix romaine*, Hachette, 1991.
Henri Hubert, *Les Celtes et l'expansion celtique*, Albin Michel, 1989.
Erik Abranson, *La Vie d'un légionnaire romain au temps de la Guerre des Gaules*, Flammarion, 1978.
Moignet & Kervran (préface de Christian Goudineau), *La Vie d'un guerrier gaulois*, Calleva, 2011.
Stephen Allen, *Le Guerrier celte*, Les éditions Maison, 2010.
Marc Landelle, *Le Légionnaire romain au temps de César*, Lemme, 2008.

**Documentaries**
*Ancient Rome*, BBC, 2007.
*Vercingétorix* de Jérôme Prieur, Arte Vidéo, 2007.

**Related Websites**
http://reconstitution-romaine.com/
http://www.romanarmytalk.com
http://www.les-ambiani.com/index.php
http://arverni.over-blog.com/
http://www.leg8.org/portal.php
http://www.legio-i-italica.it/

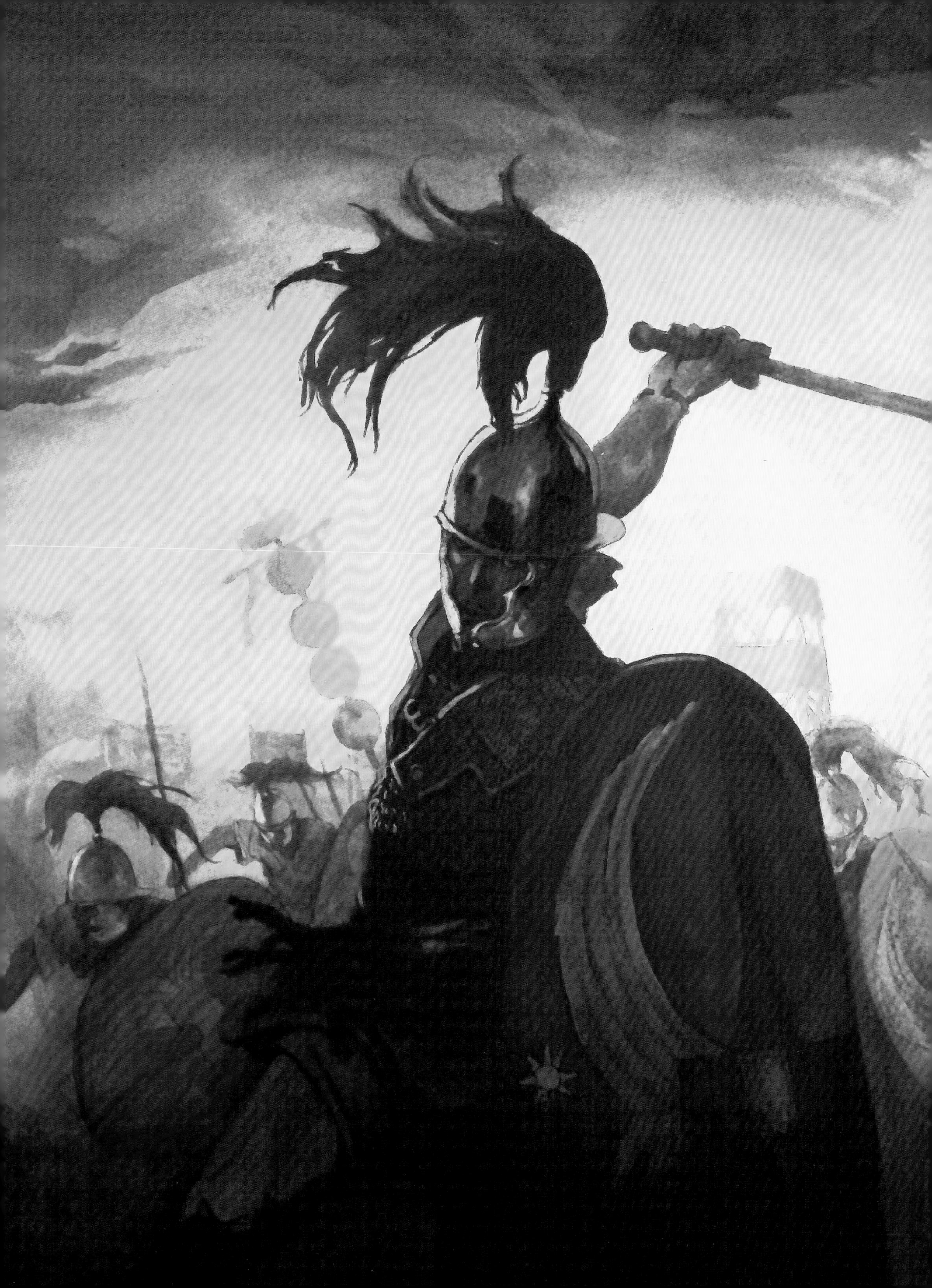